Public Universities and Regional Development

Kathryn Mohrman
Jian Shi
Sharon E. Feinblatt
King W. Chow

Sichuan University Press

SICHUAN UNIVERSITY PRESS

No. 24 South Section 1, Yihuan Road,
Chengdu, Sichuan 610065
P.R. China
http://www.scupress.com.cn

PUBLIC UNIVERSITIES AND REGIONAL DEVELOPMENT
First edition 2009
ISBN 978-7-5614-4246-3

图书在版编目（CIP）数据

公立大学与区域发展=Public Universities and
Regional Development: 英文/(美) 莫门 (Mohrman, K.)
等主编.—成都：四川大学出版社，2009.1
ISBN 978-7-5614-4246-3

Ⅰ. 公… Ⅱ. 英… Ⅲ. 公立学校：高等学院–研究–世
界–英文 Ⅳ. G649.1

中国版本图书馆CIP数据核字（2009）第007879号

Editor-in-Chief: Xiaozhou Zhang
Executive Editor: Jing Zhang
Proofreader: Lingling Jing
Cover Design is by Felipe Ruiz, Director of Strategic Marketing & Design, ASU College of Public
Programs; and Hongying Yang, Art Director in MECD Studio, Chengdu, P.R. China.

PREFACE

Kathryn Mohrman and Jian Shi

Public universities today see their mission as reaching outward to the entire world but also connecting with the geographic region in which they are located. Knowledge based economies call for new levels of cooperation, collaboration and human synergy. In this context, Arizona State University (ASU) and Sichuan University (SCU) have focused on their social, international and regional responsibilities to work together to achieve new levels of contributions to society. In 2003 the then Chinese Vice Minister of Education, Wu Qidi, first encouraged ASU and SCU to become strategic partners. She felt that these two public institutions had much in common—large size, comprehensive curricula and, most importantly, the will to make dramatic changes within university systems in the face of the unprecedented challenges of the 21st century. The result is an unparalleled Sino-American collaboration in knowledge creation, knowledge transfer and university-community development.

The common element that unites these two universities is "university design," a conscious focus on the ways in which higher education institutions organize themselves to achieve their expanded missions most successfully. But university design is not just a name for rearranging the units within a university; it also involves rethinking the goals of higher education in light of both local and global challenges today and in the

i

future. Innovations in university design mean new units being created to foster collaboration among professors, students and staff to address these new goals. New degree programs study indigenous peoples and biodesign; research institutes address sustainability and school leadership; partnerships with entities outside the university create new solutions to high altitude health problems and water resources in times of scarcity. And the list of higher education innovations goes on at length.

One outcome of the partnership between SCU and ASU is the University Design Institute(UDI), a bilateral research and action unit with a mission to understand and guide the ongoing evolution of creative models in higher education worldwide. UDI staff members in Chengdu and Phoenix collaborate internally on activities that enhance the ability of the two universities to pursue their common commitment to innovative change, and externally to create projects that challenge other higher education institutions in China, the United States and around the world to address important societal needs. Projects include implementation of strategies on university arrangements, management practices and new systems of collaboration. To date, nine other universities have joined UDI: University at Albany (State University of New York), Louisiana State University, University of Utah and the University of California system in the United States; and Chongqing University, Huazhong University of Science and Technology, Nanjing University, Xiamen University and Xi'an Jiaotong University in China. More institutions have shown interest in joining.

This case study volume is one of the first tangible products of UDI, demonstrating the priority that both ASU and SCU place on regional engagement. While not formally a land grant university, Arizona State embraces the ethos of the public institution in service to its state. ASU's current vision statement highlights community embeddedness and use-inspired research as important institutional priorities (http://www. asu. edi/newamericanuniversity/). Sichuan University, as the leading university in western China, strongly feels its responsibility to rapidly develop the region as a whole, improve quality of life and address the growing gap in China between urban and rural communities, coastal and interior regions (http://www. scu. org. cn/home/home. asp).

Given that university-community partnerships have existed for many years, why has UDI chosen to publish yet another book on universities and regional development? Certainly in the United States there is an abundance of such work. Most American public universities since their founding have focused on the needs of their regions; the establishment of land grant institutions in 1862 placed special priority on the application of knowledge to the practical needs of the citizenry. In recent years many universities worldwide, not just in the United States, have given greater emphasis to their service mission. These efforts have been "sporadic rather than systematic," however, according to a recent study by the Organisation for Economic and Co-operation and Development (OECD 2007,12).

The focus of this volume goes beyond the American experience to take a broad international perspective, as befits an institute with two founding partners on opposite sides of the globe. In its study of European policies toward regional development, OECD (2007) states, "In the past, neither public policy nor higher education institutions themselves have tended to focus strategically on the contributions that they can make to the development of regions" (11). Today, however, most governments around the world look to universities as engines of economic growth and social development. To achieve these policy goals, many nations are expanding higher education dramatically, increasing research investment and setting high expectations for research applications to flow from universities to the citizenry of these nations.

Effective and sustainable engagement requires a number of factors, including appropriate public policies, leadership, institutional change, new incentive systems and a culture that fosters university-community partnerships. Different universities in different regions face different opportunities and constraints as they pursue engagement with the societies around them. The experiences of higher education in different cultures with different histories provide both theoretical and practical value.

This volume takes a multi-national look at the subject of universities and their contributions to regional development. It brings together case studies to demonstrate the many and varied ways in which 15 universities in 7 different countries serve the people who support higher education. Increasingly, institutions are finding that community engagement is not simply a peripheral "do-good" activity but a significant contributor to the university's core missions of teaching and research. They are re-discovering the validity of John Dewey's belief that advances in knowledge are best developed when universities seek to solve the problems of their communities. In a speech given in China in 1920, Dewey (1973, 211) said:

> The end of education is not just the cultivation of scholars or bookworms who are satisfied to spend all their time reading, but rather it is to cultivate useful members of society. Ability to read is not enough to make a good citizen, if by good citizen we mean one who must make real contribution to society.

This volume is the result of the effort of dozens of people in many places around the world. The 44 authors, both participants and observers of university-community partnerships, have worked hard to tell their stories in ways that will inspire and inform others. Less obvious to the reader is the effort of others behind the scenes—Fang Jiang, Alison Dalton Smith, and Jing Wang in Phoenix and Chengdong Yang, Songyan Wen and Yu Zhang in Chengdu. Most important, of course, are the many unnamed actors determined to achieve the highest levels of university contribution to advancing the well-being of their communities and regions.

Public universities often struggle in their efforts to contribute to regional development. The work is difficult and the rhetoric of engagement often exceeds the reality. The universities featured in this volume, however, demonstrate that higher education institutions can make a difference for the people and the societies they were created to serve.

Kathryn Mohrman
Phoenix, Arizona, USA
Jian Shi
Chengdu, Sichuan, PRC

Table of Contents

INTRODUCTION

Sharon E. Feinblatt

Commitment to community is a global higher education standard today. This volume illuminates the growing commitment to regional development by presenting case studies through the context of public universities in the United States, China and five other countries. Through this book, we provide an opportunity for learning and sharing across borders and cultures, ultimately benefiting the worldwide community.

Key questions drive the stories of our case studies and aid in providing a framework for comparison of a variety of projects and programs spanning the globe. Though locale, size and cultural differences abound in the case schools highlighted in this volume, universal ideals related to our topic can be examined. These include:

- How university leaders articulate their regional development vision and strategies
- What strategic actions university leaders can effectively use to manage the interactive relationships between university goals and regional development
- How public universities effectively promote, direct and reinforce regional development internally as well as at the local and/or national level through specific regional partnerships
- What outcomes are important when evaluating public universities'

performance in regional development

• What issues and challenges arise from regional development activities

While each chapter highlights a specific example of regional development, community engagement or university-community partnerships, the driving questions above allow for comparison and consideration across continents, state lines and cultural values.

Defining the Landscape of Commitment

As we consider a variety of regional development issues within the volume, it is important to also clarify the different terms that describe this body of knowledge. Universities, government officials and the general public use different terms to describe the relationship between institutions of higher education and the citizens they serve. In this volume, we use "regional development" as our subject; however, "community engagement" and "university-community partnerships" are also used to define a general commitment of higher education institutions to the localities in which they reside, most often to social and economic improvement. Identifying the subtle differences in the definitions of these terms can help us better recognize and understand the many ways in which universities are involved within their communities.

As we take a closer look at the specific definitions of these terms, we can see the slight differences in the level, scope and depth of involvement by key stakeholders in the relationship. The connection established by leadership to the university mission, involvement of individuals at various levels of the partnership and institutional scope of the partnership all take on different roles in the examination of these terms. The spectrum below provides a visual interpretation of the spectrum of university outreach and engagement.

Table 1.1 *Continuum of commitment and involvement*

COMMUNITY OUTREACH AND ENGAGEMENT	UNIVERSITY/COMMUNITY PARTNERSHIPS	REGIONAL DEVELOPMENT

→Increasing level of commitment by university leadership ———→

→Increasing involvement of number and variety of stakeholders ———→

→Increasing scope of involvement from within the university ———→

Community outreach and engagement is defined as connecting with the local or regional community in a meaningful and beneficial way. Multiple projects connect to an overall mission to improve the civic health of the community and increase the university's significance as a community institution. Ongoing conversations with multiple segments of the community act as a guide to strategic decisionmaking. (http://www. nationaloutreach. org/engage/community. cfm). In examples of community outreach and engagement, a tie to university mission is apparent, with basic interest by university leadership. *Outreach* indicates some level of one-way action, typically from the university to the community, rather than a two-way, mutually involved process.

We define *university-community partnerships* in this publication as problem-focused community outreach where each stakeholder, having enlightened self-interest, takes part in the development, contribution of effort and rewards of the partnered project. This term defines a relationship around a project that is mutually beneficial, but also mutually developed and led. Typically there is support and interest from leadership and a clear connection to mission. Stakeholder involvement can be seen at a variety of levels, but most important is equality in stakeholder decision making and participation in the endeavor from beginning to end.

Regional development is an outward and visible sign of the third or public service role of higher education through which the institution can demonstrate its contribution to civil society (Goddard, 9). This is the term we use in the title of this book and the most broad, far reaching term on the spectrum. Within regional development, we see more institutional

3

commitment from leadership in action as well as in words. University leadership has a clear, consistent message of continuous vested interest and responsibility to the region in the work of the institution. In this right third of the spectrum above, we see the generation of knowledge and outputs of the university directly answering the needs of the region. We see evidence of this as community issues are integrated into academic courses and faculty research. University-wide messages speak of a clear commitment as a public steward in many realms of the academy's work. There is also a broad view of what is considered "community" within examples of regional development, often reaching across city boundaries. Commitment to state or national issues is more apparent in examples of regional development.

Evident in the work of regional development is direct collaboration with other leaders within the region from the highest levels of office. Cooperative work in improving a region often involves higher education with mayors, governors, regional civic leaders and industry CEOs to develop and implement a large scale, long term agenda. This critical feature of a common long term agenda sets the tone for the entire community. Regional development is not a single project between an internal university unit and an outside entity, but rather a long term commitment to a public agenda benefiting the greater region. This collaborative action in regional planning is evident in many chapters in this volume.

The Historical Context and Contemporary Lens

One early example of university commitment to the public good is the creation of land grant universities in the United States. Beginning with the Morrill Act of 1862 the national government created publicly supported universities to assist in the development of the economy. As engaged institutions, land grant universities have the mission to respond to the contemporary needs of students and communities, focusing knowledge and expertise in solving problems facing their regions. The National

Association of State Universities and Land Grant Colleges (NASULGC) defines this idea on its website as "institutions that have redesigned their teaching, research, extension and service functions to become even more sympathetically and productively involved with their communities." (http://nasulgc. org/NetCommunity/Page. aspx? pid =224&srcid =183) This definition embodies the ideas and practices of sharing, reciprocity and mutual respect among partners.

The relationship between higher education and government can be described as an ongoing series of "social contracts" with an expectation that a commitment should be made by colleges and universities to focus on service to their public in recognition of the mission of these institutions (Perorazio, 2000). This is further supported by the March 2000 Kellogg Commission report as it states:

> The obstinate problems of today and tomorrow in our nation and world—poverty, family and community breakdown, restricted access to health care, hunger, overpopulation, global warming and other assaults on the natural environment—must be addressed by our universities if society is to have any chance at all of solving them. (Kellogg Commission, 2000, 20)

Various leading universities are committing new human and capital resources to the idea of community engagement. David Maurasse, like others in this field, recognizes the growth of this relatively new concept in higher education. "The community-building and community development movements have been gaining steam; add to the mix the knowledge, facilities, person power, and influence of academia and we have great possibilities for effective partnerships" (Maurasse, 2001, 5).

The literature about university-community partnerships is primarily anecdotal—case studies and observations of particular settings—rather than theoretical. However, general themes about this body of literature certainly emerged by leading researchers in the field. A selection of authors who have written about topics related to university-community partnerships includes John Goodlad, Ernest Boyer, Ira Harkavy and Wim Wiewel. A common theme addressed by these authors is the social responsibility a university has to its community, a foundational concept to the idea of regional development. Other contemporaries have documented various cases highlighting methods to achieve successful university partnerships including structure, function and purpose.

Though a scattered history of community engagement practices existed beginning in the late 1800s, it was during the 1980s and 1990s that a small number of universities in the United States began to verbalize commitments to their surrounding communities. In an issue of *Metropolitan Universities* focused on university-community partnerships, Harkavy and Wiewel recognize this "sea of change" occurring across our nation, "toward becoming genuinely civic institutions devoted to solving the pressing problems of society" (1995, 7). Continuing these thoughts, Boyer, a proponent of social and civic responsibility, argued that the ivory tower mentality that plagued many colleges and universities in the past can no longer have a place in the academic marketplace (1991, A48). Now more than ever, the institution has a direct connection to the positive social, economic, technological and environmental success of its community.

The current decade has witnessed another resurgence of commitment to regional development with a more pronounced international presence. The idea of a socially responsible university is found throughout examples in this book as well as more recent compilations by Maurasse, Maureen Kenny and others. Puukka and Marmalejo comment that, "in addition to teaching and research, higher education institutions are expected to play a key role as agents of economic, social and cultural development" (2008, 223). More widely recognized than before is the fact that social awareness and responsibility to the community reside at the heart of university community partnerships.

The International Perspective

Other nations agree with this responsibility. The Organisation for Economic Co-operation and Development (OECD), an international organization with members primarily from Europe, has committed itself to the study, analysis and growth of regional development on a global level. In 2004, OECD's Programme on Institutional Management of Higher Education began a series of comparative studies in 12 European countries on regional development by institutions of higher education. Ministries of education and other top governmental agents in these countries often act as "champions of the role of higher education and research in meeting national and international aspirations" (Regional engagement, 2007).

Just as is evident in many educational institutions in the United States, however, engagement with the community remains a third assignment, not necessarily linked to the mission of these international universities. In a 2007 policy report, OECD recognizes that in order for higher education to play a role, universities must not only teach students and perform cutting edge research, but they must "engage with others in their regions, provide opportunities for lifelong learning and contribute to the development of knowledge intensive jobs which enables graduates to find local employment" (OECD, 2007), all advancing the economic and social condition of the region.

Another example is the People's Republic of China which is investing massive resources in higher education because it sees universities and colleges as drivers for economic and social development of the nation. In 2007, President Hu Jintao commented that "Education should be developed as a priority to help train more professional and skilled people for building a moderately prosperous society and propelling socialist modernization" (August 2007, www. chinaview. cn). According to the Chinese Ministry of Education website (http://www. moe. edu. cn/english/higher _ h. htm), in addition to a dramatic increase in access to postsecondary education, Chinese institutions have engaged in reforms in various areas such as higher education management and financing, student curriculum, student recruitment and teaching models. Universities have been granted greater autonomy to adapt their research to the demands of society. Institutions have taken part in the development of science parks and establishing high tech enterprises run by universities to combine industry, teaching and research to ultimately benefit the greater society.

Challenges in Practice

Universities in the United States, as well as institutions in other countries, face significant challenges in pursuing regional development goals. Often the central administration does not place a high priority on regional development and many universities lack sufficient financial resources to meet their goals. On many campuses, faculty members do not get "credit" for community work when being considered for promotion and/or tenure. To alleviate such difficulties, a few universities have established internal grant competitions and formal connections to tenure and new administrative structures; however, a long road exists to turn this challenge into an opportunity.

The level of commitment by universities to their communities certainly varies. As an example, Barbara Holland used information from 23 case studies completed between 1994 and 1997 to prepare a matrix of levels of commitment to service (Kenny et al., 2002). At each level of relevance shown on Table 1.2, you can see the changes in institutional commitment to community engagement, moving from a singular or peripheral role in the institution to a more central place within the context of institutional purpose and action.

Table 1.2 *Levels of commitment to community engagement*

	Level One: Low Relevance	Level Two: Medium Relevance	Level Three: High Relevance	Level Four: Full Integration
Mission	No mention or undefined rhetorical reference	Engagement is part of what we do as educated citizens	Engagement is an aspect of our academic agenda	Engagement is a central and defining characteristic
Leadership (Presidents, Vice Presidents, Deans, Chairs)	Engagement not mentioned as a priority; general rhetorical references to community or society	Expressions that describe institution as asset to community through economic impact	Interest in and support for specific, short-term community projects; engagement discussed as a part of learning and research	Broad leadership commitment to a sustained engagement agenda with ongoing funding support and community input
Promotion, Tenure, Hiring	Idea of engagement is confused with traditional view of service	Community engagement mentioned; volunteerism or consulting may be included in portfolio	Formal guidelines for defining, documenting & rewarding engaged teaching/research	Community-based research and teaching are valid criteria for hiring and reward
Organization Structure and Funding	No units focus on engagement or volunteerism	Units may exist to foster volunteerism/community service	Various separate centers and institutes are organized to support engagement; soft funding	Infrastructure exists (with base funding) to support partnerships and widespread faculty/ student participation
Student Involvement & Curriculum	Part of extracurricular student life activities	Organized institutional support for volunteer activity and community leadership development	Opportunity for internships, practice, some service-learning courses	Service-learning and community-based learning integrated across curriculum; linked to learning goals
Faculty Involvement	Traditional service defined as campus duties; committees; little support for interdisciplinary work	Pro bono consulting; community volunteerism acknowledged	Tenured/senior faculty may pursue community-based research; some teach service-learning courses	Community-based research and learning intentionally integrated across disciplines; interdisciplinary work is supported
Community Involvement	Random, occasional, symbolic or limited individual or group involvement	Community representation on advisory boards for departments or schools	Community influences campus through active partnerships, participation in service-learning programs or specific grants	Community involved in defining, conducting and evaluating community-based research and teaching; sustained partnerships
External Communications and Fundraising	Community engagement not an emphasis	Stories of students or alumni as good citizens; partnerships are grant dependent	Emphasis on economic impact of institution; public role of centers, institutes, extension	Engagement is integral to fundraising goals; joint grants/gifts with community; base funding

The Holland factors listed on the left column of the chart are related to issues of commitment to regional development discussed in this introduction and expanded upon in later chapters of this volume. This matrix discusses service learning commitment by institutions with a continuum of methods, showing a greater institutional commitment as the schools move through the levels and stages of service learning.

The Holland matrix provides a succinct and comprehensive view of the graduated levels of service learning commitment within a university and the various factors involved in the process. It includes the important factors of leadership involvement, faculty initiative and student engagement, all critical to successful university partnerships. In addition, core institutional practices of tenure (faculty incentive), fundraising and curriculum are all included as essential factors. Holland is illustrating investment and action as being directly related to integration and success to service learning in an institution.

We can examine a university's obligation to regional development in a similar fashion. Translated to our subject, this chart illustrates the graduated commitment necessary throughout the university structure and system to make partnerships an integral part of the fabric of the institution. This idea is also discussed in the spectrum of definitions above which indicates various levels of commitment, scope and leadership when describing university involvement with the community.

Origins of this Volume

The initiative of publishing this book provides context and insight into the ideas presented in future chapters. Arizona State University and Sichuan University in China are partners in the creation of the University Design Institute, a think tank and a "do-tank" engaging universities worldwide in innovative strategies for addressing the complex issues of the 21st century. The scope of current social, environmental and economic challenges necessitates changes in the ways universities approach their work and understand their responsibilities to their students and faculty—and to the needs of society on local, national and international levels.

This book is one of the first efforts of the University Design Institute to address important challenges facing higher education institutions in China, the United States and elsewhere. In selecting the case studies to include in this publication, we sought a wide range of cases representing different aspects of public universities including size of school, regional location and rural/urban distinction.

In addition, the publication team identified specific categories of regional development to include in the volume. The overview of the literature available on regional development, primarily based in the United States, identified overarching categories including the four themes we are using in this volume.

- Universities engaged in *Economic Development* include are not limited to partnerships with business, industry, retailers and/or government to improve the growth potential or sustainability of the region. Project outcomes often included growth of local student retention post-graduation, downtown development, retail or business enhancement in the region and community revitalization.
- Within the category of *Communication and Technology Development*, examples included rural technology development, technology transfer, business corridor development, commercial development and interdisciplinary innovation.
- *Social Development* programs in a region included strategic faculty-student engagement, social entrepreneurship, local educational development, community building programs, student citizenship and civic engagement (catalyzing student and community commitment).
- *Sustainable Environmental Development* is defined as a university project which would include working with contemporary scientific development and the regional community to build sustainable environmental practices.

With this background, we turn to the heart of the book, the case studies. The bulk of the book is separated into chapters focusing on a variety of regional development case studies showcasing schools from across the United States, China, Europe, Mexico and Australia. Some of the chapters provide examples of the categories of regional development discussed above. Other chapters take a more comprehensive look at regional development within a specific community. In all of the case studies, you will gain a sense of similarities and differences in working with regional communities to solve problems, based on culture, location and the international communities.

In chapter 2, the **University at Albany (State University of New York)** presents a social development example for improvement in youth and family support and elder-friendly communities. Drawing on lessons learned from two four-county collaborative efforts with the aging and families and children, the authors focus the discussion on engagement principles and pinnacle achievements on partnerships with United Way as well as public sector stakeholders. Recommendations based on Albany's findings are offered for academic units and universities who partner with their communities.

The next chapter focuses on **Arizona State University** and the economic revitalization of the city's downtown, creating an economic stimulus while providing more educational opportunities and new ways of engaging the community. The case study examines the history of the partnership development, challenges of "embeddedness" and lessons learned as the nation's fifth largest city and third largest university work together to create ASU's vision of a New American University.

Chapter 4 investigates the challenges facing the **Portuguese higher education system** by the Center for Research in Higher Education Policies (CIPES). The expansion and delivery of higher education in all regions of Portugal was an important public policy issue in the 1970s and 1980s. Today it continues as an issue of concern, especially because of the inability for higher education to deliver greater economic prosperity to peripheral regions of the country. This chapter analyzes data on student placement, suggesting possible explanations for discrepancies in the regional supply and demand of public education. This chapter is an example of a regional developmental program and its changes over time.

Taking a comprehensive viewpoint, chapter 5 looks at **Chongqing University**'s contribution to regional development by strategically matching its own development objectives to the needs of the region, the key to successful partnerships worldwide. The chapter explains how CQU uses university researchers' work with local businesses to meet regional challenges and maximize public benefit. Primary stakeholders working as partners throughout the development process are at the core of these successful programs.

Chapter 6 introduces the reader to an example of social development through the discussion of **Cornell University**'s Urban Scholars Program. The case study outlines its creation and evolution of the program in attracting accomplished students to participate in research and direct service with non-profit leaders in New York City's most economically distressed communities. The chapter discusses strengths and weaknesses of the program and its success in encouraging two-thirds of its participants to pursue public service positions after graduation.

Chapter 7 looks at an environmental crisis facing the Ayuquila-Armería river basin in Jalisco, Mexico. The **University of Guadalajara**'s challenge was to work with the community to solve pollution problems affecting an important water source for farming, and sugar cane production and human consumption in the state. In this example of environmental development, we learn how the university effectively worked in partnership with the communities in the river basin through an established university institute to reverse the pollution crisis and create regional, systematic governance structures.

Chapter 8 discusses another environmental development contribution by **Louisiana State University** in the wake of Hurricanes Katrina and Rita. The focus is on service learning in which LSU students, from landscape architecture to environmental science, worked with local communities to understand environmental hazards and their impacts, as well as strategies to minimize future losses. Complementing these efforts were community education initiatives that combined LSU's Agricultural Extension and Sea Grant field staff with campus researchers to deliver beneficial projects to the region.

Many universities define regional development through their successful partnerships with local business and non-profit sector organizations. **Luleå University of Technology** in Sweden provides an example of its own work in this area in chapter 9. The authors identify challenges involved in cross-sector collaboration between academic institutions and external partners in industry, business and public sectors, specifically, a center for development of innovative solutions for the engineering and IT companies in the two northernmost counties in Sweden.

Chapter 10 focuses on **Monash University** in Australia and its work in balancing regional initiatives and development with its recent international outreach activities. This chapter looks at regional development through a different lens, a local university going global with the establishment of international campuses, facing particular challenges of multi-national, multi-campus research initiatives. This chapter and the case covering the University of Newcastle give a solid review of the bigger picture of regional development and set the stage for the comprehensive issues surrounding our topic.

As the place of higher education in China changes over time, **Nanjing University** discusses its regional development work in chapter 11 as an institutional partnership with the governing body of the province. For ten years, more than 400 scholars and government leaders have come together to form the highest level policy consultancy for Jiangsu Provincial Government. This example highlights how universities have moved to a more central position in social development in this country. Key issues such as sustainable development, rule of law and the development of a modern service industry are offered.

Chapter 12 tells the story of the **University of Newcastle** and its transformation into a key leader in regional development. The university focused on its medical and science expertise along with its cultural and social strengths, utilizing the university's intellectual capital for the benefit of the region in matters of health, environment and quality of life, alongside the creation of employment opportunities. The concept of regional development in a global context, similar to Monash University, is presented.

As discussed in chapter 3 with the ASU case, economic development in many urban regions is grounded in the involvement of a large university which makes its home in a city. In chapter 13, **Ohio State University** discusses its major contributions to urban revitalization through its program, Campus Partners. The university worked with the city of Columbus and residents and organizations of the University District to improve neighborhoods around the campus. Their approach includes a shared vision, market-based revitalization, multiple sources of funding and a focus on long term results. Another perspective on urban and economic development is highlighted in what is becoming more prevalent community engagement for large public universities.

Sichuan University is a premier university in western China, committed to poverty reduction in order to promote positive development in the region. Chapter 14 reviews the poverty problem in western China and SCU's work to incorporate strategic action items for long term improvement of this crisis. Cases of the university's institutionalized efforts are presented as an example of a university in a developing country contributing to regional development.

Chapter 15 focuses on **Texas Tech University**, the largest comprehensive higher education institution in Texas serving a region larger than most of the states in the U.S. Because of the large region that it serves, Texas Tech has implemented the use of online classes, video conferencing and DVD instruction, among other resources at off-campus locations. This case study, an example of communication and technology development, examines adaptation of pedagogies to address regional development, mutuality and reciprocity agreements between partners, technology as an enabler of partnerships and financial infrastructure required for sustainable delivery of hybrid academic programs. In light of the growing need to deliver education to a greater number of individuals, this example of the use of technology is a modern solution to a longstanding issue for public universities.

The **University of Utah** case study provides another comprehensive perspective of regional development, emphasizing a full continuum of engagement. Vehicles for university-community engagement include student directed projects, service learning courses and community based research. The successes of such partnerships are attributed to a focus on leadership, resident empowerment and community capacity building, all of which can be seen in many of the cases in this volume. Issues of reciprocity, sustainability and the continuing role of the university in the community are analyzed to provide models for success and to ignite the discussion on the future trajectory of university engagement.

The **Conclusion** looks at the topic of public universities and regional development through the examples provided by these case studies. It parallels this introduction in seeking to draw together the many threads presented in the volume.

The final case study concludes our examples in a most poignant fashion. Regional development and, more specifically, universities' role in the burgeoning issues of our planet is critical to solving challenges being faced by local communities, regions and nations. An institution's involvement is not relegated to only research based solutions, but action based collaborations. In all cases of regional development, we see action oriented, leadership based and stakeholder generated solutions blossoming from a commitment to community improvement. These principles are at the core of successful, long term regional development initiatives, and are recurring themes throughout our international collection of cases.

In the spectrum of university outreach and engagement discussed at the beginning of this introduction, we outlined three primary definitions of engagement and their place within the field of these types of programs. As you read through the volume, and more specifically the cases which follow, consider this spectrum as a lens through which these programs can be analyzed.

· Where do these examples reside on the spectrum?

- What are the key differences and similarities which place them in these categories?
- How do a university's or community's location, size, culture and history shape the type of engagement, which they participate within their region?
- What type of foundation must be in place for a community or university to be an active member of a partnership?

We encourage you to use this volume as a foundation or continuation to your own regional development goals and aspirations. An overarching and standing commitment to this field of involvement within our global community will be the ultimate contribution that our communities and universities can make to humankind.

FOSTERING REGIONAL PARTNERSHIPS FOR CHILDREN, FAMILIES AND THE AGING

Katharine Briar-Lawson, Philip McCallion and Bruce Stanley
University at Albany (State University of New York), USA

Universities play many roles in community-building partnerships. For example, economic and social development is part of a long heritage of university-community partnerships. These partnerships have focused on priorities such as land development (Perry & Wiewel, 2005), K-12 education reform (Percy, Zimpher & Brukardt, 2006) anti-poverty strategies (Soska & Butterfield, 2004), disaster relief, workforce development issues (Briar-Lawson & Zlotnik, 2004; Lawson et al., 2006), and creating elder-friendly communities (Bronstein, McCallion & Kramer, 2006). Location often matters in these partnerships; notably, urban universities have assumed joint responsibility for urban revitalization and renewal.

The impetus for community engagement is often the self-interest of the university. This may involve pressing needs to avert crime, to expand the footprint for more student housing or research facilities and to create opportunities for service learning and pilot projects (Benson, Harcavy & Puckett, 2007). Other university-community partnerships are less about construction and expansion of the campus with self-interest at the core and are instead about building new programs and services for a region. This reflects the altruism of the university, schools and individual faculty, moving beyond self-interest to being engaged in solving the problems of the day.

In this chapter we present two case studies of university engagement in social development. The University at Albany (UAlbany) has a strong tradition of service, first rooted in its origins as a state normal school in 1844 and over time manifested in a wealth of activities and partnerships in fields ranging from social welfare to nanotechnology. UAlbany's community engagement is an important function of its research, teaching and service mission and is advanced through the leadership and commitment of the president and various senior administrators, deans, department chairs and faculty. The President's Office plays an increasingly coordinative role to help identify, connect and leverage efforts across nine schools and colleges. As a research university, UAlbany pairs such outreach work with data driven and evaluative activities.

UAlbany's strategic location in the capital city of New York State makes it well positioned to work closely with regional and state partners focusing on critical needs in New York. UAlbany's College of Nanoscale Science and Engineering, ranked the No.1 college in the world for nanotechnology and microtechnology by *Small Times* magazine in 2007, is transforming and revitalizing the economy of the state with government and industry partners. At the same time, UAlbany continues its historic legacy in public service and engagement with public and non-profit sectors.

Capital Region as Design Lab

The Capital Region is a century-old test market for " Madison Avenue" media and marketing because of the unique geography of the area. Given such market research and the development of new commercial products, the region has a parallel opportunity to incubate new programs and services that might inform public policy.

The School of Social Welfare (SSW) has sought to have greater community impact and to advance the region as a test site for possible program and policy innovations addressing unmet social needs. The president and provost made this engagement agenda an explicit part of the work of the SSW dean when she was recruited and hired in 1999.

SSW faculty and administrators play a myriad of community-building roles as brokers and facilitators of service development. They serve on boards, work as collaborative facilitators, conduct research and co-design new programs and services. They also serve as grant writers, trainers and consultants. In addition, they provide services as liaisons to field agencies where students do internships. SSW is a community-building resource providing $4 million annually of in-kind services by student interns in field placements in non-profit and public sector agencies.

SSW has also engaged in a number of community-building projects that integrate service learning and internships while advancing strategic agendas that generate cross-county collaborative projects to improve community and individual outcomes. Two case examples of such community building are profiled in this chapter. In both cases these regional development opportunities emerged from crises, unmet needs and emergent opportunities. The first involves children and families fostering family support and economic development. The second focuses on the aging, initiating the first steps toward creating an elder-friendly community in response to the dramatic growth in the aging population and the need to redesign communities to support meaningful and high quality-of-life initiatives. This chapter will provide an overview of how SSW faculty and partners executed their regional development vision and strategies for these two initiatives. In addition it will briefly highlight some outcomes and evaluation challenges as well as lessons learned.

Family Support Network

The work of SSW to address the needs of the most vulnerable children and families emerged with the opportunity to cooperate with an elementary school of largely disadvantaged students next door to the downtown campus. The SSW helped build assets and provide more supports to children and families, teachers and administrators. Outreach to the principals at the elementary school led to grant proposals developed by faculty and staff to address poverty, violence and the perplexing non-involvement of many parents. Faculty and administrators of SSW met with teachers at the school and co-designed a 911 rapid response system, so that high-need children in the classroom could be triaged through an array of school based and school linked services. In essence the collaboration helped create "a full service school." Paralleling this work with SSW, the elementary school embarked on a literacy campaign. With help from SSW's university-wide Community and Public Service Program, an AmeriCorps Vista grant was secured promoting a parent-led family resource center. Faculty developed grants to foster more rapid response to high-need youth in the classroom through mental health interventions. A time dollar store was established for the children to buy school supplies, computers and other goods. To earn time dollars, children and their parents volunteered in an array of service projects in the school and neighborhood. Each hour of volunteering became a redeemable time dollar. Children who had been identified as delinquent began to earn time dollars and each good deed helped to overshadow the tarnished image that had plagued them in the past. In the first three months of the time dollar project, more than $11,000 worth of time dollars had been earned.

Some "restorative justice" of sorts occurred when a SSW faculty member who had been knocked down in the parking lot issued the first computer to a child and his mother. Together, the mother and child had earned 100 time dollars, sufficient to pay for the cost of a computer in the time dollar store. The culmination of all the successes led to the school board citing the elementary school as the most improved school in the district. Fourth grade test scores demonstrated that academic achievement had improved along with dramatic declines in fights, suspensions and expulsions (Austin et al., 2006). Special education students were maintained in the classroom and school and the "push outs and pull outs" declined precipitously.

The United Way (UW) focused on the work at the elementary school in its search for new opportunities for strategic investments. Parent development and family support were the priorities selected by the United Way Community Building Committee and Board. United Way formed a partnership led with SSW called the Family Support Network. The mission of the Family Support Network is to improve outcomes for vulnerable families by building capacity, resources and supports. This initiative sustained and replicated elements of the elementary school pilot in more than ten sites. Several are in public schools and others are agencies in a five-county region spanning urban, suburban, rural and small town communities.

In addition there are more than 50 other agencies that are part of this Family Support Network. Key features in these sites are parent-led family resource centers, case management and family team facilitation in which families and service providers convene to develop more empowering, coherent and integrated service plans. Such team meetings are needed given the fact that many public sector families receive service from up to 14 agencies. Yet service providers often do not coordinate services or communicate, due to a range of barriers including confidentiality issues. Other features of FSN include economic self-sufficiency and time dollar programs, micro-lending and micro-enterprises, financial education, assistance with earned income tax credits and, most recently, early child development and literacy services.

Students from SSW do internships at United Way and at the key sites. They also have course work that focuses on these initiatives especially in community-building and economic development classes. Their internship projects include grant work and cross-site program development. Several students have been hired by United Way upon graduation to advance the Family Support Network and the Earned Income Tax Credit (EITC) Program. This EITC initiative provides income tax preparation assistance to the working poor who can then receive tax rebates. These rebates may help lift some out of poverty.

Faculty involvement is also notable. One faculty member collects data annually on the financial support needs of families and individuals claiming EITC. Others undertake board training and grant development.

This SSW-UW partnership has been underway for six years. The Family Support Network and agenda have developed to the point that six sites now receive special "high impact" investment funds to advance these services and programs. Family support has increasingly been seen as an investment arena for United Way. In the past year, two United Ways have merged in the region; now this Family Support Network serves a five-county area. Because the new United Way has embraced the Family Support Network, the program has a strong likelihood of continuance.

Elder-Friendly Community

The second partnership centered around early efforts to create an elder-friendly community, begun with a grant awarded to SSW by the John A. Hartford Foundation in 2000 to train students to be leaders in the development of new services for the aging. The SSW Internship in Aging Program became a national model that is now being adapted and replicated in most graduate schools of social work. Students do internships in agencies using a rotation model and undertake leadership projects that build new services to foster more relevant supports to the aging and their families.

Several years into this grant, the John A. Hartford Foundation came to SSW and the New York State Office for the Aging (NYSOFA) suggesting the need for a pilot program for an elder-friendly community in the region. It was to be one of two pilots nationally for the foundation. Two grants were subsequently awarded to the SSW and its Center for Excellence in Aging Services (CEAS); one was for planning and the other for implementation.

During the planning phase, more than 600 representatives of state and local governments, foundations, health networks, insurers, caregivers, employers, aging services providers, faith communities, and the aging persons themselves contributed to the design process. Another 80 agencies and faith communities committed to participate in the implementation plans. The planning process used a mixed methodology of interviews with aging consumers, key decision makers and opinion shapers including political leaders, aging advocates, faith community leaders and health system administrators. Focus groups and interviews were held around such issues as transportation, discharge planning and underserved communities. These focus groups explored the need for an information and referral system, reviewed existing data bases and service delivery and identified barriers to continued community living. Meetings were held with national experts as well as those least likely to be heard from, such as the frail elderly, the most impoverished and those living in remote rural areas.

A community advisory committee was convened to oversee the elder-friendly community-building initiative. Its members consisted of commissioners of the Area Agencies on Aging in the region along with business and community leaders. This committee wrestled with the fragmentation in a region with more than 80 different elected governmental bodies.

The region faced dynamics such as unnecessary hospitalization and institutionalization occurring because diversionary community and related services were not easily found or accessed by frail elders. Health promotion initiatives were designed to expand the supportive services mix by first, identifying critical needs and then offering evidence based programs targeting disease management, exercise and nutrition. A key component has been the building of cadres of volunteers, often older volunteers, to expand caregiver supports in a cost-effective manner. In particularly stressed communities in the region there has also been an emphasis on developing health navigator programs and in promoting health screenings.

A centerpiece of this collaborative work has been the building of a web-based data base, ElderNetworkNY. org, with information on all available services for older persons. After 18 months of design and development work, this web-based service now gets more than 10,000 hits per week. Hundreds of older persons and their caregivers are served annually. Such web-based information is linked to in-person assistance through each county Area Agency on Aging and supports the statewide NYConnects information and assistance system. In the next iteration, the web resources will be embedded in a statewide NYConnects web-based resource modeled on this and other pilot work in the state.

The collaboration to develop ElderNetworkNY.org was a first for the four counties in the region as the commissioners created a cross-county and regional strategy to address the needs of the aging. Other regional attempts had failed so this pilot, along with the Family Support Network, served as evidence that the regionalization of initiatives, including shared resources across many counties, could be a viable option for community building. Next steps involve a pilot social work intern program, funded potentially through Medicaid. This pilot internship will test which competencies are required to help seniors navigate the long term care system. It will help to inform a state-wide replication so that all counties have coordinators who can provide discerning help including in-home supports required to remain independent. Such services thus help to divert seniors from unnecessary nursing home placements and attendant high costs such as Medicaid expenditures.

Common Elements

Despite being two disparate community-building initiatives, these two projects share common features. Both have had to overcome the county and small town "divides" that have historically impeded cross-county and regional work. Other commonalities include the cost sharing involving staff members both at United Way and with NYSOFA. Both initiatives relied on collaboration involving community partners and funders. The newly hired staff member facilitating the FSN had served as the key person building the web-based information and assistance services for the Elder Network. She will play a crucial role in helping the Elder Network database become a resource to the newly developing United Way 211 system for information retrieval and disaster response. Moreover, she brings her knowledge of building regional initiatives to the FSN and can offer lessons learned from an intergenerational service perspective to the Family Resource Centers.

Both regional projects have increasingly focused on financial education and literacy. This is a re-emergent area of interest in social work as a profession. The cross-cutting, intergenerational nature of financial education is particularly timely given the U.S. policy shift to reform welfare and to the growing economic, employment and income challenges faced by many, including impoverished elders.

Both regional initiatives have used trial-and-error inventive strategies to attain goals. Revisioning and strategic improvements have also been continuous design elements. Both projects have been guided by logic models (see Figures 2.1 and 2.2 below). These have been helpful conceptually as well as from an evaluative standpoint due to the absence of comparison counties and sites for more traditional forms of evaluation (Weiss, 1995).

Visions, Strategies and Evaluation Issues

The visions and strategies that launched the two community-building initiatives have been informed and guided by key stakeholders, not the university alone. In fact the university did not espouse a regionalization goal that might have guided the work—and might actually have impeded the programs that evolved. Thus, for example, in the early stages of the

Elder Network, "regionalization" or the "r" word, as it was called, was replaced with the term "collaboration."

The Family Support Network has been shaped in part by an oversight collaborative of partnering agencies, public schools, staff, volunteers, student interns and funders. All have been keys to making the visions realistic and developmentally appropriate to the constraints and opportunities in the region. For example, several years into the work, AmeriCorps Vista funding requirements changed from an emphasis on the use of residents from neighborhoods to run the parent resource centers to a national pool of college graduates. Thus it was determined by the Family Support Network that this grant funding was not in keeping with the social and economic development mission of the sites. Program goals include laddering people out of poverty and into jobs in their own neighborhoods. Moreover, these AmeriCorps Vista volunteers were prohibited from providing direct services and, in several cases, such services were critical to the well-being of children and families in crisis. Thus this grant source was not continued, with the FRCs depending more upon volunteers rather than funded staff. Volunteers may bring creative resources to their posts but are often less able to devote as much time to the labor intensive roles involved, for example, in overseeing a time dollar store, an operation similar to a small business operation requiring intensive fiscal management.

Figure 2.1 *United way of Northeast New York Capital District family support network*

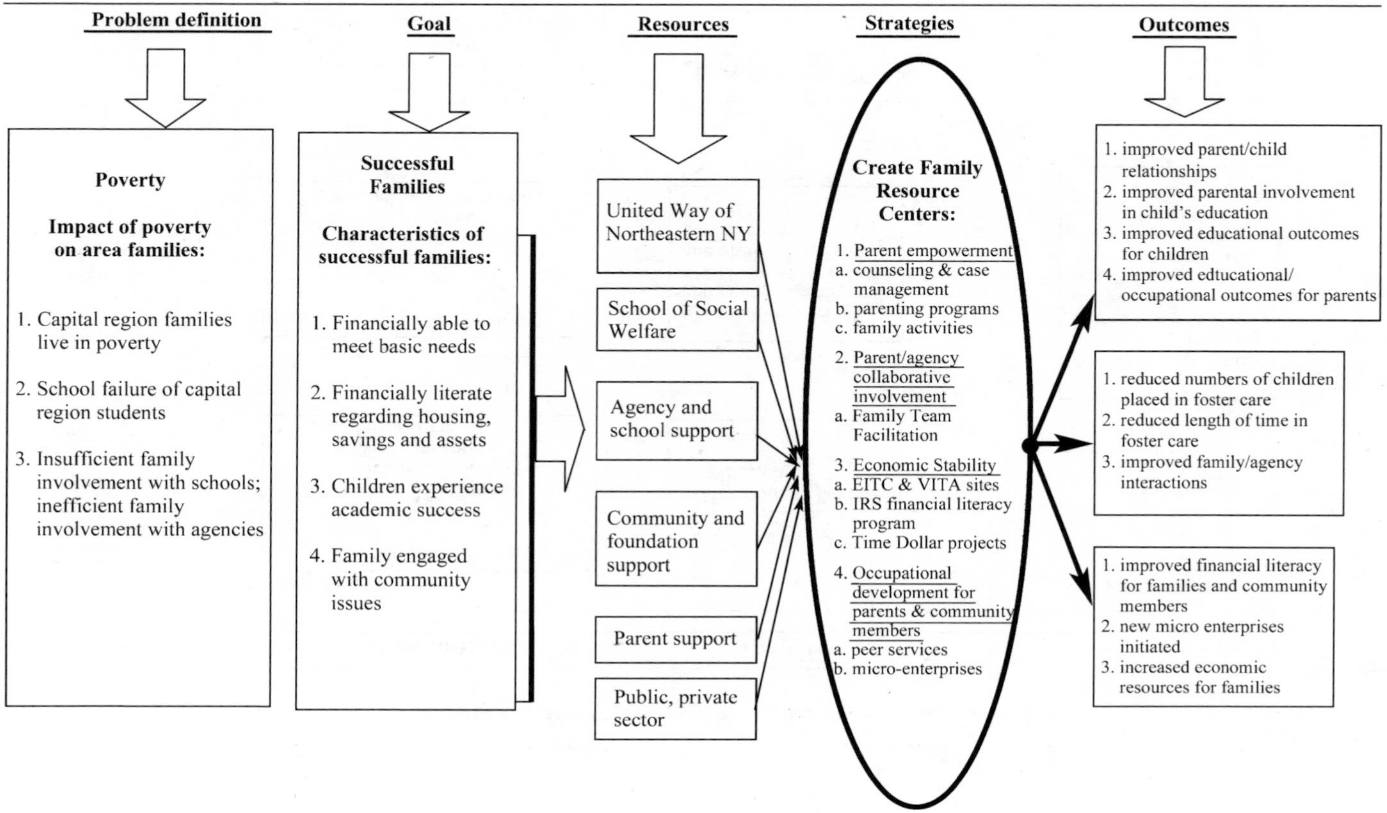

Problem definition

Poverty

Impact of poverty on area families:

1. Capital region families live in poverty
2. School failure of capital region students
3. Insufficient family involvement with schools; inefficient family involvement with agencies

Goal

Successful Families

Characteristics of successful families:

1. Financially able to meet basic needs
2. Financially literate regarding housing, savings and assets
3. Children experience academic success
4. Family engaged with community issues

Resources

United Way of Northeastern NY

School of Social Welfare

Agency and school support

Community and foundation support

Parent support

Public, private sector

Strategies

Create Family Resource Centers:

1. Parent empowerment
   a. counseling & case management
   b. parenting programs
   c. family activities
2. Parent/agency collaborative involvement
   a. Family Team Facilitation
3. Economic Stability
   a. EITC & VITA sites
   b. IRS financial literacy program
   c. Time Dollar projects
4. Occupational development for parents & community members
   a. peer services
   b. micro-enterprises

Outcomes

1. improved parent/child relationships
2. improved parental involvement in child's education
3. improved educational outcomes for children
4. improved educational/ occupational outcomes for parents

1. reduced numbers of children placed in foster care
2. reduced length of time in foster care
3. improved family/agency interactions

1. improved financial literacy for families and community members
2. new micro enterprises initiated
3. increased economic resources for families

Figure 2.2 Information and assistance initiative logic model

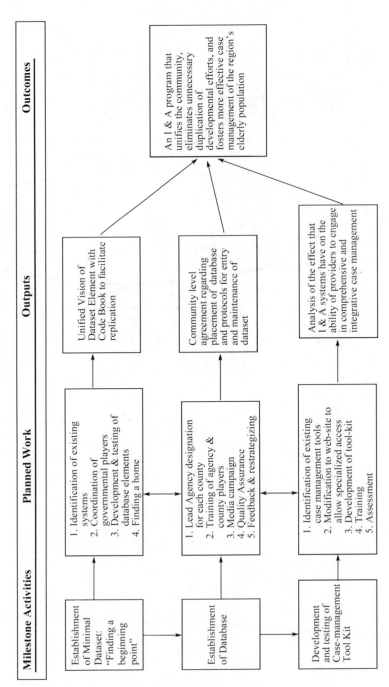

Visions and strategies have also been enhanced by special funds from numerous sources ranging from foundations to the U.S. Department of Health and Human Services. In addition, non-traditional partners including the business community have provided donations and services. Moreover, FSN sites were also able to apply for special pilot funds from United Way in a major investment strategy to deepen impacts. Six of the current 13 sites were selected.

Other strategy and ongoing capacity-building issues involve the variability of services at the sites. For example, case management services are provided in all the FRCs but not all sites offer the EITC refund service for the working poor or the time dollar program. In addition, family team conferencing is offered to a more limited number of families, depending on funding.

Outcomes for the FSN include the establishment of a five-county collaborative involving non-profit organizations, public agencies, school districts and business partners. More than $700,000 in private and public funding has been leveraged. A series of financial literacy training and asset-building strategies have been advanced to help families make better informed financial decisions. In addition, an economic development training program provided training and business plans for economically disadvantaged individuals participating in the Family Resource Centers to help individuals with micro-enterprise and micro-loan opportunities. Finally, the Family Resource Centers in the schools are helping children succeed (Austin et al., 2005). Student misconduct referrals and suspensions have been reduced and the attendance rates have increased. Time dollar service hours have increased and more businesses have become involved in the program. Family team conferencing programs and early childhood development services have been added to new sites.

Vision and strategy issues have also been pronounced with the Elder Network. The original grant of $300,000 from the John A. Hartford

Foundation helped to leverage an investment of $800,000 from the NYS government, making it possible to expand health promotion into several community agencies, but all these grants have now ended. Therefore the SSW has provided bridge funds to support the Elder Network and its data base. The SSW Center for Excellence in Aging Service has sustained a forum for collaboration among the four county offices for the aging and found continuation funding for programs targeting older persons in distressed communities. In addition the center has sustained a program of health education and promotion throughout the region and supported the continuation of several aging focused community boards and organizations. The center continues to offer technical assistance to local providers to support and expand aging services. Center leaders worked closely with the NYS Office for the Aging and the NYS Department of Health on the design of the next stage of information and assistance. The center works closely with the NYS Office for the Aging and the NYS Association for Area Agencies on Aging to share lessons learned with other regions of the state.

Outcome goals created for the Elder Network have been achieved, including the web-based information and assistance system. Health promotion initiatives have been sustained, another goal of the funders; the Elder Network collaborates with the NYS Office for the Aging to expand health promotion offerings and to begin a nursing home diversion initiative. The Center has helped develop an aging focused public relations and media campaign supporting the launch by Albany Guardian Society of *Capital Commons Quarterly*, a periodical focused on aging issues in the Capital Region of New York. The region now has a comprehensive database integrating demographics, health and social service utilization and health information for the aging population of the Capital Region forming the basis for local planning by the county offices for the aging. Ongoing grant development and partnerships of the center for Excellence in Aging Services are keys to the sustainability of the Elder Network.

Interactive Relationships between University
Goals and Regional Development

Universities can play key roles in the regionalization process as many initiatives span county boundaries and unite an area. The full service school model is now having some impact beyond the Albany City Schools as requests are coming in from several other superintendants in the region for replication; yet the model continues to develop. The concept had to be proven in several sites. One of the two principals in the original pilot school adjacent to the university was moved into the most unsafe middle school in the district where he replicated the full service school. As it demonstrated its effectiveness in addressing fights, truancy and disciplinary actions, the middle school was removed from the NYS unsafe school list. Meanwhile other principals were asking the SSW and UW for help with similar full service school developments. The Albany City School district recently passed a school levy (a tax increase) that added another $450,000 into the full service school project. This funding provides stipends for parents and interns, a cross site supervisor and key service providers with resources to expand their behavioral intervention programs. In addition, the SSW Center for Human Services Research helped to write a successful Safe Schools grant to promote more full service schools.

In more recent years the university, under the leadership of a former president, developed the UAlbany-Albany High School Alliance for Young Talent (Alliance). This is a university-wide project to help advance student success and college access at the school. Core programs include university-sponsored mentoring and tutoring, freshmen visits to the campus and faculty "teach togethers" at the high school. Now the high school will be developing a full service school with special programs focusing on the ninth grade repeaters and youth transitioning from an alternative ninth grade program. SSW is integral to the Alliance and is helping to foster the scale-up of the full service school to the high school. Several faculty members from the SSW are also advancing the Alliance by providing cultural competency training with teachers. The United Way FSN will also be a major collaborator in the process.

The creation of an elder-friendly community has led to a number of additional developments at the university and in the community. A seminal inner city development promotes a faith based, neighborhood lay advocate program. Begun with funding from local foundations, this outreach program helps frail elders stay in their own homes and relies on volunteers from inner city ministries and churches to help with this care. The program has now grown with a Practice Change Fellowship award from Atlantic Philanthropies and the John A. Hartford Foundation to provide a lead staff member in the Center for Excellence in Aging Services. The effort focuses on a community collaborative targeting neighborhood-wide health addressing some of the violence issues plaguing this community. Another by-product of the regional planning process in aging was the cross-county investment by county Commissioners of Aging to oversee the development and delivery of education on Medicare Part D drug prescription program.

A parallel community-building initiative has involved the promotion of a Neighborhood Naturally Occurring Retirement Community (NNORC). Like other initiatives, SSW faculty as well as students and community leaders have been involved in grant development, evaluation, and needs assessments. The success of this first SSW-assisted NNORC has helped encourage the development of an investment by United Way in planning for a second NNORC in the region.

Other major developments involve local banks investing in elder abuse and financial fraud prevention with a growing group of investors including the state legislature, banks, foundations and the United Way. The Center for Excellence in Aging Services is developing an intergenerational financial literacy tool that will be used in the United

Way Family Resource Centers and at other United Way agencies.

Key features of this iterative, interactive work involve a shared sense of mission and passion for the initiatives with a "whatever it takes" attitude about making progress. Also critical has been the ongoing collaboration on grants, the teaching of relevant courses, providing strategic learning experiences for student interns and advocacy to advance fund raising.

Each of these community-building activities and programs is accompanied by relevant academic and educational innovations. Curricular developments in aging alongside new grants to support such educational enhancements are keys to the furthering of community building work. For example, several students in the Internship in Aging Program do their field placements in the projects developed by the Center for Excellence in Aging Services.

Financial education and economic development are areas of growing emphasis in SSW, a direct result of these two community-building initiatives. The SSW is now attempting to undertake an 11-county initiative in cooperation with the UAlbany School of Business and the Small Business Administration to advance micro-enterprises and micro-loans in conjunction with several of the United Ways that cross the multi-county region.

Lessons Learned

Ongoing needs assessment and consumer and community guided feedback are essential to the community-building process. This developmental approach has informed more of a shared, inventive and even trial-and-error journey rather than a formal, prescriptive work plan. Since the university has historically been known to descend on communities to collect data and then leave, it was essential that community partners saw the university as working with and for them. This "bottom up" rather than university-directed "top down" strategy has been essential in building collaborative cultures for problem solving and goal setting.

The development of collaborative culture was fostered by:

1) grants that were secured for the community, not just the university;

2) collaborative and shared leadership;

3) the shifting of decision making to bodies like the United Way Family Support Network, Community Building and Board Committees;

4) faculty and MSW interns involved in evaluation and service delivery;

5) evaluation activities that demonstrated the value and cost effectiveness of programs such as an early child development pilot program resulting in expansion to FSN sites; and

6) education, training opportunities such as grant writing workshops.

In the case of the Elder Network, there was an array of similar stakeholders who provided ongoing feedback such as the Senior Issues Forum, a consumer group. Thus, being consumer and community guided seems to be an essential component to the partnership-building process.

Success indices and outcome measures were critical to the charting of progress. Because both case vignettes depict complex change initiatives, multiple measures for charting progress have been warranted. The fact that there may be no comparison or control group for the multi-site work adds to the complexity in evaluation and progress charting. For this reason, logic models (Figures 2.1 & 2.2) helped to depict the key variables in the change plan. As these desired outcomes were evidenced with discernable short and long term impacts, then the logic models and theory that undergirded them proved to be a helpful tool in the progress charting. Logic models also help with goal achievement by specifying desired outcomes and then "backward mapping" with the essential inputs, activities and outputs required to achieve these goals.

The Family Support Logic Model (Figure 2.1) depicts such problems as poverty, school failure and lack of family involvement that are to be addressed along with the goals of financial and related school success.

The resources to be mobilized are specified including those of United Way, the SSW and agencies, schools and families themselves. The strategies to solve these problems are specified, including family resource centers providing an array of empowerment, family capacity building and strategic economic supports. Outcomes depicted include improved parent and child relationships, reduced needs for foster care and out of home placements, educational success, financial literacy and occupational development for parents.

The logic model for the Information and Assistance program of the Elder Network (Figure 2. 2) provides conceptual frames using different schemas. In this case the logic model specifies the planned activities which include the building of the data base and case management tools. The planned work comprises the identification of the systems and collaborators to test the data and provide the case management tools as well as quality assurance. Outcomes include access to and utility of the I and A system as well as improved case management for elders.

Influencing public policy, another desire of the university and our partners, has taken time. In some cases the community-building agendas are aligned with the interests and priorities of policy leaders and well positioned to be sustained. In the case of the Elder Network, several of its initiatives have been adopted and spearheaded by the Director of NYSOFA. These include creating vital communities for productive aging, civic engagement agendas that advance new and meaningful roles in retirement as well as work to further develop NYConnects, a single point of entry into the long-term care system.

On the other hand, the work of the Family Support Network including full service schools and the use of family resource centers are not yet connected to state policy. While efforts have been launched to advance these agendas, no formal legislation or leadership from the executive branch at the state level has championed these initiatives. However, at the county and city level, the value of these services has been recognized as the city of Albany and Albany County government have been partners in this service development. In fact the Albany County Children and Family Services Department received a Substance Abuse and Mental Health Services Administration grant (written in part by the SSW Center for Human Services Research) to create a family resource center and a system of care strategy to address children's mental health.

In all of this work it has been the university's and SSW's desire to be seen as a design and development arm of the community, willing to co-create new initiatives to address human needs. In this way, the university can be positioned to be more of a long term and even welcomed partner in regional community building. In turn, such collaboration enriches the educational, research and public service missions of the university.

GREAT EXPECTATIONS:
ASU DOWNTOWN PHOENIX CAMPUS

Bonita Kline

Arizona State University, USA

Sometimes it takes a catalyst to start a reaction—a catalyst such as two new leaders working together to take a university, a city and a region to new heights. Michael Crow, president of Arizona State University (ASU) and Phoenix Mayor Phil Gordon came into their respective offices about the same time (2002-2003) with similarly high aspirations. The nation's fifth largest city and third largest university are collaborating to quickly build a new campus in central Phoenix to meet the needs of their constituencies. The state's burgeoning population and university's rapidly growing enrollment are putting pressure on both men to act swiftly. This chapter looks at the creation of the new campus and its success in meeting its goals.

Phoenix is the nexus of the region's government, business, communication and transportation networks. The city is striving to create an environment that will attract the "creative class," people who will build a knowledge industry and develop technologies to nourish Arizona in the 21st century. The downtown campus not only provides additional space, it is an opportunity for students and faculty to be closer to, and more involved in, places where new knowledge is created and applied.

Despite the city's growth and prosperity, its core has been somewhat hollow, especially after business hours. Much downtown acreage is vacant or abandoned. The city hopes that the influx of students, staff and faculty will encourage downtown merchants, attract more businesses and create a more lively ambiance.

The downtown campus project attempts to seamlessly integrate the university into the city—and vice versa. The project is noteworthy for the extent of the partnership between the university and the city, and for the speed and magnitude of construction. In less than five years, the partnership garnered public support and input, approved plans, purchased land, arranged funding and completed construction on the first phase. A $223 million bond issue approved by Phoenix citizens in 2006 provided essential funding.

A History of Rapid Growth

Because it is located in the Southwest's largest population center, ASU has experienced dramatic increases in enrollment greater than the growth of the other two public universities in the state. In 1958, there were 10,000 students at ASU; in 2007, there were 64,000 with plans for 100,000 in less than 15 years. The Arizona Board of Regents is considering a plan, called 2020 vision, which would increase the number of students in the state's university system by at least 60% in next 12 years in order to bring the percentage of residents with a college education up to the national average. Studies have shown that people with a college education have higher earnings, generate more tax revenue and rely less on government financial support (Ryman, 2008). Since the original Tempe campus is at capacity, ASU's attention is shifting to its other campuses: ASU West, ASU East and the newest, the Downtown Phoenix campus, the focus of this study.

Phoenix, capital of the youngest continental state, has all the drive, energy and impatience of youth. New residents flock to Arizona at a rate of 150,000 per year. Phoenix is a low-lying metropolis, spreading across the desert and merging with other growing cities to form one of the nation's fastest growing metropolitan areas. Skyscrapers jut conspicuously along a five mile stretch of Central Avenue and around the core of the city. In the last 30 years, projects to attract people downtown have included a civic/ convention center, a ball park, a sports arena, museums, performing arts centers and retail/dining complexes. Each new structure has been another piece in the revitalization effort.

A crucial element of a successful downtown—and campus—is connectivity. In 2000, Phoenix citizens voted 2-to-1 in favor of a $1.1 billion multi-modal transportation system with increased bus service and light rail. The rail system's initial 20 mile route passes the valley's major entertainment and sports venues, museums, medical centers, the airport, the Central Avenue business district and two of ASU's four campuses. Light rail's route was a deciding factor in ASU's site selection for the downtown campus.

Also approved by state voters in the 2000 election was Proposition 301, allocating $1 billion in funding to the three state universities for research, technology transfer and new business development (City of Phoenix, 2004, 2). This investment is already paying dividends as Arizona attracts new research programs. In 2002, an Arizona BioInitiative Task Force secured $90 million in pledges and contributions to bring the Translational Genomics Research Institute (TGen) and the headquarters of the International Genomics Consortium (IGC) to Phoenix. Arizona's universities and colleges promised faculty support and resources, the state committed $430 billion for genomic research, and the city of Phoenix agreed to donate land for a 15-acre research park and to construct the research facilities.

As TGen settled in, ASU got a new leader with a vision for a new type of university. Michael M. Crow came from Columbia University, where he was a chief strategist who specialized in bridging the gap between research and application of knowledge. From the beginning, Crow said he intended to remake the university. In his 2002 inaugural address, he declared that many universities pattern themselves after the top universities—the "gold standard"—but it is the standard of the past, not the future. Nineteenth-century-style universities are less relevant in an age in which new technology and knowledge are the currency. In an ASU Alumni magazine he stated, "My vision for Arizona State University is to pioneer a new model for the American research university, one that breaks the mold that I believe has constrained these institutions for decades, if not centuries... This will be an institution that does not just engage in community service, but rather takes on major responsibility for the economic, social, and cultural vitality of its community" (ASU Vision, Fall 2003, 3-4).

In 2003, as Crow was formulating his ideas, he met with Phil Gordon, then a candidate for mayor in Phoenix. The two discussed how a downtown campus could help both the city and the university. As Gordon tells it, "It had been a longstanding community ambition to have a major university campus located downtown, but ASU's presence was minimal until one morning over breakfast five years ago. It was then that new ASU President Michael Crow and I changed the future of both the university and downtown Phoenix, by outlining his plans for expansion on the back of a napkin" (Crow, 2008). Gordon is a strong proponent of better education at all levels and included it as one of three issues in his campaign platform: education, public safety and jobs. In the fall of 2003, he was elected mayor of Phoenix with 72% of the vote—a strong indication that he had public support for his priorities.

The Planning Process

One of President Crow's design imperatives is to embrace the university's cultural, socioeconomic and physical setting, to learn from local experience and contribute to it. Especially relevant to the new Phoenix campus is the concept of "social embeddedness" in which the university becomes part of the community to learn of its needs, and then direct its intellectual strengths to meet those needs. The university has an impact on the community, but also allows the community to effect changes in the university so it can meet changing requirements of the region (ASU, 2004a, 16).

In spring 2003 Crow assigned a university design team to develop a strategy for handling enrollment growth with multiple campuses. Among the questions contemplated were: how to differentiate among the four campuses; whether each should have a distinctive mission and program; and how much autonomy each campus should have. Input was sought from students, ASU personnel and the public through several meetings at various campuses and off-campus sites. Consultants were asked to consider how the university should interface with the community, how to blur the boundaries between the community and university, and how to leverage strengths of the institution in the community.

In April 2004, the university design team proposed that the university would have four campuses, including a downtown campus to accommodate 15,000 students studying journalism, mass communication, nursing and health, public affairs, social work and community development. The campus would also house University College with extended education programs and KAET-TV Channel 8 (ASU, 2004b). These programs were selected because of their direct relationship with the urban community.

In Spring of 2004, ASU outlined its goal of a full university with 30% to 40% of students living downtown. Phoenix Futures, a group of developers, also showed its plan for the downtown featuring a diversity of housing, mixed-use districts, innovative retail and enhanced historic and existing uses. A study by an independent planning consultant stated that Phoenix needed to develop a vital, dense and truly urban downtown to attract educators, artists, writers, architects, designers, technology workers and business people, all mobile professionals who can live wherever they choose. The consultants saw the elements of a vibrant downtown coalescing in planning for the expansion of the convention center, light rail, a new 1,000 room hotel, several significant residential developments and ASU's downtown campus.

Assimilating suggestions and concepts from ASU, consultants, citizens and stakeholders, the city of Phoenix developed *Downtown Phoenix: A Strategic Vision and Blueprint for the Future* in 2004. The study states that "downtowns are hot again" and "the cornerstone of regional economic development" because government, universities and medical facilities tend to locate in the heart of cities. City planners concluded that future efforts should concentrate on emerging strengths: university collaboration, biosciences and high wage science and technology enterprises. The report calls them the region's "Three Big Bets" because they have the greatest potential for boosting economic growth.

The city's vision statement predicted that the downtown campus would create 7,700 jobs, generate more than $500 million per year in spending and provide $7 million a year in revenue to the city. Phoenix also invited the other two state universities to expand into the city and encouraged collaborations, such as the Phoenix Biomedical Campus (PBC), especially since there was no medical school in Phoenix or central Arizona. This project has been recognized as an economic engine and was appropriated $470 million by the Arizona Legislature in June 2008 (Arizona Board of Regents, 2008).

The $90 million investment in TGen is already providing dividends in the biosciences industry; TGen has spun off three new companies, opened a branch facility in northern Arizona and formed partnerships with Mayo Clinic and the Arizona Autism Center. A five year plan for the region calls for increased efforts in fields such as cancer therapeutics, neurological sciences and bioengineering (City of Phoenix, 2004, 2). The city invited all three Arizona public universities to locate programs in Phoenix, an invitation that ultimately led to the creation of the University of Arizona College of Medicine-Phoenix. The city renovated historic structures to house the medical school as part of a partnership among local and state governments, the Board of Regents, valley hospitals and both ASU and the U of A. Mayor Gordon's dual alumniship at both schools helped in getting them to set aside decades of rivalry and to work together to provide a medical school for Arizona's largest city.

The third goal is industry clusters in technology. The region is targeting five knowledge intensive clusters in high technology, software, biomedical, aerospace and advanced business services (City of Phoenix, 2004, 2). In successful high technology centers, such as California's Silicon Valley, critical components include a distinguished research center, access to venture capital, a skilled labor force, an international airport, cultural and natural amenities and a high quality of life (Arbo & Benneworth, 2007). ASU contributes by creating a skilled labor force, conducting research and attracting venture capital. Arizona has been weak in the availability of venture capital, but hopes to attract investment from outside the state as the region builds its reputation for research (Hill, 2006).

The city wants to knit these three big projects together with "small wonders" such as gathering places, neighborhood restaurants, galleries and shops to create round-the-clock activity. The city will be a more inviting place for students, residents, tourists, conventioneers and, perhaps most importantly, the creative class. The report cites Harvard University scholar Edward Glaeser who observed that the density of cities provides the perfect milieu for the driving forces of the knowledge economy: idea fermentation and technology innovation (City of Phoenix, 2004, 9).

Getting It Done

Phoenix leaders recognized that reaping the full benefit of a university campus in the downtown would require a long term commitment and a close partnership with ASU. The Vision statement says that Phoenix is hindered because "Arizona does not provide its cities with a full 'toolbox' to deal with urban revitalization" (City of Phoenix, 2004, 56). Unlike many states, Arizona does not allow tax increment financing (TIF) through which bonds are sold to cover the cost of infrastructure and other development expenses and repaid with the increased tax revenue generated by the improvements. Despite the absence of this tool, however, Phoenix was committed to building the university and improving the downtown.

The city expects the presence of 15,000 students and 1,800 personnel to have a significant impact on the economy, housing and neighborhoods of downtown. Residents and business people welcome potential employment and educational opportunities of ASU, but others fear the loss of residential areas as non-residential uses expand. A few neighborhoods, favoring quiet streets with single family residences, want to preserve their character and worry that students won't maintain the homes (City of Phoenix, 2004, 20). If the university was coming, it would be best to have a mutually agreed-upon plan.

Although the city had developed guidelines and mission statements as it tried to revitalize the downtown, there was no comprehensive master plan for the whole area, so ASU offered to create one. In June 2005, the university entered into an Intergovernmental Agreement (IGA) with the city of Phoenix to develop the Downtown Phoenix campus.

Most universities finance large real estate projects by the sale of bonds issued by the university or a state board of regents (Perry & Wiewel, 2005, 209). But in this case, the city of Phoenix agreed to provide the land and construct the buildings and infrastructure. The city planned to cover all its costs for the campus with a bond issue, but it had to be approved by Phoenix voters in March 2006. In the interim, the city would pay interest only on the first $100 million necessary to open Phase I of the campus by fall 2006.

ASU agreed to pay 50% of the interest cost for up to three years or until revenue became available from the March 2006 bond program. The university would bring some of its schools and programs to the campus and pay the operating costs, including utilities, maintenance, classroom and office supplies and salaries. While the city could provide funds for construction through the issuance of bonds, money for operating costs for new facilities would be a challenge for the city to work into its budget. ASU would also provide fixtures, furniture and equipment. Some facilities, such as dorms, parking and retail, would be handled by private companies. ASU also agreed to transfer the Mercado, a small development that had been used for offsite classes, to the city and engage in fundraising to reduce the city's debt (http://phoenix. gov/2006bond/ bondfaq. html).

Throughout 2005, members of the city and university worked jointly on the design/build process. Even before funds were obtained from the bond issuance, the city started acquiring the land, negotiating property exchanges and entering into public-private partnerships. City planners thought it was necessary to do this before the exact campus location was disclosed and caused property prices to escalate. It was not as much a leap of faith as it first appears. If things went awry, the property could be sold again.

The bond proposal totalled $878.5 million for homeland security, education, parks, libraries, streets and other city infrastructure and amenities. Of those funds, the ASU campus was allocated $223 million. ASU helped to promote the city's "Building Our Future" campaign. Rallies, public presentations, websites and publications explained the bond program to voters (http://phoenix. gov/2006bond/). The campaign emphasized the area's runaway population growth and rapidly increasing number of students who must be educated. The bond passed easily on March 14, 2006 with 66% of the votes.

One of the key factors in location choice was the new light rail system linking the campus with Tempe to transport students and faculty downtown from throughout the valley. A site was selected along Central Avenue, a transit center where light rail and bus routes converge. Another benefit was the proximity of Arizona Center, an attractive shopping center with restaurants and a theater. Taking advantage of what was already in place, ASU leased an upstairs suite as a student center and used a former Ramada Inn as a temporary dormitory. Space at a historic post office was rented for student services.

In August 2006, only five months after the bond election, the Downtown Phoenix campus welcomed more than 3,000 full time and 6,000 part time students. The first colleges to open at the new location were Nursing & Healthcare Innovation, Public Programs and University College.

The College of Public Programs

At the Tempe campus, the schools, centers and institutes of the College of Public Programs were in different buildings. Located together at the new campus helps collaboration and focus on ASU's mission and their work in the community, says Debra Friedman, dean of the college and university vice president of the ASU Downtown Phoenix campus. The College of Public Programs concentrates on interdisciplinary study of public and community issues. Locating near Arizona's government offices was logical since the students have or seek careers in public administration, elected office, community development, non-profit leadership, social work and community development. Meetings with government officials and community leaders are now easier and take less travel time. Friedman finds the number of meetings and organizations with which she and others serve have multiplied. Proximity has increased opportunities for communication and the ability to be attuned to the needs of the region (Friedman, 2008).

As an example of how both the city and the students benefit, ASU and the Department of Economic Security and the Division of Children,

Youth and Families/Child Protective Services collaborate on the Child Welfare Training Project. With funds from the Child Welfare Field Education and Student Support Project, master's students in social work receive scholarships in exchange for an agreement to work with DES. This better satisfies the state's need for more well trained social workers and the community benefits.

College of Nursing & Healthcare Innovation

Bernadette Melnyk was sold on President Crow's concept of the New American University when she accepted her position as Dean of the College of Nursing in January 2005. When she saw the older facilities at Tempe, she thought, "I am going to have to build a really big dream to recruit people." Moving to newly renovated facilities with up-to-date technology has helped. She and staff members designed the space and an innovative nursing program. The college was given a new name to emphasize its changes—the College of Nursing & Healthcare Innovation. In 2005, the school recruited 23 new full time faculty and increased enrollment. In 2002, ASU graduated 160 nurses; in 2007 it graduated 320 (Berry, 2008). Funding was also dramatically improved. A business advisory group composed of alumni and community leaders was formed to create business plans and assist with raising funds. A local executive and philanthropist matched donations in a series of challenge grants that raised almost $56,000 in 2005. A solid research infrastructure was developed and grants submitted to the National Institutes of Health increased by 225%.

Educational partnerships were developed with Mayo Clinic Hospital, Banner Healthcare and other medical institutions. New centers of excellence were created, such as The Center for Advancement of Evidence-Based Practice. As an integral part of their community, nurse practitioners and 200 students provide healthcare services at a ground level clinic to students, faculty and staff, as well as nearby residents who often have little or no health insurance. One existing program, Breaking the Cycle Community Health Care, is now administered and partially funded by the ASU College of Nursing & Healthcare Innovation. It was operating in Phoenix before the downtown campus was started, but now is easier for staff and students to reach.

The school is also helping to fulfill the state's increasing need for nurses as baby boomers reach their golden years in this popular retirement state. By the time Dean Melnyk manned a backhoe at the groundbreaking for the second building, the College of Nursing & Healthcare Innovation had become the largest nursing program in the country. The new five story building will provide additional classroom space for nearly 2,000 students. Dean Melnyk is already thinking about phase three—a larger community health center that will provide additional training opportunities for students.

Walter Cronkite School of Journalism and Mass Communication

In preparation for the move to a new campus, the Walter Cronkite School of Journalism and Mass Communication became an independent college of ASU and doubled the number of faculty and staff, recruiting highly regarded journalists from the nation's top newspapers and media services. The move was an opportunity to design a building suitable for technology of the 21st century and to locate closer to major media providers where students can intern. Within a couple of blocks are the state's major daily newspaper, *The Arizona Republic,* NBC and Fox affiliate television stations, radio stations, public relations firms and magazine publishers. Journalism students are encouraged to practice their skills in the neighborhood.

As online journalism erases the line between broadcast and print disciplines, media professionals need experience with the latest technological tools. Increasingly, they will multi-task: interviewing, writing, editing, reporting, recording video and audio and preparing it all for presentation online or on camera. At the school, students use two TV studios, production and audio control rooms, editing suites and a transmission center. Students provide news coverage and hone their abilities through programs for the community such as Cronkite News Service.

Students are closer to where news, decisions and history are made. Downtown Phoenix may not have been a lively place after dark, but it has always been the heart of its business sector. The legislature and governor's office are less than two miles away. City Hall, federal, state and county courthouses and government agencies are within walking distance. As Mayor Gordon said, the downtown location "will allow journalism students to essentially have a laboratory that is as big as downtown Phoenix itself" (Cronkite School, 2007, 6). In the spirit of community integration, the spacious First Amendment Forum hosts weekly public events with officials, leaders, television personalities and faculty discussing journalism, news and regional issues like immigration. The college's radio station hosts musical events, and postings about local events encourage students to interact with community members. KAET, the university owned public broadcast station, also moved to the new building. With its own studios, production suites and transmission center, it acts as a "teaching hospital" where journalism students can gain experience.

Lessons Learned

Communication

When ASU and the city of Phoenix worked together to seek the support of voters for the bond, communication was good with meetings and forums where various parties could provide input and receive information. Once the bond was passed and the project was underway, interest and attention seem to have turned to other matters, perhaps because participants were no longer in the same positions or because staff members were busy putting the plans into action.

Although the overall experience of working together has been positive for both the city and the university, at City Hall and with a few community members there is a feeling that communication between partners was not as good as it could have been. The design of the second nursing building did not fit with the city's concept. City planners thought the ASU representative missed the idea of open, welcoming buildings and a pedestrian-friendly environment. Although Phoenix controlled the purse strings, city personnel say they tried to be as cooperative as possible and perhaps could have been more firm. The situation came to a head when the public spoke up. Somewhat ironically, ASU planning students became involved in the design process to ensure that proposed community-friendly standards were met (Downtown Voices, 2008).

In some cases, the city and the university had different ideas about how to develop an area, such as the Civic Space across the street from the University Center and Cronkite Building. ASU originally envisioned that it would be used mainly by students. But the city's parks department took a strong stance on public usage and hired an architect. The result will be a park and a restaurant with facilities for the general public, including students.

One planner noted that ASU did not participate fully on projects such as streetscapes. Stakeholders were e-mailed copies of various plans with a request for comment, but response was seldom received from ASU architects, designers or planners. Perhaps in an urban partnership, more participation and visibility is necessary, particularly with the New American University and the concept of embeddedness, requiring transparency and trust.

Leadership

Mayor Phil Gordon was re-elected as mayor in 2007 with 77% of the vote, a strong measure of confidence for his leadership and programs. In 2008, he won a commendation in a project called World Mayor, organized by the urban affairs think tank, City Mayors, coming in fourth in a field of 820 nominees. His profile included these comments: "The majority of Phoenix residents support the mayor's efforts to build bridges" and "He doesn't just see our city as his domain, he sees Phoenix as a global citizen, partner and player. " An ASU alumna wrote, "the City of Phoenix has no official responsibility for education, which is the responsibility of local school boards and the State of Arizona. But Mayor Gordon has made education a priority and is rebuilding our community around education... most impressive is what he has done at the university level" (http://www. citymayors. com/). Viable partnerships require commitment and Mayor Gordon has proven to be a staunch ally of ASU's efforts, particularly during the 2006 bond election.

Getting wide acceptance for new concepts, such as "The New American University" and "One University in Many Places, " takes strong leadership. President Crow has been a dynamic force at ASU, making big changes and taking quick action. That potential is what drew some new personnel to ASU. As one person pointed out, there is no dean of a college at ASU who predates President Crow's arrival; they have all been hired or promoted by him. The university has hired more than 400 new faculty and administrators, targeting scholars with prestigious credentials. In the first five years of Crow's presidency, ASU has recruited more members of the National Academies of Sciences, Engineering and Medicine than in the previous 45 years combined (ASU, 2007).

Nursing Dean Bernadette Melnyk says that Crow is deliberate in who he hires, choosing the right person for a position and selecting strong leaders. She is a case in point. Melnyk had no thought of coming to ASU, but accepted the position as Dean and Distinguished Foundation Professor in Nursing after meeting President Crow and learning about his goals and concepts. She says there are many dreamers, but Crow is one of the visionaries who make things happen by inspiring others. The school has been able to accomplish more in three years than most do in ten or twenty. Dean Friedman came to ASU for the challenge of building a critical institution in one of the nation's largest cities.

Opportunities and Challenges

Change brings opportunities, but also challenges and a need for adaptation. Creating the New American University has required restructuring of colleges, departments, institutes and centers. A major reorganization took place in 2004 to reduce duplicate programs and offer new opportunities. In 2006, administrative services were centralized, placing the deans on all campuses under one provost. The "One Campus in Many Places" plan shuffled schools, institutes and programs to best fit the four individual campuses. Most recently, at the start of the fall 2008 semester, Provost Betty Capaldi announced that several schools would be combining or moving to strengthen ASU's academic offerings, while tightening the administrative structure and reducing costs.

When schools were moved to Downtown Phoenix, not everyone was happy about relocating to a different campus. For some, it required a longer commute. A few felt the move was "imposed" upon them and expressed trepidation about leaving behind the more traditional form of campus. Some students and employees worried they would no longer be in the mainstream of the university if they were not at the Tempe campus. Time helps people adjust to new situations. After working at the downtown campus for a year, one staff member told Dean Friedman that she was now a believer and had never enjoyed better working conditions. With more than two years advance notice, people at the journalism school had time to plan their new building in the new location. New employees and students know what to expect before they start. In the first semester at the downtown campus, only 120 students, rather than the anticipated 270, chose to reside at the downtown campus, but in 2008, residencies at the new dorms were at the expected level.

Timing can be a tricky thing. Some people expressed frustration with the tight construction timeline. As one person said, additional time would have allowed a more thorough discussion and participation by the general public, an appropriate effort since the school is using almost $300 million in public funds. More input might have prevented the disagreement about the design of the second nursing building. On the other hand, consultation slows down the design process; in Phoenix the public was expecting quick action after the bond election.

In this age, when people expect instant results, the challenge for ASU and Phoenix will be fulfilling these high expectations. Only two years after the campus's opening, despite rapid construction and plans proceeding on schedule, local citizens are asking when they will feel its effects on the economy and in their lives. The Phoenix community made a huge investment in the Downtown Phoenix campus, so people are eager to see direct impact on local businesses and increasing numbers of students eating, shopping, and living downtown.

A 2004 economic impact study projected that, during construction, 1,300 jobs would be created annually with an economic output of $166.8 million and $8.4 million in taxes paid to the state, county and city. At build-out, the output would be $569.5 million with $44.0 million in tax revenue. With the current weakening of the economy and the majority of downtown students just starting in 2008, however, it is difficult to determine the long term economic impact. There has been constant activity, however, as cranes swing, jackhammers pound and workmen come and go. A hotdog vendor under a colorful umbrella caters to construction people. Students, faculty and staff form waiting lines at the new Starbucks in the residence halls, and university people are more visible in the downtown. As one merchant said, the mood is cautious optimism.

The Future

Growth will continue to be a challenge for ASU and Phoenix.

Economic growth will need to keep pace with the burgeoning population. Growth creates jobs which will attract yet more people. The Phoenix metro area is expected to grow by 50%, from approximately 4 million in 2006 to 5.9 million in 2017. The Downtown Phoenix campus expects enrollment to grow from 7,500 to 15,000 students by 2020 (ASU, 2006).

The dynamic partnership between Arizona State University and the city of Phoenix is achieving its goal of building a new campus. It has spurred new collaborations among cities, universities, hospitals, governments, organizations and businesses. In his 2005 "Future of the City" address, Mayor Gordon explained the need to move quickly, saying that the world today moves at cyber-speed. Cities that "foolishly rest on their laurels will lose ground to ambitious cities like Phoenix. " He said, "We are a city of opportunity and we haven't even begun to tap into our full potential. But we will. Because Phoenix is a city determined to be the best and to have the best..." (Gordon, 2005)

ASU will be part of the equation, educating students and doing research, but also continually adapting to meet new needs and demands. President Crow intends to grow the university, not only in size but in impact, influence and contribution. He believes that a research university, particularly ASU, can be a powerful engine for societal transformation as it generates new knowledge and influences almost every aspect of the future (ASU Vision, Fall 2003, 3-4).

The new Phoenix campus is an ideal case study for the concepts of the New American University because there is a baseline from which to measure progress. Until 2006, there was no downtown campus and very little community in the center of the city. The two will evolve together. It is an ideal lab to test the concept of social embeddedness since ASU seeks to be an integral part of the city. Mixed use is the new *modus operandi*. In addition to academic space, university buildings have shops, restaurants, offices and clinics that serve the public. Decisions, resources and responsibilities are shared to some extent between university and city. There is some push and pull between partners as details are worked out in this ongoing joint project—and that is what partnership is all about.

This century will be faster paced, more crowded and full of technological and economic challenges. Other universities and other cities will be faced with the challenges of population growth, a turbulent economy and changing educational needs. They will need to step outside the comfortable traditions and move quickly to stay in touch with society. Communication, leadership and willingness to partner with various entities are lessons to be learned from Phoenix and ASU's downtown campus. It is an ongoing effort in which the city and university will continue to draw upon each other's strengths and support.

A REGIONAL MISMATCH?
STUDENT APPLICATIONS AND
INSTITUTIONAL RESPONSES IN THE PORTUGUESE
PUBLIC HIGHER EDUCATION SYSTEM

Pedro Teixeira, Madalena Fonseca, Diana Amado,
Carla Sá and Alberto Amaral
Center for Higher Education Policy Studies, Portugal

Until recent decades the Portuguese higher education system was markedly elitist, with a strong regional concentration in a few major cities. In the 1970s when the system took its first steps towards massification, one of the most important developments was the wider geographical distribution of public higher education institutions (HEIs). Subsequent governments have explicitly stated that geographical diversification is a major objective of the expansion of higher education. In the late eighties, greater institutional autonomy was granted to promote public HEIs' responsiveness to local demands from both students and employers.

Since almost two decades have elapsed since the system moved to a mass level, we seek to assess the capacity of institutions to adjust to local demands. In this paper we analyze the data on the number of candidates to higher education programs and the number of places available, to assess the effectiveness of Portuguese HEIs in mapping student demand. We discuss possible explanations for the mismatches between regional supply and demand.

The Expansion of the Portuguese HE System
and Its Regional Dimension

Traditionally, Portugal has had very low levels of literacy, resulting in a poorly qualified labor force. In the beginning of the twentieth century, around 90% of the Portuguese population was illiterate (Reis, 1993) but the situation started to change in the 1960s. The country was able to address part of its deficit, though the average educational level remained low when compared to other European countries. In this context of poor qualifications it is not surprising that the Portuguese system of higher education has remained strikingly elitist (see Nunes, 2000). One of the most important dimensions of the system was its high regional concentration, with public institutions only in the three major cities of Lisbon, Porto and Coimbra. Thus it is hardly surprising that the major higher education reforms of the early 1970s focused on the expansion of the higher education network into all regions of the country in order to speed Portugal's economic modernization. It was expected that this expansion would be an engine of growth in those regions, by improving the qualification of the labor force and providing an important stimulus for economic activity. In particular, it was expected that higher education would provide the type of graduates needed by local industries, including ceramics (in the center of the country), the textile industry (in the northwest and parts of the center) or even agriculture, husbandry and wine sectors (in inland regions).

Throughout the seventies there were important steps towards regional expansion and diversification. The 1973 reform created new universities and university institutes in several medium size cities across the country, as well as polytechnic institutes and teacher training schools. However, the main change in the regional distribution was the creation of the so-called vocational sector, with polytechnic institutes and schools being established in almost every provincial capital (Crespo, 1993). The pressures for rapid expansion accelerated after the democratic revolution in April of 1974; the promise of a more egalitarian society created an explosive demand for higher education. This placed a severe strain on many institutions and eventually the Ministry of Education introduced a system of *numerus clausus* to control the expansion, which remains in place today.[1]

Because the development of the public polytechnic sector was slow, students unable to enter university had no acceptable alternative. This situation forced the mainstream political parties to agree that increasing the rates of participation in higher education should be given priority on the political agenda. Faced with significant restrictions regarding the financial and human resources needed to promote the necessary levels of expansion through the public system, however, policy makers used the emerging private sector to increase availability while at the same time expanding the public polytechnic network.

Table 4.1   *Growth of enrollments, total and by sub-sector*

	1971		1981		1991		2001		2007	
	No.	%	No.	%	No.	%	No.	%	No.	%
Public Universities	43,191	87.3	64,659	76.8	103,999	55.7	176,303	44.4	175,998	46.7
Public Polytechnics	2,981	6.0	12,195	14.5	31,351	16.8	108,486	27.4	108,335	28.7
Private Institutions	3,289	6.7	7,319	8.7	51,430	27.5	111,812	28.2	92,584	24.6
Total	49,461	100.0	84,173	100.0	186,780	100.0	396,601	100.0	376,917	100.0
Gross enrollment rate (%) (20-24 yrs)	7.9%		11.0%		24.4%		50.2%		47.7% (census 2001)	

Note. From Barreto (1996); Simão et al (2002); OCES.

As Table 4.1 demonstrates, the system doubled in size each decade, moving steadily away from its original elitist character. Until the early 1980s, public universities overwhelmingly dominated the higher education system. A decade later, the public polytechnics were already absorbing a significant proportion of enrollments; today this sector represents more than a quarter of the total system. On the other hand, the expansion was also significantly fuelled by the private sector, representing about one-third of enrollments although declining (Teixeira & Amaral, 2007). This rapid growth has been a challenge since it meant not only a larger student population, but also a more diverse one. Moreover, this diversification of the student cohort included bringing into the system groups that were traditionally under-represented (Teixeira et al., 2006).

In the years after the democratic revolution in Portugal, this concern with social inclusion became very relevant in higher education debates and regional diversification was obscured by equity issues. The geographic distribution launched by the 1973 reform was postponed due to suspicion that the creation of different types of institutions could create segmentation within the system that would reproduce social inequalities. Many policy makers argued that the development of a binary system would preserve universities for the middle class and divert most working class students to the vocational sector.

With time it became evident that geography was a source of social inequality. For many low-income students, geographical concentration of higher education institutions was an additional barrier in their access, not the least because of the additional costs associated with leaving home to attend university. Thus, in the eighties there was an enhanced attention to the link between geographical diversification and equality in access to higher education. This geographical expansion was particularly visible in the polytechnic sector, which had a strong regional orientation and was regarded as the primary instrument for providing higher education to the more remote areas of the country.

In addition, some vocational colleges were integrated into recently established polytechnic institutions, especially in the larger cities. Some of the earliest vocational institutions were transformed into universities and the public university network expanded with the establishment of three new universities in the south (Algarve) and in the islands of Azores and Madeira. Thus, the supply of higher education changed significantly, reaching all regions and breaking with a secular pattern of strong spatial concentration (see Table 4.2).

Table 4.2 *Distribution of enrollments by region*

Region	1967	1991	2001			2007			Population 15-24 years
			Public	*Private*	*Total*	*Public*	*Private*	*Total*	
North	18.5%	26.8%	27.5%	37.1%	30.3%	27.5%	41.7%	31.0%	38
Centre	24.6	18.0	26.3	8.3	21.0	26.3	7.1	21.5	22
Lisbon	56.9	49.6	33.2	51.4	38.5	34.6	48.1	38.0	24
South	—	4.2	10.8	2.8	8.5	9.4	2.6	7.7	11
Islands	—	1.4	2.2	0.4	1.7	2.2	0.5	1.8	6

Note. From INE various years; OCES.

Curiously, the private sector did not contribute much to the regional diversification of the system, contrary to the expectations of many observers. Private institutions invested in the main urban areas of Lisbon and Porto, almost ignoring other important cities in the center of the country (Amaral & Teixeira, 2000). Hence, the regional distribution of the higher education network is much more concentrated in the private than in the public sector.

By the mid-1990s, however, there were concerns that this growth of the system was becoming unsustainable. Several observers commented that strategies of diversification had more to do with institutional interests than student and labor market needs. These fears were especially critical in the case of recently established institutions located in more peripheral and sparsely populated areas of the country. These concerns gained momentum from the late nineties onwards, when the previously robust levels of student demand gave way to stagnant and even decreasing numbers of new applicants.

These lower enrollments are associated with the decline in birth rates since the 1980s onwards finally reached higher education. Moreover, the reduction in drop-out rates at elementary and secondary levels was insufficient to offset the demographic decline. Since then, Portuguese higher education institutions have been facing a much more demanding context that has tested their strategies of growth and diversification.

Demand and Supply of Higher Education: A Difficult Match?

In this section, we present the current situation regarding the balance between supply of and demand for new candidates into the public higher education sector, including regional differences. We then compare how HEIs have been performing regarding student enrollments and the attractiveness of their various academic programs.[2]

The General Situation in Terms of Demand and Supply

In 2006 there were more than 30 public higher education institutions in continental Portugal and in the islands of Azores and Madeira: 14 universities, 1 open university, 15 polytechnic institutes, 3 specialized schools of nursing and some schools affiliated with the military and police sectors. Some institutions include both a university and a polytechnic, while other institutions have created branch campuses where they offer some degree programs.

The Portuguese higher education network tends to reproduce the pattern of distribution of the population and economic activity, with the highest number of institutions, as well as the largest and most prestigious, located in the two major metropolitan areas. Second tier cities remain with the universities or polytechnic institutes of smaller size and doubtful sustainability in most of their courses or programs.

On the demand side, it is important to remember that access to higher education is selective, since there is a *numerus clausus* system annually defined by the Ministry of Higher Education for each study program. To enter higher education, students compete nationally for places by choosing up to six combinations of study program/institution in decreasing order of preference, being placed according to the weighted average of high school grades and admission exams. Each study program/ institution decides the weights attached to each component, within the limits defined by the Ministry. The first application phase, occurring in July/August, includes all places for new students in the system. The second phase takes place in September, with only the remaining vacancies available. The polytechnic institutes may define quotas for their study programs (up to 50%) for candidates residing in the same region.

The Portuguese higher education system has evolved from scarcity to excessive supply (Portela et al., 2008). In the academic year 2006/2007 there were 46,528 vacancies in the public sector and the number of new enrolled students was 40,400. [3] Thus, 87% of the available places were occupied by new students. Only about half of the candidates were placed in their first preference regarding the combination of study program/ institution.

In order to assess the potential unbalances between demand and supply we have analyzed statistical indicators of two major types. On the one hand, we analyzed the occupation rate, that is, the ratio between the number of enrolled students and the number of offered vacancies in the whole system. This indicator reflects not only the balance between supply and demand, but, more significantly, shows the extent to which there is a match between supply and demand for each degree program. We also looked at the students' priorities, namely their first options regarding institution and program. This second aspect is relevant in order to assess if some programs are attracting students interested in that program or merely attracting students that could not enroll in their first option. Thus, it will provide valuable indications regarding any program's attractiveness and its vulnerability or strength.

In 2006/2007, the average occupation rate for the whole public system was 87% and the first choices corresponded also, by coincidence, to about 87% of the vacancies. Those numbers, however, hide major differences between universities and polytechnics in the public sector.

The former seem to enjoy, on average, a better situation. Public universities offered 58% of all available vacancies and collected 64% of all student first choices in the first phase of the annual process. In contrast, public polytechnics offered about 42% of all the public vacancies, but they collected only 31% of the first choices in the first phase,[4] with an average occupation rate of 81%. In the following sections we analyze those differences in more detail and the possible reasons for their existence.

A Diverse Institutional Landscape

Besides these general differences between the university and the polytechnic sectors, there are significant differences within each of these sectors. This situation is particularly relevant since the overall demand is lower than supply. In order to assess the potential imbalances across institutions, we use two indicators. First, we look at the abovementioned occupation rate for each degree program. In Figure 4.1 we show the institutional differences regarding this aspect for academic year 2006/2007. At the institutional level, there are a few cases of public HEIs that achieve a value close to 1 or even slightly above that value. This means that these institutions are able to fill almost or even all of their vacancies in all degree programs offered. By contrast, some institutions struggle to fill even half of their *numerus clausus*.

The best performance regarding occupation rates is obtained by schools of nursing, although they represent only a small part of the system. Very good performance is attained by most universities located in major cities. There are a few exceptions to this pattern, namely the university and the polytechnic of Lisbon, possibly because Lisbon has an excess of supply. The poorest performers are overwhelming in the polytechnic sector, although universities located away from the coast also have lower occupation rates. Overall one can say that, according to this indicator, universities are performing better than polytechnics, schools of nursing are performing very well, and urban institutions perform much better than those located in peripheral areas.

Figure 4.1 *Occupation Rate, 2006/2007 (National Average 0. 87)*

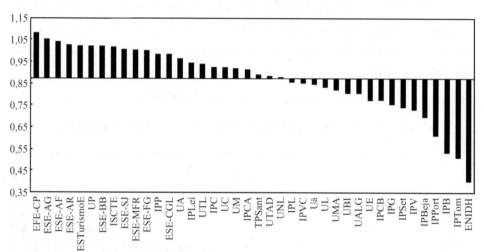

The other indicator used in the analysis is the *weakness indicator*, which uses the information provided by the first choices of the candidates.[5] This is the ratio between the number of vacancies filled with candidates that were not placed in their first choice of program/institution and the total number of vacancies offered. This ratio was calculated by taking into account only the first phase of the access process and it is bounded between 0 and 1 (the closer to 1 the larger the proportion of students who did not choose that program as a first option). This indicator assesses the attractiveness of each program. Moreover, it provides valuable elements on each program's outlook, since it suggests the percentage of students that could be lost in favor of other institutions and/or programs if there was a change in the access system that allowed students to look for a better match with their first preferences.

The average value of the weakness indicator for the whole system was 0. 50. This means that 50% of all vacancies were filled with candidates that placed that combination of program/institution as second and higher order choices for the year 2006/2007. Also in this respect we find an interesting picture, with very diverse institutional situations even when occupancy rates are high (see Figure 4. 2). Some institutions show a high degree of attractiveness, filling their vacancies with high grade point average students that place their programs as a first option. Other institutions fill their vacancies at a high rate but with students who did not choose the institutions or programs as their first option.

Figure 4.2 *Weakness Indicator, 2006/2007 (National Average 0. 50)*

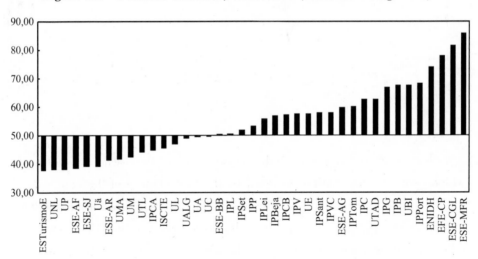

In general, universities tend to perform better than polytechnics in attracting first options. The best performers according to this indicator are universities located in the main urban areas. The schools of nursing, which perform well in the first indicator, provide a varied picture in their ability to attract first options. Among the worst performers we find a mixture of urban and more peripheral institutions. In the former case it may be that a large share of their students had tried unsuccessfully to enroll, as a first priority, in a more prestigious institution located in the same region.

The institutional analysis of both indicators suggests some interesting regional differences. In general universities perform better than polytechnics in both indicators, and urban institutions perform better than those located in more remote areas. However, there are a few caveats. Some institutions located in more populated coastal areas perform poorly on attractiveness because they tend to be regarded as a second (or higher) option than a more prestigious institution (normally a university) located nearby.

A few of the newer institutions, mostly universities, achieved good scores in both occupation rates and attractiveness. Also, the differences among institutions in the same sector and sharing several characteristics (age, location) suggest that other factors need to be examined to explain differences in institutional performance. One of the main factors may be the type of programs offered, to which we turn now our attention.

Programmatic Preferences and Tactical Options

Since students choose a combination of program/institution, it is also relevant to analyze these two indicators for each specific program. Of the 991 programs offered in 2006/2007, 469—almost half of them— registered an occupation rate of 100%; and 640 programs—about two thirds—presented an occupation rate above the national average. The program's occupation rate alone, however, is an insufficient indicator since in certain disciplines demand is still above the available supply. In such cases the candidates' decision making processes are complex; often student choices do not match their preferences for knowledge fields or professional objectives. Some students who do not expect to be placed in their first choice follow diverse strategies. Some will look for placement in the same degree program but in a location further away from their residence. Most of them, however, will look for other available programs close to home.

We need to look not only at the capacity of programs to fill a high proportion of their vacancies, but also to their performance as a top choice for a significant number of candidates. Some programs may appear to be good performers in the first instance just because they benefit from an excessive number of candidates in a similar program at another institution. They may also benefit from an excessive demand in a related field. Thus, we need to combine both kinds of information to identify different groups of programs.

One set of degree programs is outstanding in the sense that they have an extremely strong demand and attract a high number of very good students. These programs compel other institutions and other programs to reorganize to absorb the unmet demand. This is the case of medicine programs that attracted more than 4,000 first choices, 3,000 of them in the first phase, but offered only 1,300 available vacancies. Another example is nursing, which received more than 5,000 first choices, 3,700 of them in the first phase, competing for 1,400 vacancies. Another relevant case is law with 1,700 first choices for 1,200 available places. Other highly attractive programs are psychology, civil engineering, economics, management, pharmaceutical sciences, sports, architecture and design.

The popularity of certain programs may be a combination of several factors. In some cases like medicine, civil engineering and economics, the persistent strong demand may be a combination of good expectations regarding employability and future income and high social prestige of those professions. In the case of medicine and nursing one may add stability of employment since many graduates will secure jobs in the public sector.

The pharmaceutical sciences may be benefiting from social prestige and high income associated with a restricted access to the profession and strong regulations. Although these may be nowadays unrealistic, due to the expansion of the number of graduates and to the liberalization of the sector, this information may be underestimated or only slowly apprehended by new candidates. This may be an example about the problems of information, and the lag in its transmission, and the opacity in the higher education market. Some areas like architecture, sports or psychology may be explained not so much by good prospects of employability and income but by the attractiveness of those fields. Students seem to underestimate the difficulties in the future transition to the labor market vis-à-vis high expectations of intellectual and professional fulfillment. These examples show that prospective students may choose with an implicit cost-benefit calculation that includes non-pecuniary types of returns such as professional and intellectual rewards.

Programs with excess demand will "feed" other programs that students may consider as substitutes or alternatives. They can be in the same institution or others, though in general students tend to go for programs that are disciplinary and geographically close to their unsuccessful first choice. This is the case of all degree programs in the health sector, since many candidates who are unable to enroll in medicine try dentistry, pharmacy or nursing, either at the same or a nearby institution. It is revealing, for example, that all degree programs in pharmaceutical sciences present high values for the weakness indicator, which effectively corresponds to a high percentage of second and higher order choices of enrolled students.

Another interesting example is the case of the dental medicine program at the University of Porto, presenting an occupation rate close to 100% in 2006. Although the initial number of candidates that had placed dental medicine as their first option was higher than the number of vacancies available, the program had 92% of its enrolled candidates that did not choose this program as their first choice. Students with very good marks who do not find a place in their first preference program (e.g., medicine) will enroll in other programs (e.g., pharmaceutical sciences or dental medicine), displacing candidates who chose this program as their first preference but have lower marks. Therefore, the system creates a "wave" of preference mismatches that travels across the system.

The opposite situation occurs in a small number of cases where students choose a specific program and look for vacancies wherever they are available, moving mostly geographically but not so much across disciplines. These are programs that in many cases do not have very high occupation rates but the number of enrolled students corresponds essentially to first choices, presenting a low weakness indicator. In some cases, these programs may correspond to a situation of an excessive *numerus clausus*. Many examples of this behavior are to be found in institutions located in peripheral areas in the interior of the country. This may help to explain why some programs offered by peripheral institutions present a national recruitment pattern, while the recruitment in metropolitan areas is more geographically concentrated.

Finally, there are many degree programs clearly surviving as "last chance" programs. These programs may present high occupation rates in the most popular institutions but lack demand at more geographically peripheral institutions. Students unable to get the place of their first preference decide to enroll in an available vacancy in their area of residence in order to get a degree in a more prestigious institution. The same situation prevails in some engineering and technological fields and seems to have a negative effect on many polytechnic institutes.

The mismatch between supply and effective demand is more evident in the case of a large number of degree programs that have simultaneously low demand—the number of vacancies on offer being obviously excessive—and occupation rates below the national average. In some cases, these programs were important in the past for the institution or for the local economy, but seemed doomed unless they are adapted. In some cases the changes in the local economy have reduced the demand for certain kinds of graduates. Also, students may think that their employability prospects will be poor as the number of specialized graduates available in the labor market increases.

Economic adjustment is certainly relevant for higher education institutions. While they can enjoy some advantages by targeting local employment needs with specialized programs, they need to monitor the labor market and revise when necessary. Moreover, they should not approach their program supply in a static manner, but must be willing to change or even discontinue programs when student demand declines significantly. This will also require flexibility in the use of resources, namely human resources, to move people from declining programs to new ones.

The reverse is also true as new industries emerge. In some cases students do not immediately realize the employment potential represented by those new areas. This again highlights the poor level of information available to students and/or their inaction in searching for relevant employment information. Institutions need not only to identify the emergent areas where they may offer new degrees, but they also must be effective in marketing those new offerings.

The balance of supply and demand is a shared responsibility between higher education institutions and the government, since the institutions may propose new programs and changes in the *numerus clausus*, though the government has the final word. Thus, the current unbalances in the system are partly the institution's responsibility and partly the government's, since the latter could reduce the *numerus clausus* or even reduce the level of funding for certain programs that persistently failed to attract a sufficient number of students.

A Regional Perspective on Supply and Demand

A careful look at spatial patterns helps to assess these mismatches. Figure 4.3 gives us the number of vacancies and the number of candidates who have chosen that institution as a first option for each major university and polytechnic for 2006. The circles with the grey area larger than the black lines represent institutions in which the demand is greater than supply, whilst the circles with a white rim represent institutions in which the supply is greater than demand.

Figure 4.3 *Number of vacancies and first-options by public HEI (2006)*

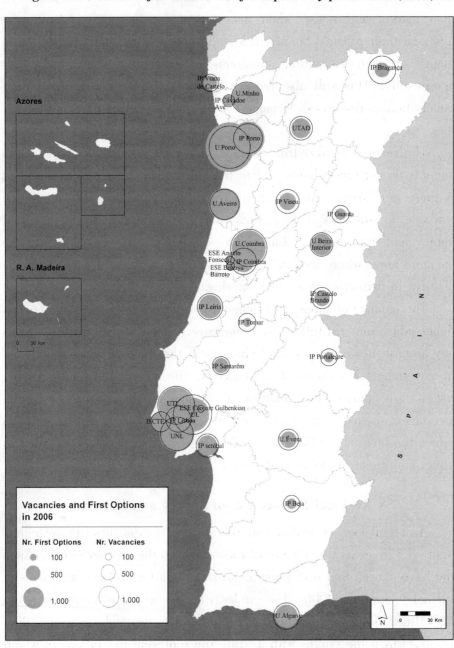

Figure 4.3 shows the weaknesses of institutions located in areas with low or aging populations. Institutions in regions with smaller populations fill a large proportion of their vacancies with candidates from outside their region who could not enter their first option. The number of such candidates has declined, due to demographics and the expansion of prestigious and urban programs, increasing the vulnerability of more peripheral institutions with shrinking markets. The situation has been even more problematic for polytechnic institutions located in peripheral areas, since these tend not to be students' first options.

One of the striking lessons of the regional origin of candidates is the fact that Portuguese higher education institutions, above all, recruit their students locally. This explains that Portuguese higher education public institutions have recruited on average, in the year 2006, 49% of their new students from the Educational District (CAE) in which they are located. This percentage varies between a maximum of 94.7% and a minimum of 23.6%. Thus it is reasonable to say that the regional expansion of higher education—especially of the public network—has contributed to decreasing student mobility, as the more recent institutions tend to attract a growing number of candidates living in their region. Therefore, distance to the institution is one of the main determinants of students' preferences. Since only polytechnics can establish a regional quota in the access system, one may conclude that regionalization of demand has been stimulated by the availability of higher education locally and by the costs associated with enrolling into an institution away from home.

Although public institutions do charge tuition fees, their level is not very high, especially when compared to North American standards. Thus, the major costs that students and their families need to bear are the subsistence costs and the opportunity costs of being a full time student. The former will tend to increase significantly if the student enrolls in an institution located in another region, because that will mean that students will need to pay for additional accommodation and transportation costs. It is noteworthy that a very high proportion of Portuguese young people continue to live with their parents well into their adult lives, hence the relevance of studying close to their parents' home.

Institutions in peripheral areas face a double weakness. On the one hand, these regions are weaker from an economic point of view, thus having difficulties in creating and maintaining employment. On the other hand, they have difficulty in attracting and retaining young people, especially in a context in which students are less mobile. Over the last few years, there has been a progressive increase of the regional unbalances of the occupation rates per district. Therefore, we may conclude that population aging and the decrease in demand will naturally penalize the areas less densely populated and economically more peripheral.[6]

Conclusion

In recent decades the Portuguese higher education system has expanded significantly, changing its regional concentration. From the seventies onwards, several governments have used geographical diversification as a major drive for the growth of higher education. From a regional perspective, the establishment and consolidation of a binary system of universities and polytechnics was important, with the latter playing a crucial role in a more geographically dispersed system.

The slowdown of student demand has created an overall problem of excess supply, since the occupancy rate is presently below 100%. In addition, we have identified significant differences, with institutions in populous areas performing better, probably because those regions also have the most prestigious institutions and most attractive employment opportunities. Thus demand for higher education seems to reflect more general patterns of population and wealth concentration in those urban coastal areas.

Since the students apply for a specific program in a specific institution, we find that some disciplines seem to enjoy a very favorable position, attracting more candidates than their number of vacancies while others struggle. Examples of this latter situation can be found in many of the programs in teacher training and veterinary sciences, and in some cases of environmental engineering and biology.

This has left many of the more recent regional institutions in a fragile situation and seems to undermine many of the original purposes of regional diversification. The expansion of the system was aimed at improving the equality of opportunities by making higher education more geographically available to students living in more peripheral areas. However, the persistent trend towards concentration of population in large coastal urban areas has significantly reduced the demand for education at the newer inland institutions. As a consequence, the hopes of economic development and regional equality are not being realized.

This fragile situation also points out that many institutions have been slow to adapt to changing circumstances. Although the government has the ultimate power to set the *numerus clausus* and the level of funding for each program, institutions have reasonable autonomy to propose new programs and to change existing ones. Moreover, there was nothing preventing them to propose changes in the existing number of places attributed to each program.

This lack of responsiveness may be due to organizational structure and rigidities. Both academic and non-academic staffs in public institutions are considered as civil servants and therefore their labor contracts are strictly regulated nationally. It is very difficult for many institutions to reduce staff in some areas or to move people to new and expanding areas.

However, it may also be the case that institutions have been incapable of developing a robust strategy. Many institutions associate size with prestige and seem more willing to establish or expand programs rather than to reduce or extinguish them. There are also clear signs of insufficient organizational leadership, since some institutions with similar characteristics present different occupation rates and attractiveness. Thus, it suggests that some institutions have been more effective at targeting market opportunities and adjusting to student demand than others.

These findings also suggest that simplistic changes in policy, including regional adjustments, may not be effective. The resistance of students to move to another region, even when they are frustrated in their first priority choices, suggests that any geographical reorganization of program supply will not necessarily be successful. For instance, increasing the supply of certain programs in peripheral institutions may not attract candidates interested in that area from other regions. The data suggest that the regional factor may prevail in their choices.

These results indicate that both institutions and policymakers need to think harder about the factors hindering regional mobility and contributing to some distortions in the system. It may be that the available mechanisms of financial support are not sufficient to overcome the additional costs related to mobility. On a different note, it may be also that students do not consider that it makes a big difference which institution they attend. This may be a result of strong credentialist views among students who believe that the labor market will value the existence of a degree more than its specific content. It may even be that students are not particularly well informed about the quality, content and employability prospects of each program/institution.

In any case, we conclude from our study that there are some significant and complex distortions in the Portuguese match between supply and demand that need to be addressed in order to enhance higher education's contribution for individual and social progress. These distortions also indicate that higher education is one part of a broader and deeper problem in Portugal of a growing concentration of population and wealth in the largest urban areas.

Although the geographical dispersion of higher education was aimed at promoting a more balanced distribution of economic opportunities, its impact was insufficient to break or even to slow down that trend significantly. To a large extent this was not so much a failure of the regional role of higher education institutions as of the whole strategy of a more balanced country from a regional point of view. The reversal of the problems faced by more peripheral higher education institutions requires a change in regional policy to challenge the current patterns of distribution of population and wealth across the country.

Although the problems are significant, the remedies are not obvious. The trend of desertification of inland areas seems hard to reverse. Moreover, the regional actors are rather weak. Portugal is centralized administratively, without strong regional authorities. In the mid-nineties a national referendum rejected the establishment of a regional level of government, though the current political mood suggests that it is likely that a new referendum will take place in the near future. However, at the moment the local political power is mostly restricted to municipalities, which can only have a very limited impact in this respect.

There are three areas that require more attention. First, the government should create stronger stimulus to strengthen the interaction between higher education institutions and local businesses. This should not be restricted to teaching activities, but should also focus on technology transfer and the development of activities to strengthen local economies. Second, higher education institutions should be more candid in their assessment of their strengths and especially of their weaknesses and show a greater willingness to respond to external needs and demands. This change will require more effective modes of governance and leadership and better instruments of public accountability. Finally, the regional role of higher education policy should not be regarded as a separate policy, but rather as part of the whole set of regional policies that may promote a less unequal and more cohesive country.

Notes

[1] This means that the number of vacancies in each program in all higher education institutions (public or private) was restricted and defined annually.

[2] In the analysis we will focus only on the public sector for several reasons. First, the private sector has a much more concentrated regional pattern, thus limiting the range of analysis. Second, the development of the private sector has been mostly motivated by forces other than regional development concerns. Finally, the degree of influence of the government in the public sector is far more explicit than in the private one.

[3] All indicators presented in Section 3 are computed based on administrative data, provided by the Ministry of Science, Technology and Higher Education, for the academic year 2006/2007. Data on all study programs and institutions, such as requisites and vacancies, as well as data on student preferences are available.

[4] Percentages of first choices do not add up to 100% as some colleges, e.g. the nursing schools, are not considered universities or polytechnic institutes. In the year analyzed those colleges received 5% of the first choices.

[5] This indicacor has been adapted from Portela et al. (2008).

[6] However this indicator—occupation rate per district—can be partially misleading in some areas due to recent improvements in accessibility. For instance, the districts of Viana do Castelo, Santarém and Setúbal present low occupation rates, and the local offer is rather low, but the proximity to the largest metropolitan areas (Lisbon and Porto) facilitates the mobility of potential students.

CONTRIBUTIONS TO DEVELOPMENT THROUGH SUPPORT AND INTEGRATION

Hua Li and Chengping Zhao
Chongqing University, China

Chongqing University (CQU), located in Chongqing Municipality in the western part of China, is directly under the State Ministry of Education. It is one of the key national universities receiving significant financial support from the 211 Project (designed to develop 100 top universities for the 21st century) and the 985 Project (created to promote a group of first-class universities in China, now numbering 39). CQU operates with the service oriented position of "taking Chongqing as a home base, finding a foothold in the southwest area, facing the west region, servicing the country, and moving toward the world."

One of the important functions of modern higher education is serving the society, and an integrative approach of production, education and research is a good way for the university to accomplish that goal. CQU considers regional development as an important responsibility, and believes that the institution must keep in mind what business enterprises are thinking in order to focus on the needs for socioeconomic development. To advance this goal of regional development, the university makes contributions for support and seeks integration for development. As a result, both the quality and efficiency of its education are greatly improved in this process. The university has become an important talent pool in the economic construction and social development of Chongqing Municipality, an engine of technological innovation and a think tank for governmental decision making.

This paper takes CQU as a case study of the ways in which a university should serve regional socioeconomic development in order to win support from the local government and thus to realize self-development. This paper briefly introduces the development process of integrating production, education and research, explores the effective model of university serving local economic development and summarizes the basic concepts of higher education serving regional development. Then with detailed facts and data, this paper gives an overall explanation of the experience and achievements made by CQU in actively serving regional socioeconomic development by developing comprehensive superiority, adjusting its disciplines, cultivating student talent and the like. In the end, this paper analyzes the basic experiments made by CQU in serving regional socioeconomic development and shares its experiences with other universities.

Adherence to Serving Regional Development

Taking the wide view of the history of the world higher education, especially ever since Humboldt built Berlin University in the 19th century, the three social functions of higher education have been talent training, scientific research and social service, and have played an increasingly important influence in society, politics, economics, culture and education.

The integration of production, education and scientific research is the basic developmental experiment of world higher education. Early in the 1980s, CQU had clearly realized the importance of these three functions as effective ways in which the university could actively promote regional socioeconomic development. It took the first step in practicing the integrative approach of production, education and research at home, proactively exploring effective models of social service, promoting the close combination of scientific research and talent training with the developing demand of the local and the state and winning self-development and achieving its social value.

In 1982, CQU took its first step in exploring the combination of teaching and scientific research with production by gradually establishing close cooperation with more than 200 large and medium-sized enterprises, local governments and scientific research institutes and by signing agreements with them on personnel training and science and technology cooperation. In 1992, the university proposed and implemented a strategy of integration of production, education and research in terms of points (cooperate with more than 30 large enterprises), lines (extend along the economic zone of the Three Gorges of the Yangtze River), and areas (base in Chongqing, Sichuan, Southwest China, and open to the whole country). In January 1994, CQU established the first university board among the universities in China, with the approval of the former State Education Commission (now the Ministry of Education). The board provided a legal guarantee for pushing the cooperation in running the school with the combination of production, education and research, a practical platform for proactively serving regional economic and social development (Wen 2004).

Chongqing University Board is an organization for consultation, assessment, and evaluation organization for important issues such as institutional management, education and technology. It is a bridge, a tie and a coordination body to keep a long term, comprehensive and close cooperative relationship between the board member units and CQU. The board plays an important role in raising school's educational development funds, and supports the reform and development of CQU. It is a result of the university's adaptation to the socialist market economy system of China. Its main purpose is to explore a new school-running mechanism, with a macro-management government, extensive participation of the society, an independent running of schools and strengthening universities' capacity for serving regional socioeconomic development (CQU Board

Statute, 1997).

In order to function well, the Party Secretary General of Chongqing is elected as honorary president of the Board, the Deputy Vice Mayor of the municipal government as president and some famous academics both at home and abroad as honorary chairmen, such as Feng Yuanzhen, a member of the American Academy of Engineering and the Academy of Medicine, as well as a Fellow of Technology and Ma Lin, a biochemistry expert and former President of the Chinese University of Hong Kong (CQU, 2003).

After more than twenty years' practical exploration of production, education and research (PER) cooperation, CQU came up with a clear concept, that is, firmly taking the road of PER cooperation and servicing regional economic and social development. PER cooperation requires adherence to the guiding principle of "complementing in advantages, pursuing mutual benefits and seeking common development." CQU follows two propositions of thinking what enterprises are thinking and accurate identification of the idea of combining production and research to optimize resources with proper allocation, making the best use of the living resources. Production and research cooperation must pay attention to the three areas of university responsibility for scientific and technological projects, personnel training and the needs of the upcoming research as a link. PER cooperation requires constant innovation and adaptation to maintain effective models and means of cooperation. Moreover, attention must be paid to the following four combinations:

- close combination of undergraduate education model of PER cooperation and the construction of research universities with the improvement of education quality and the cultivation of qualified talents
- close combination with the expansion of scientific research fields and the improvement of academic standards
- close combination with exertion of one's own potentials and

strengthening school-running capabilities

- close combination with the western development and service in regional economic and social development

Among them, "the serving principle" is the guiding principle of universities serving regional development, so as to achieve the "win-win" goal; "two propositions" is the practical foundation and driving source of universities serving regional development, that is to say, the development of the university must meet the demands of the region, company and state strategy; "three focal points" is the basic means and practical carrier of universities serving regional development, that is, to implement it by means of allocating resources and adopting proper cooperative ways, and through concrete scientific exploration, personnel training project and so on; and "four combinations" is the fundamental aim of universities serving regional development and the essential embodiment of devotion for development, that is, achieving the developmental goal of improving the quality of personnel training and strengthening science and technology innovation capacity as well as the overall quality of the university.

Take Root in Chongqing to
Serve Regional Economic and Social Development

Chongqing is a famous historical and cultural city in China, and served as the capital of China during the Second World War from 1937 to 1946. It is also one of the four Chinese cities marked on the world map of the United Nations Hall, and it is one of the four municipalities of China after Beijing, Tianjin and Shanghai. Chongqing is known as a "Mountain City" because of its steep terrain. Located between the more developed eastern cities and the western region with greater natural resources, it is the largest economic center in the upper reaches of Yangtze River, the significant industrial and commercial city of the southwestern region and the hub of communications by land and sea (Introduction of Chongqing, n. d.). The world famous scenery of the Three Gorges of the Yangtze River is mainly located in Chongqing. Chongqing covers an area of 8. 2 million square kilometers (3.17 million square miles) and governs 40 administrative districts (autonomous counties). By the end of 2007, its population had reached 32 million. Chongqing is megacity with the biggest administrative area, the largest population and the greatest number of administrative units of any province or municipality in China. In 2007, the total productive outcome of Chongqing reached 411,182 million yuan or US$ 60.4 million (Chongqing Statistical Bureau, 2008).

Higher education is the driving source of regional economic growth and the essential element of improving regional competitiveness. Higher education must adapt to regional economic circumstances, form local characteristics and serve regional economic and social needs. Ever since the founding of CQU in 1929, it has been closely associated with the construction and development of Chongqing.

Most importantly, in order to let high level universities play their role in the development of China and its regions, the 985 Project provides support for top universities under the jurisdiction of the Ministry of Education and the provincial/municipal/autonomous regional government where the university belongs. More specifically, the Ministry of Education signed a protocol with the Chongqing government in support of CQU, making clear each other's responsibilities and obligations, with the key point of matching contributions of construction funds. This agreement further strengthens the responsibilities and obligations of CQU for the economic and social development of Chongqing.

In recent years, through fully exerting its advantages in personnel training, comprehensive disciplines and scientific and technological innovation, CQU served the regional economic and social development in a number of ways:

1) *Exert its comprehensive superiority and provide support for the decision making of the local government.* According to the basic development concept mentioned above, CQU insists on taking local needs

as the basis for action. Giving full play to its advantages in comprehensive disciplines as well as cross-disciplinary strengths, it provides significant intellectual support in a series of important strategic decisions of Chongqing. For instance, after Chongqing made the decision to speed up its urbanization strategy in 2003, CQU took the initiative to apply discipline advantages in such fields as architecture, planning and municipal administration. It also undertook the task of urban planning and design in more than 40 new rural construction projects totally for free and sent experts to give instruction whenever necessary.

Shortly after the municipal government declared a priority on promoting the construction of a new type of industrialization in Chongqing Municipality, the university began to organize experts to engage in systematic research around important strategic subjects relating to technology platform, industrial structure, industrial layout and comprehensive utilization of resources included in the four key industries, namely automobile and motorcycle industry, equipment manufacturing industry, resource processing industry and the high technology industry. In a timely manner, it made recommendations to the municipal government.

Responding to the local governmental policy of new countryside construction, CQU assumed responsibility for three poor areas as an effort to alleviate poverty. Meanwhile, it called for a group of experts from the CQU Development Research Center and the Sustainable Development Research Institute to study the theories and policies relevant to building of the new socialist rural areas thus laying a solid theoretical foundation for the government to develop correct policies.

In the sphere of promoting environmental and economic development in the Three Gorges reservoir area, many experts were asked to do research on such issues as reservoir management, solid waste treatment, returning farmland to forest in marginal sloping areas and pollution control. Scholars at CQU have completed feasibility studies on such topics as "The City Proper Drainage System Safety and the Sources Control Technology," "Reservoir Medium-sized City Wastewater Treatment Plant Upgrading and Function of the Quality Improvement of Urban Water Technology Research," "The Optimal Operation of Sewage Plant Technology Research on Small City Reservoir Water Drainage Networking," "Wastewater Treatment Research of Key Technologies in the Three Gorges Reservoir Area Food Industrial Park," "Water Pollution Control Technology in the Small Mountain Town" and "Water Pollution Control and Urban Governance Integrated Technique of the Three Gorges Reservoir Area." These research reports provide important technological support for decision making of the municipal government.

What's more, Chongqing University has appointed more than 30 scholars as senior advisers for policy analysis and decision making of the Chongqing municipal government. At the same time, these scholars also make suggestions and proposals, giving full play to their roles as a think tank. As a result, CQU has made a positive contribution to the local economic construction and social development.

2) *Adjust the discipline layout and provide scientific and technological support.* Insisting on responsiveness to the state's strategic need and the region's business demand, CQU has actively adapted to changes in the regional industrial structure through reform and adjustment in its curriculum. For example, it has created more than 30 urgently needed undergraduate majors in fields related to the new type of industrialization and the construction of a modern city, such as vehicle engineering, pharmaceutical engineering and landscape architecture design. In the meantime, it optimizes and promotes the traditional advanced disciplines such as mechanical engineering, architecture, electrical engineering, civil engineering, mining engineering and materials engineering, all of which are closely related to the development of the pillar industries of Chongqing.

CQU also puts forth effort to build 12 principles related to the sustainable development of Chongqing, such as urban planning and architecture in mountainous areas, the development and utilization of mineral energy resources, the environmental protection of Three Gorges reservoir area and economic growth studies in less developed areas of China. It has set up corresponding scientific research bases and provides powerful support for new forms of industrialization of Chongqing.

For instance, in order to support the development of the automobile and motorcycle industry, CQU helped to accelerate the application of new materials and the upgrading of existing products by organizing scientific and technological personnel to form a joint magnesium alloy research group. This group has made a breakthrough in a number of forefront core technologies and key technologies of industrialization in the processing technology and industrialization of magnesium alloy. Therefore, it enables the magnesium alloy products to be widely used in the production of automobiles and motorcycles, military products, hand tools and many other industries in an advanced manner. In 2007, the national magnesium alloy engineering technology research center was set up at CQU.

Chongqing can be called a Bridge Capital because of the large number of bridges spanning the rivers of the area, so the safety of the bridges has become a major social problem. A group of academicians with Prof. Huang Shanglian, member of the Chinese Academy of Engineering, as the leader, has invented and patented a variety of sensors to measure deformation structure/displacement and stress/strain. Based mainly on lasers and fiber optic technologies, the research of structural health monitoring sensors has conquered many critical problems such as sensor accuracy, reliability and engineering applications and integration. The findings have been successfully applied to the Chongqing Dafoshi Bridge and the Shibanpo Yangtze River Bridge and more than ten other bridges. The research team has built the first international long distance monitoring group system of bridge structure, which has provided effective technological support for the monitoring and control of the security of the bridges.

China has a national power development strategy focused on west-east power transmission and north-south networking. In response to this national priority, CQU has confronted a series of challenges for high voltage power transmission, such as large-capacity, long-distance, high-altitude, snow-capped and environmental insulation choice. The laboratory for "High-voltage electrical engineering and new technologies" of CQU accelerates independent technical innovation. After conquering the difficulties of high altitude, filthy, ice, acid rain (fog), dirt and other complex environmental challenges, the laboratory research has made significant high level achievements in insulation and the mechanism of AC-DC discharge. These theoretical accomplishments have been applied widely to the Qinghai-Tibet railway and other key national electrical engineering projects requiring highly effective external insulation of electrical equipment.

3) *Education of highly trained personnel in support of regional development.* The economic competition between the different regions today and in the future is ultimately the competition for human talent. Thus universities should be the cradle for new brainpower and the source of intellectual support for regional economic construction and social development. On the one hand, CQU has been expanding its enrollment scale in Chongqing. In 2007, it enrolled 1964 undergraduate students from Chongqing, an increase of 141%, comparing with 1997. Over the decade, it trained more than 2,500 postgraduate students for Chongqing, occupying 45% of the total number of graduate students, and also trained more than 10,000 undergraduate students, accounting for over 30% of the total number of undergraduates. It is 10% more than the enrollment rate in Chongqing and it plays an important role in the net flow of high level talents in Chongqing.

On the other hand, CQU actively explores new models of school-enterprise and institution-local cooperation in training personnel. According to the demand of regional economic development and enterprise development, CQU has worked with local businesses to operate sub-baccalaureate schools and offer degree and non-degree programs in fields relevant to the local economy. Through these joint efforts, CQU has optimized the personnel structure and enhanced the qualities of staff in those enterprises. Over the decade, CQU has trained more than 1,700 engineering postgraduates in manufacturing, architecture, software and other fields, and more than 3,000 high level talents in economics and management. By offering the machinery engineering and industrial engineering program, construction supervisors training program and 300 other courses, more than 20,000 people have graduated and become the backbone of the economic construction in Chongqing and even in the west (Keep pace, 2007). Meanwhile, CQU also appointed 70 excellent teachers and leaders to take temporary positions in Chongqing district (counties) government; more than 20 young doctors and professors function in such positions as deputy general managers, assistant general managers, deputy directors of technical management division and assistant chief engineers of branch factory in Changan Company, Silian Group, Jianshe Group and other large state-owned enterprises.

CQU Experience

Through its service, CQU has won the appreciation and solid support of the Chongqing municipal government. The future reform and development of CQU is also in the overall planning of Chongqing's economic construction and social development. Chongqing Municipality has given full support and has created an unprecedented good external environment for CQU's development. In the development of 211 Project for the 11th five-year plan (2006-2010), the Chongqing municipal government has invested 82 million yuan for the construction of key disciplines, which is far more than the formerly promised 1:1 ratio with the Ministry of Education. And in the first and second phase construction of 985 Project, the Chongqing municipal government promised to input 240 million yuan matching funds with $1:0.8$ ratio, and 300 million yuan with $1:1$ ratio respectively, which has reached 400 million yuan so far.

In reflecting upon the experiences of CQU's commitment to serving regional economic development, there are some lessons to be shared:

1) *Universities should firmly establish the idea of serving regional development.* CQU's history demonstrates that the development of the institutions cannot be achieved without the support from the regional government, and support from the government greatly depends on the devotion of the school to regional development. Only by correctly handling the relations between service and support, devotion and joint construction and cooperation and development can the university promote its administrative management, service competence, overall capacity and social reputation. Therefore, universities should give priority to the idea of serving regional development, strongly emphasize the establishment and development of good cooperative relations with the local government, and develop a relaxed and harmonious atmosphere.

2) *Set up special units to provide organizational support for regional development.* To guarantee the close cooperation of the university with business and society, the university should establish special institutions to provide overall coordination for related projects within the university. It should specifically manage the cooperation of the university with enterprises, scientific research institutes, financial institutions and local government, and form a comprehensive model of the combination of PER. It should establish a long and stable relationship of complementing strengths and advantages, pursuing mutual benefits and seeking common development. It should carry out cooperation in scientific research, scientific and technological innovation, technical consultation, personnel training, cooperative training and other aspects and make the service develop in depth.

3) *Strengthen disciplinary development that is matched to regional needs.* Effective discipline construction provides the chief strategic

position in the university's development. In an academic institution, disciplines are the basic units of the university, and the development of the university depends on the growth and advancement of its academic programs at the disciplinary level. In a sense, the level of sophistication of the disciplines also determines the level service to regional development that the university can provide. Thus, to meet the important strategic demand of the state and localities, the university should strengthen coordinated academic development to provide intellectual and curricular support that is closely linked with regional needs.

4) *Continually strengthen the capacity of scientific and technological innovation to provide a solid foundation for serving regional development.* Scientific technology is a key productive force, and scientific and technologic advancement and innovation are vital driving forces of economic and social development. Only by continually strengthening scientific and technologic innovation power and capacity can the university maintain its capacity to contribute to the economic and social development of the region in which it is based.

TRANSFORMING URBAN NEIGHBORHOODS THROUGH INSPIRED CIVIC LEADERSHIP: CORNELL URBAN SCHOLARS PROGRAM

John Nettleton, Sarah Smith and Kenneth Reardon
Cornell University, USA

New York City's Challenge

As ongoing corporatization of the world economy generates and sustains increasing transnational investment, the significant shifts in local and regional economies that result propel natural resources, business opportunities and people across national borders at an unprecedented scale. New York and other global cities with advanced business service sectors stand at the heart of this global economic system. As such cities develop and refine financial service industries and related investment mechanisms to retain their economic primacy, the resulting direct and associated economic activity has attracted significant numbers of new immigrants from across the nation and around the globe. In New York City, this influx of new immigrants has dramatically increased the city's total population, which grew from 7.3 to 8 million between 1990 and 2000 and is projected to reach 8.4 million by 2010 and more than 9 million by 2030!

The energy, labor and entrepreneurial activity of the many new immigrant households from Central and South America, the Middle East, Africa and Asia have together helped to revitalize and repopulate many of the city's older and outlying residential neighborhoods, especially those in

The Bronx and Brooklyn that experienced losses during the 1970s and early 1980s often exceeding 10% of their total population. South Bronx neighborhoods at risk from depopulation have risen again, with housing stock rehabilitated through New York City's investment in *in rem* (city-held) properties and the accompanying construction of new townhouses and small, multi-family units. While this trend has revivified sections of neighborhoods throughout New York, such growth has also bolstered demand and highlighted the need to develop and maintain public health, education, housing, transport and cultural services for newly arrived New Yorkers and longstanding residents alike. Mass transit service, while improved, is strained and utility networks in many neighborhoods are increasingly subject to brownouts and service interruptions, the result of increased reliance on telecommunications and a lack of long term investment in essential infrastructure.

This new (and not so new) demand for services presents real challenges for local elected officials and managers, especially senior leadership of the city's public agencies and non-profit organizations. The city's broad network of human service and community based organizations face these challenges, newly constrained by limits in public sector and charitable support. With both New York City's and the state's revenue base overly reliant upon highly paid Wall Street positions, job cuts, consolidation and closure of institutions in banking and finance are causing multi-year budget shortfalls and corresponding cuts in services, social programs and state spending. Such rapid and unbalanced growth masks a growing disparity in household income between the richest and poorest New Yorkers that is among the most pronounced in the U.S. In fact, a subway trip on the #6 train of only five stops (2.4 miles, from Manhattan's 96th Street Station—located in the top-ranked Human Development District in the country—to The Bronx's 3rd Avenue and 138th Street Station in the 16th CD, ranked 422 of 436 among all districts) reveals a gap in mean earnings from $117K (Manhattan) to $35K (The Bronx).

In an environment where available public resources are held steady or declining and need is clear and growing, social service agencies and NGOs in New York City and across the nation continue to confront issues of succession and transfer of leadership brought on by the retirement of a generation of activists and professionals. These individuals' early experience within the social and political movements of the 1960s era has provided a rich base of experience and political education on which their advocacy activities on behalf of the poor and disenfranchised was built. These public servants, both in and out of government, have dedicated their careers to the promotion of neighborhood wealth and a "double bottom line" incorporating economic as well as community indicators and metrics. This mission has proven essential to holistic development and the long term resolution of access to the essentials of human development: a long and healthy life, access to knowledge and a decent standard of living.

A deep concern regarding the retirement of this committed generation of activists who have served the many non-profit and civic organizations providing essential human and social services for New York City's poorest households and communities, led the leadership of The Heckscher Foundation for Children, a major funder of direct services in low-income New York City communities, to take steps to directly address this emerging situation. In 2001, the foundation challenged Cornell University, New York State's land grant university, to establish a public service program that would encourage the best and brightest students to consider public service careers in New York City.

As a land grant institution, committed to the generation and application of knowledge designed to enhance the competitive position of New York State agriculture and manufacturing, Cornell welcomed this opportunity to strengthen the organizational capacity of non-profits and public agencies committed to addressing the critical educational, health care, housing and job training needs of New York City's newest immigrant communities. This effort was a natural extension of Cornell's ongoing outreach programs in New York City that have, in large part, been designed to promote economic and community development in the city's most distressed communities.

Through this new program, Cornell focused significant new resources on rebuilding the social capital of select city neighborhoods by recruiting outstanding students to complete paid summer internships with non-profits serving these areas. In doing so, the campus sought to encourage these and other students to pursue public service careers in New York City following their graduation. This strategy is consistent with the social capital development ideas articulated in Pastor, Dreier, Grigsby and Lopez-Garza (2000, 1-16), Florida's (2002, 1-20) ideas regarding the role talented young professionals can play in promoting urban revitalization in economically challenged communities, and Porter's (1995) arguments regarding the untapped markets that exist within poor and working class communities highlighted in his *Harvard Business Review* article, "The Competitive Advantage of the Inner City."

Creating the Cornell Urban Scholars Program

In the spring of 2002, Kenneth Reardon, Associate Professor in City and Regional Planning, learned of an opportunity to submit a proposal related to youth involvement in public service. Working with Leonardo Vargas-Mendez, Executive Director of the Cornell Public Service Center, and John Nettleton, Senior Extension Associate of Cornell's New York City Cooperative Extension Service, Reardon devised a preliminary proposal for the establishment of a public service-focused summer internship program in New York City which he called the Cornell Urban Scholars Program (CUSP).

This proposal outlined the development of a public service internship program offering undergraduates, regardless of their majors, the opportunity to spend eight weeks each summer working full time in support of the direct service, issue advocacy and community organizing efforts of non-profit organizations and public agencies serving New York City's poorest neighborhoods. The program, as initially conceived, was designed to achieve the following objectives:

- Provide staff support for non-profits serving the city's poorest children, families, and communities;
- Deepen Cornell students' understanding of the structural causes of uneven patterns of metropolitan development and persistent poverty; and
- Inspire Cornell's most accomplished students to pursue public service careers in New York City's most economically challenged communities.

Prior to submitting the CUSP proposal to the Heckscher Foundation, Reardon, Vargas-Mendez and Nettleton met with the senior leadership of Cornell's New York City Cooperative Extension Program to elicit their feedback on the proposal. Members of the extension faculty were highly supportive of this new initiative, offering to assist in locating appropriate student internship placements and in orienting prospective students to the city's non-profit sector and the neighborhoods these organizations serve.

Shortly after the Heckscher Foundation funded the CUSP proposal, Reardon and Vargas-Mendez, who served as the program's co-directors, formed two committees to guide the program's ongoing operation and future development. First, the CUSP Governing Council was established to create policies designed to shape the program's ongoing evolution and to insure its successful institutionalization as a core element of the university's land grant mission. Among those participating in CUSP's Governing Council were the Vice Provost for Land Grant Affairs, the Vice President for Academic and Student Affairs, a Senior Program Office and Major Gifts Manager from the Office of Alumni Affairs and Development, the Executive Director of the Cornell Public Service Center and an Associate Professor of City and Regional Planning. Second, the CUSP

Advisory Board was formed to create a curriculum to prepare students for their New York City public service activities, to recruit students from across the campus for participation in the program and to encourage Cornell's fourteen separate colleges and schools to make financial contributions to the program. For the last seven years, a mix of fifteen to twenty students and faculty have met on a quarterly basis, as part of the CUSP Advisory Board, to guide its ongoing development.

Through the work of the Governing Council, CUSP's activities were brought to the attention of both Cornell University's President and Board of Trustees. They recently incorporated a planned $6 million endowment to support CUSP into Cornell's current capital fundraising campaign. A curriculum-based service learning program had never before been included in the university's capital campaign which has tended to emphasize funding for brick and mortar projects and endowed faculty positions. Over the years, the CUSP Advisory Board has made numerous important contributions to the program. Each year, board members have selected the students who have participated in CUSP's undergraduate and graduate programs. Board members have also shaped the five academic courses that have been developed to prepare students for their New York City fieldwork. Finally, several faculty of the board have contributed to these classes as guest lecturers and supervisors of CUSP students' participatory action research papers.

For the past seven summers, the Cornell Urban Scholars Program has offered 25 to 30 juniors and seniors the opportunity to devote two summer months (four days a week) engaging in public service activities in New York City's most under-resourced neighborhoods. Representing a wide variety of disciplines, these Urban Scholars devote additional time each week to a daylong seminar, focused on the causes, consequences, and alternative strategies for reducing social inequality conducted by a Cornell faculty member. The students, few of whom are initially familiar with the daunting challenges facing New York City's poor and the agencies that serve them, begin their summer as Urban Scholars by participating in a three-day orientation that introduces them to the city's history, geography, politics and economic and social problems.

With startup and continuing funding support from the Heckscher Foundation for Children, CUSP has offered more than 200 undergraduates the opportunity to become participants in critical urban problem solving and community building efforts in New York City. During the past seven years, Cornell undergraduates have worked with:

- Mothers on the Move to challenge the building maintenance practices of absentee landlords in the South Bronx
- Harlem Children's Zone to determine the availability of fresh, healthy and affordable foods in central Harlem
- North Brooklyn Development Corporation to promote the construction of new affordable housing in the rapidly gentrifying Greenpoint community
- Added Value to introduce children to the joy of gardening and the benefits of green building and design
- Growing Up in Cities to support the environmental research and action projects of middle school children
- Cornell's New York City Cooperative Extension Service to design and implement child development courses for new parents
- ACORN to assist residents of the Red Hook Housing Project in remedying a long list of building code violations and public safety grievances
- City Councilwoman Gayle Brewer on a series of land use issues confronting residents and businesses in her Westside district
- City College of New York's Community Design Center to redesign a Robert Moses-era public park in the Highbridge neighborhood of The Bronx and to create a cultural tourism map of Harlem in support of local economic development efforts

The transformative impact of working with New York City's most inspired and committed non-profit and public sector leaders, who are engaged in critical urban problem solving, community building and policy change efforts, has prompted more than 65% of these students to either pursue public service careers in underserved communities upon graduation or enter graduate programs preparing them for such service.

CUSP's Expanding Mission

Encouraged by the program's success in stimulating interest in critical social justice issues confronting New York City and nurturing students' interest in public service careers, participating Cornell faculty have, in recent years, expanded the program in a number of important ways by:

- Establishing a freshman immersion program that introduces undergraduate students with little previous public service experience to the impressive poverty reduction efforts of New York City's most innovative non-profit agencies through a week-long Alternative Spring Break Program.
- Creating a mandatory pre-field preparation course for those accepted as Urban Scholars. This course helps students gain a deeper understanding of the political economy of social injustice, acquire skills needed to support resident-led change efforts and become oriented to the non-profit community of organizations and activists engaged in social justice issues throughout the New York region.
- Developing a web-based mentorship program for students attending the Urban Assembly School for the Urban Environment. Now beginning its second year, this collaboration matches each participating Cornell undergraduate with an 8th grader from the School for the Urban Environment. Roughly 30 Cornell students trade visits (to Bedford-Stuyvesant in Brooklyn and a follow-up visit for 8th graders and their parents to the Cornell campus). A two-

semester progressive education course for Cornell students adds curricular resources to the mix. In addition, faculty and staff from the Knight Writing Center at Cornell have designed a teacher training program and work with the entire 8th grade teaching staff to improve and enhance the writing skills of each 8th grade student. This new two-day teacher training institute in New York City was hosted in 2008 by the Urban Assembly.

- Initiating an annual non-profit career fair that attracts more than 1,200 Ithaca area college students each year, and summer and fall career events in New York City co-hosted by CityYear, Cornell's Public Service Center and the Urban Scholars Program. The first of these afternoon career events held in New York City in fall 2008 attracted more than 65 students, and featured a panel of non-profit organizational leaders and managers made up entirely of recent Cornell graduates.

- Publishing an electronic journal offering students the opportunity to explore the connections between their own service experiences and critical equity oriented public policy issues.

- Staffing the New York City Growing Up in Cities Program that has offered hundreds of middle school children the opportunity to gain a deeper understanding of the urban environment by implementing significant community improvement projects in the neighborhoods where they live.

- Creating an undergraduate concentration in Social Justice Studies comprised of a combination of lecture and field research courses designed to deepen students' understanding of the structural causes of persistent urban poverty.

The Cornell Urban Scholars Program has, in spite of its highly competitive application process, consistently attracted a large number of Cornell's most accomplished students as applicants. The typical CUSP student has an overall GPA of 3.75, has participated in more than six community service organizations and has established at least one social justice effort on campus or in the community.

The success of these undergraduate public service programs led to the establishment of the Graduate Research Fellowship in Children, Family, and Community Development Policy-Making. Since 2004, this program has offered graduate students from across the campus the opportunity to undertake participatory action research projects focused on critical policy issues facing non-profit organizations serving New York City's poor. Each of these students completes a three credit Introduction to Participatory Action Research Methods course prior to spending a summer of service in New York City. Participating students receive a modest weekly salary and housing allowance enabling them to spend the summer working with local community leaders and agency staff to complete their research. In recent years, these students have also benefited from a weekly research seminar held in New York City offered by a Cornell University faculty member.

During the past four years, CUSP's Graduate Research Fellows have undertaken a wide range of challenging research projects at the request of leaders from the city's non-profit and public sectors. Among the topics the fellows have explored are:

- Alternative Strategies for Addressing Sweatshop Conditions in New York City's Garment Industry
- Inclusionary Zoning Strategies for Expanding New York City's Supply of Affordable Housing
- Promoting Child Development through Enhanced Parental Communication Skills
- Examining the Impact of Overcrowding on Public Health Outcomes in Williamsburg, Brooklyn
- Using Advanced Computer Applications to Promote Excellence in Science Education
- Promoting Youth Empowerment Through Engagement in Urban

Environmental Action Projects
- Advancing HIV/AIDS Prevention Through Youth Generated Public Health Campaigns
- Researching Subprime Lending Practices and Mitigation Strategies to Allow Retention of Homes at Risk of Foreclosure

The contributions being made by CUSP graduates to community based change efforts are, in many ways, even more impressive. The following profiles highlight the extra ordinary work being done by a few of CUSP's many alumni.

Austin Kiplinger entered Teach for America following his CUSP experience. Working as an elementary math and science teacher in New York City, Austin decided to commit to a career in urban education. For the past four years, he has taught middle school math and science in an African American school in the Anacostia neighborhood of Washington, D.C.

Terrance McKinley entered Princeton Theological Seminary following his graduation from Cornell, where he earned his Master of Divinity degree. Upon graduating from divinity school, Rev. McKinley was appointed Associate Pastor of Allen Cathedral Church in Jamaica, Queens, where he directs the congregation's many youth and adult education programs that include two highly successful elementary and secondary charter schools. In recent years, Rev. McKinley has supervised two CUSP students involved in his congregation's economic and community development projects.

Dominic Frongilo returned home to Lansing, New York in the Finger Lakes following his CUSP experience working as a community organizer for Brooklyn ACORN. Dominic subsequently ran for Village Council emerging as one of Upstate New York's most eloquent spokespersons and effective advocates for smart growth and green building and design.

Barin Nahvi went to Washington, D.C. following her CUSP experience where she went to work for a private consulting firm focused on improving the efficiency and effectiveness of the nation's network of church-affiliated hospitals. Barin has recently completed her Masters in Health Administration and is working for one of New York City's major medical centers conducting research designed to improve patient care.

Mazie Wright entered the Teach for America Program following her CUSP internship with the New York City chapter of the Facing History and Ourselves Project. Following her Teach for America experience, Mazie joined the faculty of the Kipp Delta School for Excellence in Helena, Arkansas where she currently teaches social sciences and serves as Assistant Principal for this highly successful charter school in one of the poorest regions of the Mississippi Delta.

Program Accomplishments

The consistently large number of applicants that the Cornell Urban Scholars Program receives each year offers clear evidence of the deep, pervasive interest in public service that exists in this generation of college students. The success of the Urban Scholars Program is largely attributable to the challenging and meaningful nature of the public service opportunities that New York City's non-profit leaders have structured for these students. The experience of working shoulder to shoulder with inspired, dedicated and creative non-profit leaders has had a profound effect on each CUSP student. Many former CUSP students have maintained their relationships with their former placement supervisors and co-workers since leaving the program, and placement supervisors routinely speak of their positive experience with students they worked with in years past.

It has been possible to develop quality placements that meet the highest standards of experiential education through the efforts of a very skilled staff that has established strong working relationships with a network of more than 60 non-profit organizations and local government agencies. The staff has chosen to concentrate on developing strong and enduring relationships with a limited number of agencies whose leaderships understand the need to attract talented young people into their organizations, rather than create an extended list of agencies who may simply be looking for inexpensive seasonal help.

CUSP's ability to identify and establish contact with key leaders from the city's most innovative and effective non-profit organizations and public agencies was greatly advanced by the knowledge and relationships with local organizations that the staff from Cornell Cooperative Extension's New York City program possesses. Supported by the Colleges of Human Ecology and Agriculture and Life Sciences, extension programs were first established in New York City in 1948 with a focus on consumer education. Regarded within the national extension system as a flagship urban effort, the New York City extension program has grown and expanded to encompass nutrition and health, urban environment, family and youth development and community development initiatives. The targeted nutrition and health education program, staffed by paraprofessionals who are hired from and work in low income neighborhoods, provides hands on training for income-eligible households reaching thousands of New Yorkers each year.

For well over a decade prior to the inauguration of the Urban Scholars Program, extension staff have involved undergraduate and graduate students in a range of internships, many tied to the successful grant writing efforts that extension staff have turned to augment flat and now declining funding support from the federal government. In the early years of the Urban Scholars Program, several senior extension educators took responsibility for working with campus faculty. They found placements for as many as half of the CUSP students each year and also made significant contributions to the design of CUSP's New York City orientation program and weekly seminar series.

Student evaluations have highlighted the important contribution that CUSP's pre-field preparation courses have made to supporting students' service and learning outcomes. While initially concerned about having to dedicate four credits to such a course, the overwhelming majority of the students indicate that the exposure they received to the fundamentals of experiential education, service learning, field based research, urban ecology and city policy issues made a significant contribution to their service and learning activities in New York City. Students also stressed the important contribution that their participation in the weekly reflective seminar in New York City made to their experience. The seminar offered them an opportunity to: learn about the work being done in a wide variety of non-profits; share, in a safe environment, their placement-related anxieties, fears, and concerns; connect their placement experiences to larger theoretical, methodological and policy issues confronting those seeking to promote a more just city; and finally, to explore New York City's many neighborhoods and non-profits.

From its inception, the CUSP program has benefited from the contributions made by a very active interdisciplinary advisory board comprised of faculty, staff, administrators and students representing each of Cornell's colleges and schools. This group has played an active role in shaping CUSP's curriculum, recruiting students, evaluating applications, advising students on their research, serving as resource persons on their service projects and assisting students in securing meaningful public service jobs following graduation.

Lessons Learned

The Cornell Urban Scholars Program has made significant contributions to the economic and community development efforts of non-profit organizations and public agencies serving many of New York City's poorest neighborhoods. The quality of the organizing, policy analysis and city planning work completed by CUSP undergraduate and graduate students has prompted a significant number of organizations serving these areas to annually request students from the program. The experience these students have had working alongside highly skilled and creative non-profit and public sector managers has caused many of them to focus their undergraduate and master theses and doctoral dissertations on policy questions they first encountered during their New York public service experiences. Three recent CUSP students have succeeded in publishing policy related research papers emerging from their New York City internships in peer reviewed journals in their respective fields. An analysis of the impact of a recently proposed up-zoning of the Greenpoint-Williamsburg waterfront to accommodate new market rate housing, completed by several CUSP students, made a critical contribution to the successful efforts of a church-led coalition to secure an inclusionary zoning policy for this area that will either preserve or create 7,800 units of affordable housing.

Faculty involvement in CUSP as academic advisors and thesis supervisors has prompted several Ithaca-based to redirect a portion of their research and teaching activities to various forms of engaged scholarship in NYC's poorest neighborhoods. CUSP's positive impact on research, teaching and public service activities in the Department of City and Regional Planning, which has served as CUSP's administrative home since its inception, prompted this unit to make a three-year funding commitment to the non-tenure track faculty member who directs the program and to establish its own accredited urban public service semester in New York City during the past fall.

Finally, more than 60% of former CUSP students have either pursued full-time public service opportunities in low income communities or graduate studies to prepare them for such work. It is the profound impact that the program has had upon the post-graduation career plans of CUSP students that has maintained the Heckscher Foundation's involvement in the program.

Urban public service programs, such as CUSP, make great sense for public and private higher education institutions located in or near urban centers that are experiencing significant levels of new immigration.

Non-profit organizations and public agencies serving low income neighborhoods within these communities are being challenged to address the formidable educational, health care, housing and job training needs of new immigrant families during a time when local, state and federal spending for domestic social programs is either shrinking or static. In this context, the contribution that highly motivated and well trained undergraduate and graduate students can make to the organizing, planning, development and service delivery efforts of resource challenged non-profits and government agencies cannot be overestimated.

Future Challenges

The Urban Scholars Program has engendered a strong and positive presence on campus, and has built a national reputation that has spawned successor programs at several other colleges and universities. Despite such impressive accomplishments by the program, and the strong student and faculty support that exist for its core programs, CUSP has been unsuccessful to date in its efforts to secure campus support for its activities. Since its inception in 2002, the Heckscher Foundation has supported the overwhelming majority of the program's operating costs which have, since its initial grant in 2002, continued to ask Cornell to secure or commit matching funds to insure the program's future. The campus's inability to date to design and implement a meaningful development campaign offering matching funding for extramural patrons who might "sign on" to support this effort has put the future of the Urban Scholars Program in jeopardy, particularly given the unstinting and consistent funding by the Heckscher Foundation for the past seven years. This situation is not unusual, as a large institution—especially an educational one—considers the transition and movement of a program from "demonstration" status to standing as part of the school's regular offering and a place at the table as a full fledged academic program. Many, if not most foundations and charitable organizations, offer start-up and demonstration funding support, but such purse strings are neither unlimited nor timeless.

After seven years of growth, development and success, the Urban Scholars Program has proven its worth, mettle and relevance in both university and community settings and clearly merits the support of the wider university community. The potential loss of CUSP due to a lack of institutional funding would be a terrible blow to undergraduates seeking opportunities to explore and pursue meaningful public service careers. The death of such a widely copied and frequently cited program would also signal a withdrawal of and important resource and asset for non-profit and public agencies serving New York City's low income communities.

The Urban Scholars Program has represented an important and valued source of talented, skilled, highly motivated and youthful staff. Finally, if Cornell, as the state's land grant university, fails to find the modest resources needed to support this highly acclaimed public service program it could prove embarrassing as the university aggressively pursues, among its many civic minded alumni and allies, its current $4 billion capital campaign that allocates little to its often-cited land grant mission.

INTEGRATED WATERSHED MANAGEMENT AND POLICY ENTREPRENEURS: THE CASE OF THE AYUQUILA-ARMERÍA RIVER BASIN

Edgar E. Ramírez de la Cruz and Georgina Caire Martínez
University of Guadalajara, Mexico

Promoting rural development is a challenge in terms of both public policy making and institutional design for governance (OECD, 2007). Facing this challenge requires going beyond economic policies that promote subsidies targeted at particular economic sectors. As a response to this challenge, the regional approach to rural development proposes that natural resources must be the foundation of regional cohesion and the main element to consider in reducing rural poverty. This approach places special consideration on the relationship between individuals and property rights associated with natural resources (land, water, vegetation, aquaculture, forest etc.). In addition, the regional approach observes property rights as a result of historical, cultural, and institutional factors in order to define strategies for sustainable management of natural resources (Sepulveda et al., 2003).

In line with the regional approach, the Integrated Watersheds Management (IWM), Natural Protected Areas, and Ecological Planning are instruments for addressing environmental problems of an entire territory. The common features of these regional approach methods, including IWM, is the participatory management approach (bottom-up) which enables planning and coordinated implementation of public policies. IWM attempts to find comprehensive solutions by taking into consideration the environmental functionality of basins, the ability of its natural resources and involving key stakeholders within and outside the basin. By using the basin as a management unit, it is possible to prevent or solve problems related to water pollution, fisheries, increasing cost of water, flooding and public health issues. However, the IWM faces two important challenges. First, its implementation requires securing the cooperation of stakeholders affected. These stakeholders are social and private organizations as well as governmental agencies with shared interests for the watershed; they can also provide leadership, experience, information, economic resources, property rights or production systems that are needed for adopting IWM. The second challenge is planning and modifying human activities to make them adequate for the environmental conditions and the natural features of each area of the basin. In other words, this challenge requires achieving convergence between productive uses and conservation of resources.

This chapter presents the case of the Ayuquila-Armería river basin in Mexico concentrating on the role played by the University of Guadalajara (U of G), a public academic institution, in overcoming these challenges. In the case of the Ayuquila-Armería basin, the involvement of the university becomes important for two reasons. First, it allowed objective scientific knowledge about the particular problems of the basin to override political and economic interests of the other parties involved and provided solutions characterized by an innovative technological approach. Secondly, the university's ability to build stronger and permanent networks with the private sector and the rest of the community helped to overcome the limited networking practices developed by governmental actors. The study presented in this chapter suggests that universities can get involved in their communities not only through the production of relevant scientific knowledge and technology but also by encouraging researchers to act as policy entrepreneurs. In their role as policy entrepreneurs, researchers can facilitate the construction of agreements and adoption of feasible solutions for dealing with regional development issues.

The University of Guadalajara

U of G is the second largest public university in Mexico. According to its mission, it generates, transmits, and applies knowledge; guided by principles of social solidarity, respect for human dignity, and responsibility for communities and their environment. In order to perform its mission, U of G is structured as a network of university centers with presence in the entire state of Jalisco. This particular structure is result of a fundamental reform that took place in 1989, intended to improve the quality of education and connection of research production with the needs of the different communities in the state.

The reform attempted to address various problems identified in diverse forums (Espinoza & Medina, 1997). The main problems identified in these forums were a highly centralized administrative structure, lack of connection between research and community needs, and excessive concentration of research centers and academic programs in the metropolitan area of Guadalajara.

In order to deal with these issues, U of G created a new structure to provide more academic opportunities in the various regions of the state. In this new structure the university is divided between semiautonomous university centers of two kinds. The first kind is a thematic classification, which applies to all centers in the metropolitan area of Guadalajara. This classification created six centers that concentrate on such areas as social science natural science, and health science. The second classification of centers is by regions. In this classification there are eight regional centers that provide specific academic programs tailored to the needs of the community and are intended to produce research that corresponds with the location of the center.

It was under the dynamic of this restructuring that a laboratory, formally established in the university in 1985, was reallocated. The laboratory, a very small unit of the university, was created to perform basic and applied scientific research in biology and forest plantations, and intended to train human resources for ecological protection. The laboratory changed its location from Guadalajara city to El Grullo city with the intention of being integrated to the social and regional dynamic of the Manantlán region. The "Laboratorio Natural Las Joyas de la Sierra de Manantlán" was the foundation of what later became the Manantlán Institute, a central actor in establishing integrated watershed management in the Ayuquila-Armería River Basin. The role of researchers from this center will be discussed in the remainder of this chapter.

Integrated Watershed Management in Mexico

A watershed is the total area where surface water drains into a river, lake or wetland. Various natural processes develop in a watershed, but the hydrologic cycle is the central process. This process transfers water from rainfall towards the earth's surface, forming streams of surface water. Part of this water infiltrates the subsoil by underground streams, while other portions evaporate or feed the vegetation. Water quality depends on the physical, chemical and biological characteristics that result from the watershed and its ecosystem, transformed by human interaction. Human activities generate environmental impacts ranging from pollution to transformation of the natural balance in the watershed.

The IWM helps to avoid such problems through comprehensive solutions. In addition to planning and managing water resources, it incorporates all the processes involved in the functional balance of the basin affecting water quality. In other words, it includes a comprehensive and integrated assessment of the impact of human activities on the biophysical resources of a watershed. Otherwise, watershed management would be limited only to administering the use of available water without addressing those aspects that ensure conservation and quality as products of a hydrologic system which must include soil and vegetation.

Several studies indicate the need for improving environmental protection in Mexico. Past programs and activities have typically been disconnected and unable to curb the growing deterioration of water resources (Vargas & Mollard, 2005). Given the distribution of land ownership in Mexico, environmental protection requires social participation. For instance, communally owned land can be used for environmental conservation only if there is a consensus in the community to approve conservation projects. Since conservation frequently competes with productive uses of land, building consensus around environmental projects is a major challenge in basins where land is particularly scarce. For that reason, projects of environmental protection must be strategically focused to avoid becoming a source of political conflict in the community.

In this sense, the main advantage offered by the watershed approach in Mexico is the possibility of considering the cumulative effects of socioeconomic processes that impact the natural balance of each basin. In addition, it creates an environmental management system based on cooperation and coordination of public and private actors that takes into consideration the environmental conditions of each basin. By doing this, IWM improves the utilization of natural resources for productive purposes, and seeks to prevent and control processes of water pollution and promote the conservation and restoration of ecosystems. This instrument uses the sub-basin and micro-basin as subunits of study, planning and implementation.

In the next section, we present the case of the Ayuquila-Armería river basin in Mexico. In this case, the institutional arrangement that implemented IWM was created with substantial contribution from U of G. A major force was the Manantlán Institute of Ecology and Biodiversity (Instituto Manantlán de Ecología y Conservación de la Biodiversidad, MIEB), a unit of the university since 1985. In addition to describing the biophysical characteristics of the basin, we present the social processes that led to the adoption of IWM in the basin, highlighting the participation of academics in strengthening social networks.

The Case of the Ayuquila-Armería River Basin

The river basin Ayuquila-Armería has an area of 9,803 square kilometers which covers 30 municipalities in two states, and is home to approximately 490,000 inhabitants; Three quarters of its population lives in urban areas and the remaining 26% is distributed in 373 rural localities. Commercial agriculture and the sugar industry are the economic base of the area. The Ayuquila River is the main source of water for agriculture and domestic consumption. More than half of the basin is covered by forests and rainforest with a wide range of vegetation and biodiversity. The agricultural area is located in the lower basin with the main crops being sugar cane, agave, cantaloupe, tomato and chili pepper.

By 1985, it was evident that the economic development of a region that benefited from strong industrial and agricultural activity was exploiting existing dams in the upper basin. This development had a series of negative impacts on downstream communities that make use of water for human and agricultural consumption. For instance, high pollution levels prevented the inhabitants from fishing in the river, which impacted even more on their already high poverty levels. An increase in the number of molasses spills into the waters of the Rio Ayuquila by the sugar cane mill Melchor Ocampo was the main cause of pollution and the reason for demonstrations and protests of the villages hardest hit by its effects. However, social demonstrations were not sufficient for the mill to take actions to solve the pollution. It took a combination of local citizens and university researchers to arrive at a politically and technically feasible solution.

Three factors played a major role in reversing the problems of pollution in the river basin, but policy entrepreneurs are important in all three areas. Policy entrepreneurs are individuals willing to invest their time, resources and reputation in order to advance their ideas and convert them into public policies. In this case, researchers became directly engaged with the communities in which they conducted research and became policy entrepreneurs. In this capacity, university researchers contributed to generating solutions to regional problems of pollution caused by the absence of IWM. The three factors are the creation of the Sierra de Manantlán Biosphere Reserve (SMBR), the foundation Inter-municipal Initiative for Comprehensive Management of the Ayuquila River Basin (IICMARB, www. ayuquila. org), and the creation of the Ayuquila-Armería River Basin Commission (AARBC). These factors are presented in detail next.

Table 7.1 *Abbreviations of organization names*

AARBC	Ayuquila-Armería River Basin Commission
IICMARB	Inter-municipal Initiative for Comprehensive Management of the Ayuquila River Basin
MFB	Manantlán Foundation for Biodiversity
MIECB	Manantlán Institute for the Ecology and Biodiversity
NWC	National Water Commission
SERN	National Secretary of Environment and Natural Resources
SMBR	Sierra de Manantlán Biosphere Reserve
SSLJ	Scientific Station "Las Joyas"
U of G	University of Guadalajara

First, in the creation of SMBR, MIEB researchers were able to assist in resolving social conflicts through direct participation with local communities and introduction of an unbiased and objective perspective. MIEB promoted the creation of institutions for the preservation of forests in the upper part of the watershed and at the same time established strong links with academics, especially from the SMBR, and with local and municipal authorities. Secondly, IICMARB began as a social movement championed by MIEB researchers and other community leaders to address pollution problems arising from the disposal of solid waste in areas near the river (for more information on the IICMARB consult its website (http://www. ayuquila-armeria. col. gob. mx, and Diaz 2005). Thirdly, the confluence of legal changes provided by the National Water Act (NWA) of 1992 and the existence of academic and social networks contributed to the creation of the Ayuquila-Armería River Basin Commission (AARBC) in October 1998. AARBC was created as a forum to address issues of common interest, with legal authority provided by the NWA (Román & Silva, 2006). These factors are elaborated in detail next.

Sierra de Manantlán Biosphere Reserve (SMBR)

The Ayuquila-Armería River is born north of the watershed in the Sierra de Quila and covers a distance of 240 *km* from the top (3,290 meters above sea level) to its mouth on the coasts of Colima, forming six sub-basins. The basin covers five protected natural areas: the forest and animal protection areas Sierra de Quila and El Jabalí, the Nevado de Colima National Park, the Natural Resources Area of Las Huertas de Comalá and Sierra de Manantlán Biosphere Reserve (SMBR). The intervention of U of G was instrumental in the creation of SMBR.

Since the creation of the Scientific Station Las Joyas (SSLJ) in 1985 in the Manantlán Mountains, in the heart of the basin, university investigators established relations with communities along the river with the aim of carrying out projects of sustainable management within the region. At the same time, researchers informed governmental agencies about the nature of the problem, helping to create institutional solutions to the pollution problems and natural conflicts between economic activities, without affecting economic development in the region. As a direct result of the mediation between the community and governmental agencies, the first great accomplishment of SSLJ was the creation of the Sierra de Manantlán Biosphere Reserve in the region. SMBR was established by a presidential decree on March 23,1987, with U of G, through MIEB, responsible for drafting the Plan of Natural Resource Management.

Considering the progress and achievements of SSLJ in cooperation with the community, in 1993 the University of Guadalajara elevated the SSLJ to the rank of research institute. The new institute was named the Manantlán Institute of Ecology and Biodiversity (MIEB), and was provided with a more appropriate legal framework for achieving its goals. The new legal capacities allowed MIEB to increase its influence and involvement with the community by becoming closely involved with managing SMBR in 1994 when the federal government created the Directorate of SMBR. The director's responsibility from the beginning was coordinating the actions of stakeholders, such as other government agencies, communities, land owners, social organizations and academic institutions in the area in order to implement the management plan.

Sergio Graf, a specialist in biology, had already produced various community development projects for MIEB when he was appointed as the first Director of SMBR. Since the early diagnoses, it was clear that the situation presented significant challenges to restore the 72 *km* of the river's flow across SMBR and that the problem far exceeded the formal functions of the director's office. In order to explore the situation, researchers at MIEB conducted investigations to verify the existence of pollutants into the river, which produced evidence to support claims against the sugar cane activity and the mill. The results of these investigations provided valuable information to technical committees created during the early years of the directorate. These technical committees were formed at the community level to organize workshops and meetings to show the interaction between productive activities of the mountain communities and river pollution. This contact between researchers and communities helped organize the concerns of the population before the authorities made the institute a key broker between communities and public authorities to solve the pollution problem.

While pollution problems had prevailed for decades, the first approach taken by the coastal communities bordering SMBR was a series of participatory workshops which led to the radicalization of their position. For instance, communities threatened to block access to the mill and burn sugar cane fields. However, advice from the Directorate of the Reserve and researchers of MIEB guided them to create the Committee for the River's Defense in order to channel their frustration and to create more institutional capacity in communities to carry out actions to restore the river.

The needs for information and research that emerged at the beginning of the process were met in large part through the network of researchers from U of G. For example, in 1996 Professor Luis Manuel Martínez began coordinating a research program on water quality and conducted several studies to find evidence of water pollutants. The main sources of pollution were identified: disposal of solid waste into the river by residents and municipalities, municipal wastewater pollution, and highly toxic agrochemicals produced by agricultural activities. The chemical composition of water was causing skin diseases among the population as well as loss of aquatic biodiversity (Martínez et al., 1998; Santana et al., 1996).

Despite the community actions and agreements established with local authorities, however, there was no substantial change in water quality. The most significant source of pollution remained the mill and communities' sewage. It seemed impossible to pressure the mill's managers to take action to correct the problem, given the importance of this industry for the economy of the region. In addition, sugar cane farmers were opposed to closing the sugar mill, given the economic implications for them, in open opposition to the interests of affected communities. In March 1998, an accident caused a spill of 5,000m^3 of molasses into the river reaching nearby farmland, irrigation canals and irrigation water sources from the Ayuquila River. The environmental impact reached riverside communities of Colima who then again threatened to destroy the sugar cane mill.

The Director of SMBR decided to bring the issue before the

environmental authority at the federal level where it was decided to fine the mill under various charges of pollution. This action forced the company's managers to sit down to negotiate the need for new technologies to reduce pollution of the river caused by their wastewater. The university invited Cuban specialists to the region who proposed solutions to the problem. Surprisingly, the recommendations were not only cheap but also allowed the company to reduce costs in the short term. The recommendations created for the first time the possibility of finding a mutually beneficial solution for the pollution problem. This solution facilitated cooperation among all major stakeholders: the managers of the mill and sugar cane producers who wanted to protect their own economic interests, and the academic and other communities who championed the protection of biodiversity and the need to ensure a better quality of life for inhabitants (for more information on this, see the e-case study at http://onlinelearning. unu. edu/ayuquila/main. html).

With the intention of finding alternative models for efficient water use in the mill, meetings were held with administrators of the mill, government authorities, academic researchers and sugar cane producers from the community. The introduction of new technology and the consequential changes in the processes required the use of reclaimed water. In order for the sugar cane producers to accept changes, researchers at U of G conducted critically important investigation on the impact of using reclaimed water from the mill (Martínez et al., 2002, 31). At first, some farmers refused to use reclaimed water from the sugar cane mill for irrigation because they believed that the chemical composition of the water could affect their crops. However, research conducted by MIEB demonstrated that the water was safe (Martínez et al., 2000, 45) and showed that the new system achieved both a more efficient use of water and a decrease in pollution in wastewater discharges. The cooperation from farmers showed confidence in the work of the academic institution (Martínez, interview).[1] In the end, the impact was easily observable on the physical characteristics of water and especially in the resurgence of aquatic biodiversity.

The Intergovernmental Initiative for the Comprehensive Management of the Ayuquila-Armería River Basin (IICMAARB)

This partnership, driven by MIEB and the Directorate of SMBR, was created in 2001 with the participation of eight municipalities (now 10) and supported by the Secretary of Rural Development of Jalisco, Director of SMBR, U of G, and the Manantlán Foundation for Biodiversity (MFB). Among these organizations, FBMO requires special mention. This foundation was created in January 2000 by researchers at the U of G in order to complement the efforts of governmental and academic institutions and to work directly with the local population. Especially, this organization helps to develop and maintain the scientific, technical and economic cooperation and participation between public and private actors to achieve the objectives of biological conservation and social development. In addition, it raises funds from alternative sources, such as the Gonzalo Rio Arronte Foundation, the Mexican Fund for Nature Conservation, the World Wildlife Fund and the Nature Conservancy (Jardel, Santana, Graf & Garcia, 2008, 11).

In carrying out its duties, IICMAARB was supported by the National Water Commission (NWC) and the National Secretary of Environment and Natural Resources (NSENR). The aim of its creation was to consolidate an association to involve and support citizens and to strengthen local capacities for environmental management. So, in coordination with federal and state governments, the initiative has focused primarily on three goals: 1) reducing the negative impact of municipal wastewater, 2) improving the management of solid waste and 3) promoting environmental education in the society to prevent pollution and restore ecosystems. Researchers and students from the U of G were the main contributors to the environmental education effort.

However, as in any social enterprise that involves changes in the power structure and resource allocation, these processes have not been free from conflict. Problems associated with financing are among the most common. Since IICMAARB has no legal authority to enforce agreements or levy taxes, there has been a need to use alternative financing instruments from public and private sources, such as the IICMARB trust and the MFB. The process has also required strengthening policy networks in order to generate more certainty about the stability of funding and to facilitate a constant reassurance of the commitment of governmental authorities to informal agreements (Graf, interview). The lack of formal rules of accountability has also led to confrontations given the lack of transparency in the use of public resources.

For instance, representatives from the communities of Ayotitlán and Cuzalapa consider the land currently occupied by the scientific station and SMBR in Las Joyas taken from them without proper compensation and that the natural reserve has been managed without transparency. In addition, they consider that their opinions have not been taken into account when making decisions about management of financial resources, especially those coming from international organizations. These communities believe researchers control MIEB and the Directorate of SMBR according to their own interests and that MFB is part of a strategy to get funding for projects directed exclusively by those organizations (Gonzalez, 2007).

Despite these problems and criticisms, however, international public opinion formed by the majority of stakeholders, the U of G, foreign academic institutions, and international NGOs have provided valuable support to give continuity to the project. Among other contributors to this project of IWM, the Universities of Wisconsin and Illinois, the State of Wisconsin through the Department of Natural Resources, Credit Valley Notary Authority of Canada, and the Ford Foundation have provided valuable support (Graf, interview). In addition, the contribution of IICMAARB has been fundamental in the creation of an institutional arrangement that formally implements an IWM approach in the Ayuquila-Armería River Basin: the Ayuquila-Armería River Basin Commission.

Ayuquila-Armería River Basin Commission

The main strategy of AARBC is to coordinate efforts by defining strategic goals and objectives that incorporate priorities and social needs of participants with the environmental functionality of the basin. To ensure the existence of a shared vision among the federal government, states and municipalities, AARBC is formed by participants from all levels of government. In addition, social groups are represented by a number of organizations and foundations. AARBC has shown an important capacity to implement the principles of the IWM by facilitating the dialogue between water users and "water producers." The participation of the owners of the high sections of the basin organized through the Natural Protected Areas has successfully contributed to forest conservation and sustainable management that ensures sustainable water production in the long term.

Also, AARBC created the operational management trust, involving the federal government and Jalisco and Colima states. This organization acts as the executive arm of AARBC. The trust is responsible for executing agreements and carrying out operational activities and projects that go beyond the legal capacities of the three levels of government involved. This executive branch has become essential to the consolidation of AARBC, although its existence depends upon the annual renewal of the agreement among the funding levels of governments.

AARBC meetings take place every two months, alternating between headquarters in Jalisco and Colima. Various agreements have been made to coordinate actions and manage projects related to water management. To discuss the problems affecting the watershed, the commission set up four specialized working groups: water management and distribution, water sanitation, integrated management of natural resources, and water and forest culture.

In this group, the participation of IICMARBA has been remarkable for the development of the Integrated Solid Waste Program. This project includes important measures to promote a culture of water and forest conservation. Its website (www. ayuquila. org) also shows the results of the program and various activities to promote environmental education. The activities are part of a strategy that promotes communication across different groups to inform them about the problems and proposed solutions in the basin. The communication strategy uses a variety of media such as websites, neighborhood demonstrations, workshops, conferences, audiovisual resources, songs, plays, signs, reviews, buttons and video clips.

Since its beginning, AARBC has been aware of the need to producing reliable information for decision making (such as establishing lines of action, agreements, monitoring and assessments). The university through MIEB has contributed significantly to this cause with studies related to the ecology of the basin. Also, in order to disseminate information and to be more transparent, AARBC has created a website (http: // www. ayuquila-armeria. col. gob. mx), which lists the agreements, topics for discussion, and the results of various studies. It also reports on the state of resources in the basin and provides starting points for subsequent decisions and actions. The commission has conducted studies with the expectation of developing an instrument to guide the decisions and actions to improve water quality and assist in the management of the resource for different uses. Also, it is expected that these studies will identify critical environmental areas that require attention, establishing strategies for working with people directly involved.

Regarding the implementation of actions, AARBC acknowledges that, given the institutional framework that defines powers and duties of each governmental agency, division of labor for the implementation of actions must respect the scope of actors involved, whether they are governmental actors, water users, communities and social actors, or other professional associations (Martínez et al., 2005).

Gradually, these actions have resulted in a reduction of pollution of the river from both agro-industrial discharges and solid waste, better ecological conservation of forest resources, and development of social capital and increasing environmental education. It has also produced useful and reliable information for decision making. All these actions have positively impacted the water quality in the Ayuquila River, reinstating the native fisheries after two decades of total absence of aquatic life.

While the progress achieved by the various activities along the basin represents significant results in the regional context, it is still facing challenges in achieving the environmental balance of the basin. Among these challenges, AARBC needs to address the processes of deterioration in the high basin that increase the risk of flooding of villages and crops by the overflowing river in the lower parts. It is also important to address municipal wastewater and sanitation as well as conflicts arising from redefinitions of property rights. Finally, there is a substantial increase in the area of agave cultivation where soil conservation is not being practiced, resulting in a loss of approximately 20 tons of soil a year.

Final Considerations

The ultimate goal of integrated management of watersheds is to find ways to bring together private and public interests. This involves finding the point of balance between conservation of natural resources and productive use through participation and consensus (social feasibility). To reach this point, it is necessary to assess the various tradeoffs between actors and to create mechanisms to compensate the groups that lose with a particular form of public goods.

For instance, considering the watershed as a collective good that must be preserved for public benefit, one may apply the solution presented by Ostrom (1990) for the "tragedy of the commons": promoting institutional plans or agreements emanated from the dialogue and the commitment of the community itself, rather than resorting to attempts to impose state rules and incentives for the management of common resources (Evans, 2004; Portes, 2006). In the case of the Mexican basin, however, the law and institutional arrangements differentiate between actors when defining property rights and legal authority of governmental actors to intervene in natural resource management. Therefore, implementing IWM requires the creation of a particular institution that will facilitate governance. In designing such an institution, actors must consider how the current institutional arrangement facilitates or hinders coordination. This institutional design can only be performed by the active participation of policy entrepreneurs that understand current property rights.

The case presented here showed that public universities can create a positive environment for supplying policy entrepreneurs (in the form of researchers) with the capacity and skills needed to act as policy entrepreneurs (Mintrom, 2000; Schneider, Teske & Mintrom, 1995). With the decentralization process, the university moved the location of a laboratory from the urban metropolis to the rural community. By placing MIECB in the heart of the environmentally endangered area, U of G transformed the structure of the network of stakeholders, which led researchers to become active policy entrepreneurs (Schneider, Teske & Mintrom, 1995). The new structure of the decision making network facilitated the flow and quality of information. This network also contributed to spread the good reputation of participants, a fundamental factor for the formation of cooperative partnerships based on trust between regional organizations (Schneider et al., 2003). In addition, by promoting the laboratory to a research center, and more recently to a department, the university provided researchers with financial resources, staff and a legal framework more suitable to allow researchers to become policy entrepreneurs.

This effect is exemplified with the creation of IICMAARB, where researchers created a network that operates at different levels to implement an IWM. This network has played a decisive role both in building capacity as well as in implementing actions and projects. Investigators and U of G have transitioned from mere observers of the phenomenon and producers of scientific knowledge to active participants leading in the provision of institutional arrangement at two levels: constitutional and operating (Ostrom, 1990, 53). At these two levels, they became policy entrepreneurs who contributed to strengthening institutional capacities through persuasion and training of local authorities. Through their participation, researchers contributed to the formation of policy networks that facilitated cooperation among local authorities and allowed the adoption and implementation of projects that achieved a balance between conservation and economic development.

We mentioned that according to its mission, U of G is intended to generate, transmit and apply knowledge, guided by principles of social solidarity and responsibility for communities and their environment. U of G contributed to its mission by helping to reverse pollution in the Ayuqila-Armería river basin in two ways. First, U of G encouraged researchers to produce relevant knowledge for the community by placing research centers and institutes in geographic areas that could directly benefit from the new knowledge. Secondly, U of G provided institutes with the legal authority to establish binding agreements, which facilitated the independence of researchers and enhanced their active role as policy entrepreneurs.

In addition, this case illustrates the extent to which scientific knowledge, produced by university researchers with reputation of being unbiased and without conflict of interest, produces findings that inform debates and can be used for building consensus. These replicable research findings provided credible arguments for stakeholders. At the same time, because the new knowledge was seen as unbiased information, it encouraged cooperative behavior and forced politically motivated actors to identify common interests and revaluate their actions in the context of a broader perspective, the regional context. Moreover, the case illustrates how policy alternatives produced by research provided solutions with higher probability of being successfully implemented. These alternatives were often technically and politically feasible because they tended to incorporate the social and cultural complexity of the problem as well as the technical complexity. In addition, when the research incorporated the perceptions of the community in regard to the sources of a problem, researchers ensured that the proposed solutions balanced the need for both social and economic development.

However, resources for funding the activities within this model of governance represent a continuous struggle for researchers. U of G has provided many resources for researchers that facilitate their commitment with the promotion of this form of governance. Nevertheless, environmental conservation and IWM are not the only missions of the university. In fact U of G has multiple departments and projects with which MIEB and its researchers have to compete in order to maintain a continuous flow of resources. In this regard, the nature of IWM requires researchers to produce substantive results that encourage work and commitment of key players within the university, which is a major challenge for the survival of research institutes in public universities.

Notes

[1] Three interviews were conducted between March 7 and 9, 2006 with the following individuals:

Luis Manuel Martínez, Profesor Investigador IMECBIO-CUS de la UG.

Sergio Graf, Director of Fundacián Manantlán para la Diversidad de Occidente entrevista realizada en la Ciudad de Colima

Salvador García, Profesor Investigador, IMECBIO-CUS de la UG, Centro de Acopio Municipal, El Grullo, Jal.

The interviews were conducted for a different research project; however, the information collected was used for informing this case given the rich information they provided. In addition, these interviews provided valuable information about the role played by researchers as social and environmental entrepreneurs.

STUDENT ENGAGEMENT IN COMMUNITY DEVELOPMENT

John C. Pine, Jan Shoemaker, Bruce G. Sharky,
Elizabeth Mossop and Marsha R. Cuddeback
Louisiana State University, USA

Louisiana State University (LSU) has encouraged and supported faculty to engage their graduate and undergraduate classes in local community problem solving. Linking university classes in addressing real world problems has become increasingly important as the state of Louisiana and its coastal communities have struggled to recover from Hurricanes Katrina and Rita in 2005. Because many faculty members appreciate the value of engaging university students in addressing community problems and issues, they have structured opportunities for students to assist in the recovery process. Helping local officials to understand the nature of the problems that they have been facing and articulating alternative strategies to address these problems has helped move the recovery process forward. This chapter provides examples of how classes from LSU have been structured to combine course activities with local community recovery efforts following Hurricanes Katrina and Rita.

Hurricanes Katrina and Rita

Hurricane Katrina hit the Louisiana coast approximately 50 miles south of New Orleans in the early morning hours of August 29, 2005. The storm surge and high winds pushed water into coastal areas, overtopping levees in many areas and flooding more than 80% of New Orleans as a result of numerous breaches in the levee protection system in Orleans, St. Bernard and Plaquemines Parishes (Note that in Louisiana, the term "parish" is the same as a county in other states). Much of the population of greater New Orleans was displaced and returned to their communities to find extensive destruction. More than 150,000 residential structures were flooded by the storm in Orleans Parish and much of the commercial and residential structures in St. Bernard and Plaquemines Parishes were destroyed by the flooding. Many college students from the New Orleans area made arrangements to continue their studies at institutions throughout the United States and abroad. LSU accommodated many of these displaced students at the Baton Rouge campus.

A few weeks following Hurricane Katrina, a second powerful storm hit the western part of Louisiana, again causing extensive displacement and destruction. Rural coastal communities in Cameron and Vermillion Parishes were heavily damaged by the hurricane and the city of Lake Charles also experienced widespread damage to both residential and commercial structures from the storm.

The two storms resulted in the largest response and recovery effort to a natural disaster in the United States. Citizen and community expectations have been high but progress has been slow. Assistance from many professional and non-profit groups has been a significant factor in community recovery. LSU, along with many other higher education institutions throughout the United States, has extended assistance in many forms to coastal communities impacted by the storms. The campus opened its doors to provide a special needs shelter for displaced residents from the New Orleans area, ran a medical and mental health short term hospital in the multi-purpose basketball arena, housed numerous household pets in another arena, allowed agencies to set up temporary housing and service space on available property and provided housing to volunteers who staffed these response centers.

Many faculty and staff also supported the response and recovery efforts by state and federal agencies by supplying technical weather, remote sensing and mapping services. Finally, students and faculty volunteered to support many of the response agencies and shelters in the community. During the long term recovery process, the LSU Agricultural Extension Service has supported hazard mitigation community recovery efforts through their network of field based staff. This chapter addresses just a part of LSU's response to Hurricane Katrina and Rita by focusing on LSU students' contributions to the coastal community recovery effort as they met course requirements for selected classes.

Engagement in Hurricane Recovery and Community Development

Numerous academic units throughout LSU have provided students with opportunities to assist communities in understanding the nature and extent of the problems associated with the recovery process and in developing strategies to address these problems. Several examples of student engagement are provided here to illustrate the value of engaging students in community recovery initiatives and how this can contribute to a university educational experience. Four examples of community engagement projects are provided including:

- assessing the impacts of the 2005 storms on LSU students (Honors College) ;
- reconnecting the "Broken City" of Lake Charles (Landscape Architecture) ;
- an urban landscape laboratory (Landscape Architecture) ; and
- community planning for coastal communities in New Orleans (Architecture) .

Through the scholarship of engagement, service learning faculty and students are connecting academics to the community's most pressing problems. The vision of service learning at LSU involves advancing civic responsibility and social accountability through effective integration of academic instruction, research and community engagement. It promotes the integration of teaching, research and service to enhance learning and encourages civic responsibility and social accountability. Since January 2008, approximately 2,700 students have participated in 146 service learning classes in 35 departments, involving 75 faculty members. Service learning students have contributed to finding solutions for the systemic problems in communities; service learning courses have offered opportunities for students to gain job skills in real world settings.

The Center for Community Engagement, Learning, and Leadership (CCELL) is the primary coordinating office for service learning activities on the LSU campus. A key to its success is its Service Learning Advisory Council composed of community partners, student representatives and faculty from each college and school. The council advises the CCELL program and developed CCELL's vision, goals and operating definition of service learning. CCELL has provided a framework for each of the community development efforts to help local partners following Hurricanes Katrina and Rita. Of course, CCELL has given faculty members more than just advice in working with outside partners. It has demonstrated the value of engaging the campus with the community, facilitated financial resources to support projects, given community partners a voice on the campus and helped to document the impacts of campus and community partnerships.

Service learning emphasizes hands-on experiences that address real world concerns as a venue for educational growth. The service experience provides a context for testing, observing and trying out discipline based theories, concepts or skills. Likewise, the academic context enriches the service experience by raising questions about real world concerns and providing a forum for probing these concerns in depth. It is considered hands-on learning integrated into a course, interaction with community partners to benefit the common good and reflection to connect service to academic and civic learning goals. Service goals are aligned with learning objectives, in contrast to volunteerism and community service activities which are designed to make a difference in the lives of the service recipients but are not connected to course objectives.

Research indicates service learning has a significant impact on academic objectives. Service learning students report (Eyler & Giles, 1999):

- deeper understanding of course material
- improved ability to apply theoretical knowledge to real problems
- motivation to work harder
- enhanced college experience through stronger relationships with faculty and student peers
- improved leadership skills
- reduction in negative stereotypes and an enhanced tolerance for diversity
- deeper understanding of the complexity of social issues
- increased sense of connection to the community
- greater self-knowledge

Human Impacts of Disasters (HRNS 2000)

A unique effort to engage LSU students in understanding the impacts of Hurricanes Katrina and Rita involved entering freshmen and upper class students during the fall 2007 and 2008 semesters. The Honors College course, Human Impacts of Disasters, involved 16 faculty members in 2007 and 18 in 2008 who led sections of this class, clustered into groups of five faculty members and scheduled throughout the week. For the fall 2008 offering, five faculty members representing a broad spectrum of academic units (Architecture, Education, Environmental Studies, Oceanography and Social Work) adapted the class to engage their students in service learning by including an experiential learning course module.

The community engagement activity was designed to clarify the human impacts of Hurricanes Katrina and Rita on LSU students. Honors College students in HNRS 2000 were asked to conduct two structured interviews with upper class LSU students who were on campus during the 2005 coastal storms. Engaging the Honors College students in the interview process allowed them to gain a broader perspective of the human impacts of a disaster on families, friends, associates and home and campus communities. Through these interviews, students gained a greater appreciation of the powerful forces that accompany a disaster and came to understand that they as well as their campus should take precautionary steps to be prepared.

The interviews assessed student awareness of and engagement in campus preparedness efforts. Class members examined how well LSU was prepared to deal with student needs following the disasters and the impact of campus response activities. The interviews revealed that students on the campus following Hurricanes Katrina and Rita felt that faculty and fellow students were extremely sensitive to the stress that all felt after the storms. Students also acknowledged the role that the campus plays in supporting students during a crisis and the value of establishing volunteer opportunities for students to assist in both the response and long term recovery. Students in the class met at the end of the 2008 fall semester with LSU officials to discuss the impact of the storms on student life, how the university might support students following a disaster, and what steps might be taken to prepare students for a crisis. The HNRS 2000 faculty team and LSU's Emergency Manager agreed that gleaning information from seniors, the class that had just started at LSU in 2005, was critical in understanding how a college campus can support and assist its student community in the weeks and months following a disaster.

As part of the class, students were exposed to research methods and data gathering strategies/techniques, along with an overview of the broad interdisciplinary parameters of disaster preparedness and response. Training was provided on procedures and protocols for interviews, qualitative research methods for documenting the outcomes of the interviews, techniques for the analysis of interviews and guidelines for the analysis of current campus disaster planning and response actions.

In addition to the interview process, students engaged in a second activity that involved a simulated "crisis environment" requiring them to make decisions, work with fellow students as team members and exercise influence and lead one another. Co-sponsored by the LSU Challenge Program, the activity offered students an opportunity to become more aware of their own responses to a crisis, how their classmates deal with crisis, and how peer pressure impacts their own decision making. The simulation explored the intricacies of communication, cooperation, and trust within a safe, structured environment, and helped to form a "learning community" of students and faculty. By combining mental and physical activities within a controlled setting, the HNRS 2000 class members learned to effectively confront challenges while developing trust and teamwork.

This student engagement effort was adapted in the fall 2008 semester to encourage students to reflect on their own reactions to disaster after Hurricane Gustav struck the LSU campus on September 1, 2008. As a result, when classes analyzed the interviews described above, students were not just casual or neutral observers; their understanding was enhanced by reflection on their own experiences as a result of Hurricane Gustav.

Reconnecting a Broken City

Soon after the completion of the Interstate 10 corridor in the 1960s, the city of Lake Charles was divided with the neighborhoods north of the new interstate becoming effectively cut off and isolated from the rest of the city. A slow process of neighborhood decline resulted, leaving a large percentage of abandoned or derelict properties. The separation that followed has created two distinct areas inside the city: the area north of

I-10 and the downtown area south of the interstate. City officials provided an opportunity for citizens to discuss problems and issues confronting the North Lake Charles area following the extensive flooding and winds from Hurricane Rita in October of 2005. The community meeting revealed that previous attempts to revitalize the city of Lake Charles had failed to address the fissure caused by the interstate; as a result the deterioration of the area north of I-10 has continued.

In addition to the partition created by the interstate corridor, the devastating hurricane season of 2005 demonstrated the importance of providing immediate and affordable housing in the Gulf Coast area. The loss of property from Hurricanes Katrina and Rita has left a large number of people in Cameron and Calcasieu Parishes without housing. The need to shelter victims of natural disasters is the duty of the community, and although rarely planned before the event, was one of the top priorities for the city of Lake Charles and Calcasieu Parish immediately following the storm.

A class in the LSU School of Landscape Architecture studied the situation in the area and concluded that pre-manufactured housing was a poor choice for providing temporary housing for refugees, since such homes are not conducive to establishing a prosperous thriving community. In response, as part of a new strategy, the city planned to prepare housing sites with infrastructure that would facilitate future replacement of temporary housing with a range of permanent mixed use development and housing. Through the use of ecologically and economically based designs, it was considered possible for temporary refugee communities to become stable places of residence and commerce that would appeal to the surrounding land owners as well as its displaced inhabitants.

Figure 8.1 provides an illustration of proposed changes in the urban landscape in comparison with existing conditions prior to the storm. The images were prepared by students in the landscape architecture class after consultation with local community officials and residents. The images provide some insights into ways in which the area could be adapted to address the inherent problems that the community faced.

Figure 8.1 *Current and proposed development in Lake Charles, LA*

The city has expressed a desire to develop various sites around the city by applying standard subdivision design guidelines including building 6,050 square foot lots, roads, utilities and site amenities (including public open space with trails and park facilities). The city is also committed to applying appropriate ecological considerations including sustainable storm water management principles and, in the case of sites located in or near historical districts of the city, to promote designs in sympathy with their historical character. The recommendations from the students reinforced the city's commitment to quality housing for all residents.

The goals of this project, central to the community revitalization plans developed by the landscape architecture students, were to revitalize the area following the hurricanes of 2005 and reconnect the urban infrastructure north of the I-10 corridor to the neighborhoods and commercial districts south of I-10. Students addressed this second goal by developing a greenway system to incorporate areas of retail, mixed use, green links and housing. By utilizing undeveloped or abandoned parcels of land for new, affordable housing, the city could create a walk-able city with comfortable transitions between downtown, the historic district and the area north of I-10. The component of housing essential to the design, especially after the distressing hurricane season of 2005, was designed in such a manner that was consistent with adjoining neighborhoods. The class proposals provided a smooth transition between mature areas and the new developments that followed during the recovery period.

Furthermore, as a direct result of infilling the downtown area, the students advised that the city of Lake Charles could increase its tax base and economic prosperity by reusing mature land and limiting public costs associated with expanding infrastructure. The goal of this project is a reconnected Lake Charles, one that takes every opportunity to reuse and revitalize mature land and infrastructure to provide exceptional communities, long term housing for hurricane victims and a linkage system that will restore and maintain the integrity of the downtown areas.

The mayor and council members of the City of Lake Charles, along with staff of the planning department, met with the students to review their analysis and recommendations, which they will use in the recovery process for the community. The students' recommendations demonstrate how changes in the landscape can have positive benefits for the community. City officials also stressed that the fresh ideas from the students reinforced their own commitment to improve the quality of life for all citizens as they recovered from the disaster.

Urban Landscape Lab

The Urban Landscape Lab is a research and service learning center at the School of Landscape Architecture at LSU. The center's mission is to design and build projects in distressed urban areas that promote the development of innovative, healthy and environmentally sustainable landscapes and provide hands-on learning opportunities for LSU students. There are four ongoing projects within the lab: the New Orleans Schoolyard Project, the St.Roch's Neutral Ground Revitalization, the Viet Village Urban Farm Project and Donnelly Park Gentilly.

New Orleans Schoolyard Project

The New Orleans Schoolyard Project has worked with several schools, including LSU's School of Landscape Architecture, since Hurricane Katrina to revitalize devastated campuses. This work has focused on developing innovative design solutions that make children more active to combat childhood obesity, develop environmentally sustainable campuses, and engage the school children in design exercises. The Prevention Research Center at Tulane University's School of Public Health and Tropical Medicine has collaborated with LSU and the School of Architecture at the University of Louisiana at Lafayette to research the impact of schoolyard design on children's health and activity levels. Change in the landscape of schools in New Orleans is just a part of the long term recovery of the education system in the flooded neighborhoods. Funding to support these school yard projects is included in the Recovery School District's rebuilding plans. Funding to support the capital projects is now available to the school district and construction has begun on some projects.

St. Roch's Neutral Ground Revitalization

The St. Roch's project is located in a historic neighborhood in New Orleans devastated by the hurricane. This project, in collaboration with the Prevention Research Center at Tulane University's School of Public Health and Tropical Medicine, develops a design for a series of six median areas (called neutral grounds locally) along historic St. Roch's Avenue. The design process included extensive public participation and interviews with the local residents. The designs are focused on creating more physical activity in the neighborhood. Construction of the first phase of the design began in the fall of 2007.

Viet Village Urban Farm

The Viet Village Urban Farm project is located in east New Orleans, a Vietnamese-American community with long ties to this area of New Orleans. More than 90% of the pre-Katrina population has returned to this area after the hurricanes. The Viet Village Urban Farm is an urban farming project on 21 acres of land located at the center of the community. The farm supports household farming, producing crops for local consumption as well as commercial crops for distribution to local New Orleans restaurants. Educational and recreational activities are also incorporated into the design to create a project that will be the new center of this urban community. This project was developed in collaboration with the City Center at Tulane University. The American Society of Landscape Architects has given this project the Award of Excellence for Planning and Analysis.

Donelly Park Gentilly

Students and faculty have collaborated on the design of a local park in the flood-devastated Gentilly neighborhood as part of the post-Katrina recovery process. The project began before the hurricane to address serious problems related to lack of investment in public infrastructure. Developed in part to test models for the design of parks more generally, this project has received a major grant from a private foundation to support on-going efforts to assist this neighborhood in long term recovery. Because the area experienced such significant flood damage from Hurricane Katrina, the number of residents returning has been limited. As a result, recovery efforts in Gentilly and around Donelly Park has been very slow. The planning for Donelly Park, however, is a significant part of the long term recovery of the Gentilly area of New Orleans. Implementation of the Donelly Park reconstruction is considered by both residents and the City of New Orleans as a critical step for broader neighborhood development.

Community Planning, Design and Technical Assistance for Coastal Communities

The students and faculty in LSU's School of Architecture have been actively engaged in post-Hurricane Katrina and Rita reconstruction, planning, and assessment in the eight impacted parishes across South Louisiana, by providing technical and design assistance to residents, businesses and communities. This response was coordinated through the School of Architecture and the Office of Community Design and Development (OCDD), a university based, interdisciplinary, community outreach and research center.

Following the devastation of Louisiana's Gulf Coast parishes in 2005, OCDD and many of the school's design studios participated in more than 20 community development initiatives. A few of these student engagement projects are described below to reflect the faculty's belief that civic engagement enhances student learning. Each of these projects includes team efforts comprised of clients, community stakeholders, students and faculty and are structured to ensure successful outcomes for the community while meeting educational goals. Students working on these projects were presented with problems that immersed them in the social and political realities of a design-practice working in the public realm, and provided opportunities for them to apply their learning to real life problems. Students also developed their collaboration skills to meet the demands of an increasingly diverse, global environment.

Residents of the Upper and Lower 9th Ward came together in March 2006 to engage in a comprehensive community forum that sought to affirm, empower and sustain a resident-led short and long term plan for neighborhood recovery. Hurricane Katrina forced thousands of 9th Ward residents, young and old alike, to abandon their neighborhoods. These areas have historic significance as the home of such important New Orleans figures as Ruby Bridges, the 6-year-old African American child who took the first steps toward public school integration; the famous streetcar named Desire; and the early jazz great, Jelly Roll Morton. The Association of Community Organizers for Reform Now (ACORN) sponsored the community forum in collaboration with LSU's OCDD and Cornell University's Department of City and Regional Planning—New Orleans Planning Initiative (NOPI). Residents participated in nine different community input activity centers focusing on building local capacity, neighborhood stabilization, asset-based planning, and affordable housing. Community input served to direct and support the ongoing recovery assistance for ACORN's membership and local residents.

Figure 8.2 *Students and residents assess housing needs and preferences*

Students and research associates from the School of Architecture evaluated a 20-block site in the Upper 9th Ward, specifically the St. Claude-Florida area and Bywater neighborhoods. Their task was to determine where to begin repopulation of the neighborhood, the type of infill housing to replace properties damaged beyond repair, and the type of housing to construct on single or multiple pre-Katrina vacant lots and parcels.

With support from the United States Department of Housing and Urban Development, OCDD participated in a program to train individuals from a neighborhood in New Orleans to build houses, and ultimately to have the capacity to rebuild an economically stable and sustainable community. The construction site of the houses became non-traditional classrooms and utilized on-the-job training for area men and women. The participants were a diverse group from many New Orleans neighborhoods who worked alongside of 13 LSU architecture students who commuted three days a week from Baton Rouge to be on the job at 7:00AM. The effort resulted in two hurricane responsive and energy efficient demonstration homes, with financing for the project underwritten by a national financial institution.

Figure 8.3 *Fourth year architecture students providing on-the-job training to local residents*

Students from LSU's OCDD also provided consultation and technical support to a New Orleans mobile technical assistance home repair program, HomeWorks. This effort was supported by a grant from a non-profit organization formed to provide on-site instruction, repairs, design assistance and technical support for citizens of the city in restoring residential structures. The program targeted women homeowners and assisted them in assessing the needs for repairs, how to locate resources for materials, skilled labor required for more complicated repairs, and identifying priorities for repair.

With financial support from the Louisiana Department of Social Services, eighteen students from architecture, landscape architecture, construction management and interior design, along with faculty and recent graduates, worked together to assess the needs of 30 Louisiana childcare providers from coastal parishes who sustained damage to their facilities. In addition, a comprehensive resource and design manual was developed and provided to all childcare providers who may have had damage to their facilities or are opening facilities throughout hurricane impacted parishes in Louisiana.

In addition to this effort, 26 undergraduate students worked to determine strategies to improve the environments at childcare facilities in these areas. The research included examining the geo-spatial characteristics of the early learning/childcare environment before and after Hurricane Katrina. Students prepared an inventory of 107 Class A childcare facilities, developed papier-mâché props to elicit responses from 3- and 4-year-old children in selected childcare facilities regarding their spatial preferences, and conducted motion studies and on-site behavioral observation and analysis in an effort to understand how to enhance the facilities to support a positive learning and caring environment.

Based on this research, students designed a prototypical outdoor early learning play environment for 3- and 4-year-old children. Exemplary solutions incorporated opportunities for structured and unstructured learning, formal and informal performance (dramatic play) and parallel, imaginary and collaborative play. In addition, each solution was required to use low maintenance materials, harvest rainwater, provide protection from direct sunlight and integrate natural elements and plant materials.

Conclusion

Engaging students in community recovery efforts following a disaster provided an opportunity to extend learning well beyond traditional learning outcomes. Each of the LSU classes described in this chapter involved students in very different learning activities, from a qualitative research project that examined individual and organizational responses to students articulating alternative community planning designs. Each of the projects required extensive work from the students, from planning for the engagement effort to analysis of data collected from members of the community. Each of the class engagement efforts provided students with opportunities for creative reflection, teamwork and communication. The investment by the faculty and students has resulted in welcomed input into institutional policies and plans in the recovery of cities, school districts, governmental authorities and universities. In addition, students have gained from the opportunities to use their creative skills in developing inputs for their community partners. Feedback from these partners on the efforts of the students brings learning to a higher level and sets the stage for continued communication between the campus and the community.

LSU emphasizes teaching, research and service as essential components of its mission as Louisiana's flagship institution. The priority on outreach permeates the entire university and extends beyond its gates. As a land grant university and an urban institution, LSU is committed to using its extensive resources to solve economic, environmental and social challenges.

Engaging universities with communities impacted by a disaster presents both challenges and opportunities. Communities dealing with the many problems of long term recovery welcomed the possibility of help from a known and trusted partner as good news. Giving students the opportunity to learn with the community is not only helpful in generating possible solutions but also encourages students to learn from a disaster. The projects also show that the solutions generated by the students were starting points in a longer recovery process.

Opening the door to one opportunity tends also to broaden the relationship for future collaborations. As with any emerging relationship, university-community engagement is dynamic. To be successful, service learning projects require faculty members who want to help their communities. One should not underestimate the effort that is required to design these collaborations; it is much easier to conduct the class in the same way as the previous year.

The recovery from the 2005 hurricanes will require many years of work and ongoing problem solving by local, regional and state officials. Engaging students in the process of community recovery and development is part of this process. Community leaders recognized that the input from students contributed to their decision making process. The ideas evolving from the students provided local officials with new perspectives that enable them to see options beyond just repairing existing structures or neighborhoods. In most cases, the student input and designs provide local officials with an initial draft from which recovery efforts could be based.

Unfortunately, the recovery process is slow and funding for these projects will take years, since support for the projects is provided by state and federal agencies. The benefits, however, are immediate when local officials can see beyond the destruction of the storms to new possibilities for recovery, and students learn in more profound ways.

FUNCTIONAL CROSS-SECTOR COLLABORATION: THE CASE OF LULEÅ UNIVERSITY OF TECHNOLOGY AND PROCESSIT INNOVATIONS

Johan Johansson, Håkan Ylinenpää and Joakim Wincent
Luleå University of Technology, Sweden

Introduction

This chapter has two main ambitions: to illustrate how Luleå University of Technology (LTU) contributes to regional and company-based development through collaboration with external partners, and to identify challenges involved in cross-sector collaboration between academic institutions and external partners in industry, business, and the public sector. The case study looks specifically at a center for development of innovative solutions (ProcessIT Innovations) for the process and engineering industries, information technology companies, and universities in the two northernmost counties in Sweden (Norrbotten and Vaesterbotten). This chapter discusses:

- How LTU, a university in Sweden operates through cross-sector collaboration, in order to develop the university itself as well as the region in which it is located
- What challenges may exist in such collaborative activities.

We use an actor perspective to explain the organization of innovative processes and the roles of different entities in such collaborations. We present our results by considering two types of arguments—a more positive aspect, arguing in favor of synergies, institutional value advantages and complementary activities that can improve innovative results—and the more negative aspect, arguing that there are forces in this collaboration counteracting the potential for cross-sector collaboration. By empirically analyzing the importance of the respective actors for three different key activities in the development of innovations and innovation systems, we answer such questions as:

- Do the actors representing companies, universities and society ascribe different roles to one another depending on the type of activity to be performed?
- Are there any conflicts between the role that other actors ascribe and what this actor is considered best suited to perform?
- If there are such role conflicts, where are they most conspicuous?

The chapter concludes with a summarizing discussion in which we discuss in particular the challenges involved in employing cross-sector collaboration in practice with special attention to the role of universities.

Luleå University of Technology

LTU is located in the city of Luleå in the northernmost part of Sweden. The university started out as a technical university college with an explicit orientation towards the needs of the region's traditional industries such as mining, steel and paper and pulp. LTU's first department was in mechanical engineering, which recruited its initial 50 students in 1971. The following year the university started to educate mining engineers, and in 1977 a department for environmental engineering was established. In addition, the first non-technical fields were added—business administration and education. During the following years, additional new fields of education and research were established specifically in science and technology. Many of the new educational programs were offered in other cities than where the university's main campus is located to satisfy the needs for qualified labor in regional industry and businesses. [1] Parallel to this focus on the region's traditional industry, the university has diversified its activities with the establishment of departments in electronics, computer science, media and non-technical fields.

In 1997, Luleå became the first institution in Sweden to receive the status of a technical university. Today the university has two faculties (Technology and Arts and Social Sciences), with nearly 1,500 staff (including more than 100 professorships), and 12,200 students. Today LTU has more students in non-technical fields than in technical disciplines. In cooperation with local communities, the university is continuously engaged in giving courses and programs outside its campus sites, either through decentralized education or by utilizing distance-spanning technology. [2]

Universities are expected to contribute to the development of business and society. One important mission—and probably the most important—is to produce well-educated people who (traditionally) are capable of doing a good job as future employees or (non-traditionally) are capable of creating their own employment. Another important mission is to cooperate with industry and society in research and development, generating new solutions to existing needs or facilitating new solutions to needs we, as consumers, are not yet even aware of. The mission to cooperate, often denoted as the universities' "third task," has been a top priority for most governments during the recent decade. The reason behind this trend is, of course, the benefits for a healthy, dynamic economy of a close interaction between "theory" and "practice" in an increasingly knowledge based economy. LTU has a long tradition of cooperation and which is manifested by the Vice Chancellor of LTU, Pia Sandvik Wiklund, stating on the university webpage:

Cooperation with companies, organizations and actors in the public sector enriches education and research at the university. Much of the research is based on issues in the world outside the university and is carried on in interaction with the parties who have an interest in the results. In the same way, problems and questions from the surrounding community constitute useful starting points for students' projects and case studies. The University also desires to contribute to the region's development and growth and is active in regional development efforts.[3]

The practical arrangements for collaboration with industry, business and government take many different forms at LTU, such as contracted research, student assignments, training programs and courses for practitioners, guest lecturers from industry, spin-out support services, support for intellectual property rights (IPR), service by university staff in consultancy companies and on boards of directors of companies. Several of the professorships at LTU are financed through funding from industry; in addition, the governmental Technology Link Foundation sponsors several adjunct professorships where competence is shared between the business and industry sector and the university. Today there are 35 adjunct professorships, normally people allocating 20% of their working time to university research and/or education. Another important category is the industrial doctoral student, who is employed by a company and within the framework of his position attends a doctoral program at LTU. Among the 554 doctoral students at LTU there are today 110 industrial doctoral students. This category of doctoral student will expand as a result of the increasing number of industrial research projects at LTU and the increased need in industry for PhD graduates.

A significant part of LTU's collaboration with its external partners is channeled through specific centers operating in different fields of technology development and testing. Financed with external funding from industry or regional government, these centers are governed by independent boards staffed with people from the region's industry or government as well as from the university. Since the purpose of these centers is to link external needs to university research and education, the boards are chaired by representatives outside the university and then often by persons from industry. The daily operation in each center is executed by a manager or a management team that strives to implement the strategic orientation decided by the board.

Today 31 different centers are operating with a base at LTU, ranging from the Center for Distance-spanning Healthcare (CDH) to the Embedded Internet Systems Laboratory (EISLAB) and including ProcessIT Innovations. Besides these centers, mainly oriented towards research and development with external partners, LTU is also engaged in incubators, science parks, and technology transfer and commercialization organizations. The next section uses ProcessIT Innovations as a case study for illustrating how this external collaboration is organized and for discussing challenges involved in these kinds of collaborative arrangements.

ProcessIT Innovations

Many of the region's process and engineering industries are strong and well positioned in their global markets. Sweden and the region have attained a leading position in IT, particularly in wireless technology and applications, but also in general use and development of IT-based services. ProcessIT Innovations concentrates on new and better solutions for the process and engineering industries with the aim of strengthening their competitiveness. At the same time, the IT companies of the region get an opportunity to develop commercial products saleable on a global market, while the universities in the region are expected to establish themselves as leaders in Europe in the research areas related to ProcessIT Innovations' main areas as well as the commercialization of their research. In the long term this collaboration is expected to lead to improved prosperity, increased employment and greater competence in the whole region.

ProcessIT Innovations was initiated by the business community in the region, and today involves the process and engineering industries, IT companies and the universities of Umeå and Luleå. The center is supported by four municipalities and the county councils of Västerbotten and Norrbotten. In 2004 VINNOVA (the Swedish governmental agency for innovation systems) nominated the center for a national award, which means that it receives US$1 million annually for ten years in order to develop specific industry related innovations. In addition, the actors in ProcessIT Innovations contribute at least as much themselves in the form of money and their own work. Taken together this means a joint effort comprising more than 20 million US dollars during a ten year period. [4]

The importance of the three different actors in this cross-sector collaboration depends on the type of activity in question. Table 9. 1 summarizes what basic competences, "yield expectations" and prominent contributions the various actors can be expected to provide (for a more detailed discussion, see Westerberg, Wincent & Ylinenpää, 2007). In this case study, we separate the company actors into two groups—process and engineering companies and IT companies respectively. These two groups of companies play different roles in ProcessIT Innovations, but also represent two groups of companies whose nature and structure are very different: the companies in the process industries are as rule large global actors, while the IT companies are normally small and active on a regional or national scale.

Table 9. 1 depicts public actors as especially suited for ensuring public interests and universities as particularly well suited for knowledge development. The process and engineering industries possess competence concerning the end market, while the IT companies have the necessary competence required for the development of innovations.

Table 9.1 *Contributions and Rewards in ProcessIT Innovations*

Actor	Competence/resources	Expected yield	Prominent contributions
Public Actors	• Act as a customer in early phases • Financing of projects • Economic know-how	• More attractive region • New companies, more job opportunities, increasing tax receipts, etc. • Greater legitimacy	• Ensure public interests (develop visions for the whole innovation system)
Universities	• Analytic competence • Scientific knowledge	• International repute • Financing of research • Commercialization of research • Research publications • Feedback to undergraduate studies	• Knowledge development (develop basic knowledge for innovations)
Process and engineering industries	• Practical problems of relevance for research • Process technological experience	• More even product quality • Increased efficiency in plants	• Competence supply concerning the end market in innovation development
IT-companies	• Ability to manufacture/ install new products and services • Commercial competence	• Products and services that can be offered in a global market • Increasing earnings	• Specialist competence for development of innovations

Challenges and Potential Role Conflicts

Cross-sector collaboration is not trivial since it involves interaction among sectors and actors driven by different organizational logics. Functional cross-sector collaboration may be understood as an ideal image characterized by harmonious collaboration developing over time and becoming increasingly intimate. This ideal image may appear overly idyllic, as there are factors within and between different spheres of actors that can counteract or render real collaboration more difficult and prevent the potential of such collaboration from being utilized. Below we present some arguments questioning the ideal image of cross-sector collaboration by briefly accounting for the logic behind collaboration and organization as well as for the way in which norms and values differ among different sectors.

Potential conflict 1: Compromises result in a tug-of-war! [5] The logic behind cross-sector collaboration is that the potential for creating value might increase when two or more actors' resources are used together. The problem in such a constellation, however, is that the actors from the different spheres may often have different and sometimes contradictory reasons for engaging in collaboration in an innovation system as shown in Table 9.1. The actors have a variety of different technological, economic or yield expectations for what they wish to achieve. These differences may naturally lead to impatience, misunderstanding and role conflicts. The actors in each sector also have different images of reality and different time perspectives as their points of departure. As a result, a great deal of energy may have to be spent on coordinating these three different conceptions of what is important, what should be given priority and what time horizon the collaboration should be based on. In order to create functioning cross-sector collaboration, compromises are required so that everybody will get something out of the collaboration, which in turn implies difficulties in achieving solutions that satisfy everybody completely.

The distribution of costs and of future earnings is also a source of conflict. Another problem is that the expected yield is uncertain, as the result might be either a profit or a loss for all parties—or only for one of them. In such collaborations, both power and legitimacy play an important role for how to distribute resources and what activity the respective actors should engage in. The power balance among the parties may naturally change depending on what activity is to be performed, since the different competences that the respective actors contribute will carry different weights in different phases of the collaboration. Taken together these factors will probably cause the actors to attempt to control and manipulate the collaboration in directions that benefit themselves. There is also a risk of actors "overestimating" their own role in the activity in which they consider themselves best qualified.

Potential conflict 2: Differences become complexities! [6] Public administration is organized according to geography and political areas, universities in terms of academic disciplines, and companies according to business areas. This organization means, for example, that IT-related issues are handled by a number of authorities with different interests and that research on information technology is conducted by several different actors who may be competing for the same resources or for the preferential right of interpretation. Entrepreneurs working in IT, for example, may perceive both the public sector and academia as bureaucratic and inflexible. The different sectors are also characterized by different norms, values and rules, which may make communication and collaboration even more difficult.

One such conflict is different views about information. The public sector follows the principle of right-of-access which gives the Swedish people the right to study public documents when they so wish, but industry needs to protect its business secrets. Universities believe in independent research and need to disseminate and publish research results. Ownership issues in joint research and development projects may also cause problems, as academic researchers in Sweden normally own the result of their research, while researchers employed in industry do not. Actors in one area may ascribe less importance in certain activities to other actors although the other actors may be the most qualified to perform the activities.

Method

The focus of our analyses is on quantitative data based on a questionnaire that was sent to actors associated with ProcessIT Innovations in the middle of 2006. The respondents included CEOs, production managers and researchers. The questionnaire was sent to a total of 98 persons in 61 organizations. We received 54 replies from 39 different organizations yielding a response frequency of 55% (individual level) and a weighted response frequency of 64% (organizational level). We use the weighted responses (organizational level) in the section below.

As a first step in studying cross-sector collaboration more closely in practice, we analyze the extent to which the three categories of actors ascribe different roles to one another depending on what type of activity is to be performed in the innovation system. We base our analyses on three different key activities that are central to the development of innovations and innovation systems and that are characteristic of ProcessIT Innovations' working method (see Table 9.1): to develop visions, develop basic knowledge and introduce the innovations.

We analyze deviations from what could be expected according to an idyllic view on collaboration in which actors representing different sectors would ascribe different roles to one another based on synergies, institutional value advantages and so on, completely dependent on what type of activity is to be performed in the innovation system.

We look first at public actors who, it may be assumed, ensure public interest and look after the common utility so that all actors can attain their objectives. In order to gain a better understanding of the different actors' roles in ensuring public interest, we asked the participants to estimate the importance of different actors' roles in the development of visions for and planning of ProcessIT Innovations' activities. The answers are accounted for in Figure 9.1.

Figure 9.1 *Different actors' contributions to the innovation system—vision*

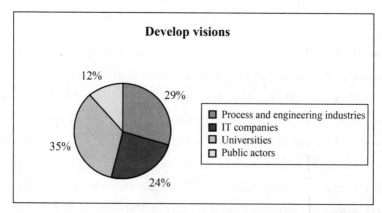

The result shows that the universities are regarded as the most important actors in the process of developing visions and planning ProcessIT Innovations' activities. The process and engineering industry companies and the IT companies occupy the second place, while actors representing the public sector are given the least importance. This is the key activity in which the public sector has its clearest and most significant role yet other actors do not agree in practice. The result shows that the actors in ProcessIT Innovations ascribe to the public sector a certain but in no way decisive role as a resource facilitator in the innovation system, but a very modest role in the other key activities in the system.

As stated above, it could be expected that universities and other educational organizations have an important role in the development of knowledge based innovations. In order to find out whether this is also true of ProcessIT Innovations, we asked the participants to weigh the importance of different actors' roles in the development of basic knowledge that can later on be put into practice as innovations. Figure 9.2 below shows that the universities clearly play a dominant role in the development of basic knowledge that can be put into practice as innovations, with the process and engineering industry companies and the IT companies in second place. The outcome is principally in accord with the expectations listed in Table 9.1.

Figure 9.2 *Different actors' contributions to the innovation system—knowledge*

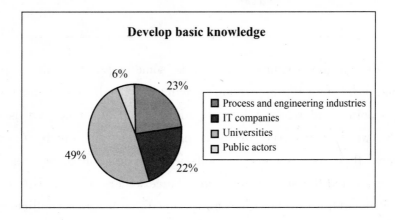

If we then focus on the key activities that are most clearly connected to commercialization (that is, introducing innovations on the market), it is reasonable to assume that the system's commercial actors hold an exceptional position in this respect. Figure 9.3 shows that the IT companies are ascribed the greatest importance when it comes to introducing innovations, but companies in the process and engineering industries are also given significant roles in these key activities. While the public sector has a very small role in this respect, the university actors are given some marginal importance. The outcome is also consistent with the expectations shown in Table 9.1.

Figure 9.3 *Different actors' contributions to the innovation system*
—introduce innovation

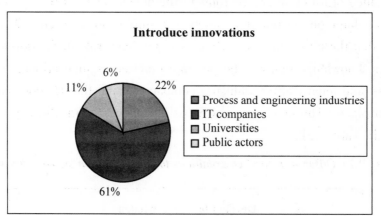

Although the outcome thus lends some support to the expected division of labor in the innovation system, our results also indicate some unclear points and role conflicts in this division of labor. We used the answers we had received to focus on the ways in which the actors evaluated their own importance (self-view) in relation to how the other actors evaluated the same actors' importance (others' view). This method made it possible to further analyze whether there are role conflicts in the innovation system. Table 9.2 shows these values, with the greatest role conflicts or causes of "tug-of-war" marked in boldface.

Table 9.2 *The actors' importance for different areas in the innovation system*

Key activities	Process and engineering industries		IT companies		Universities		Public actors	
	Others' view	Self-view	Others' view	Self-view	Others' view	Self-view	Others' view	Self-view
1. Develop visions and plan Process IT Innovations' activities	**31%**	**23%**	23%	25%	34%	39%	12%	12%
2. Develop basic knowledge to be converted into practical innovations	23%	25%	20%	24%	**44%**	**74%**	6%	5%
3. Launch innovations on the market	22%	21%	61%	59%	**13%**	**5%**	**6%**	**2%**

Table 9.2 shows several significant differences. For the process and engineering industry companies and the IT companies the self-view is to a great extent in accord with how others look upon the companies' importance in different key activities. The only exception is that the process and engineering industries are ascribed greater importance for taking part in the work of developing visions (public utility) than what they think themselves.

For the universities there is less agreement on several key activities (see the percentages in boldface). This indicates that the university actors are involved in a kind of tug-of-war, which seems to be of a double nature. The other actors either wish to push away the responsibility in certain areas or attach greater importance to themselves than the other actors think they can deliver. The university actors are conspicuous in this type of tug-of-war, as they ascribe to themselves a smaller role than what the other actors think they should have in commercialization. Perhaps the most noteworthy aspect is that the universities consider themselves extremely important for developing knowledge for innovations while not being ascribed this importance by the other actors. Generally, the results indicate that the role conflicts thus identified are primarily to be ascribed to the actors representing universities. Analyzing this in more detail reveals that the IT companies and the process and engineering industry companies have a unanimous view of the universities' importance and that it is between the universities and the public actors that the views of the universities' importance differ the most. In regards to the universities' importance in the innovation system, the table shows that there is a lack of agreement in the view of the universities' importance in all the studied areas, which might give rise to role conflicts among the actors.

The area of visions and planning is the first place in which unanimity is shattered. The largest gap is between the public actors' view and the universities' self-view, since the public actors think that the universities play a considerably smaller role than the universities' themselves think. In the key activity "providing the system with important resources" the universities depreciate their own importance markedly in comparison with the other actors' relatively unanimous view of the universities' importance in the area. In the key activity "developing basic knowledge that can later on be transformed into practical innovations," however, the universities are of the opinion that they themselves are the most important actor and that they contribute 74% of the utility in this area. The difference between the universities' self-view and the other actors' view of the universities' importance is dramatic, since the universities think that they are nearly twice as important compared to what the other actors think. The largest difference is between their self-view and the opinion of actors in the public sector. This leads to a role conflict, since universities think they are most important while depreciating the contributions of other actors.

In the area of commercialization, the greatest differences are between the universities and the process and engineering industry companies, closely followed by the IT companies. Introduction of innovations on the market is thus the fourth area where there is a lack of unanimity among the actors. The universities regard their importance in this area as fairly limited, while the other actors evaluate the universities' role two to three times higher than the universities self-view indicates. This shows that the other actors highly value the universities' indirect or direct participation in the commercialization, while the universities themselves do not feel that they have a significant role.

Concluding Discussion

LTU is well reputed for its collaboration with external partners in research and education. The focus of this chapter has been to illustrate how such collaborative activities are organized through different university related centers. To illustrate this specific form of collaboration we have presented the case of ProcessIT Innovations, a center specifically organized to develop innovations in the interface between university research and the region's traditional process industry, as well as small innovative IT companies. Besides representing a successful example of industry-university-government collaboration (at least so far), the example of ProcessIT Innovations also challenges the understanding that innovations and contributions to regional development only are found in new emerging industries, while traditional and established sectors of industry often are regarded as outdated and declining sectors of our economy, slowly facing an unavoidable death.

Our study of ProcessIT Innovations, however, also questions the idyllic aspect of harmony that is often assumed in such collaborations. Cross-sector collaboration involves the challenge to bridge actor self-interests that only partly coincide. In the studied case, we certainly find evidence that seems to support the division of labor indicated by Table 9.1, but we also have identified (potential or real) conflicts in the intricate constellation of actors that cross-sector based innovation systems represent.

The public actors were ascribed limited importance for ensuring public interest in the innovation system; instead, universities were said to be the most important actor in this area. This might be explained by the fact that the innovation system's operative management is located at LTU and by the fact that the public actors, more or less consciously, have assumed a low profile. This may be a wise strategy, since they themselves lack both technological knowledge and the ability to act as customers in early stages. Hence the public actors function more as a supportive than a driving force trying to control the direction of the innovation system. Some role conflicts between the public actors and the other actors are discernible, however, when the public actors ascribe to themselves considerably less importance than the other actors together ascribe to them in the innovation system. The public actors are probably not suffering from low self-confidence, but rather from a poor understanding of their own importance for the functioning of the innovation system and of the expectations that other actors, in particular the companies, hold for their role.

The universities' highly restrictive attitude to the public actors also points to a role conflict. The attitude can to a great extent be explained by the underlying aim of the innovation system precisely being innovations and by the universities being of the opinion that they are more important than the public actors in this area. Talks with researchers working in projects within ProcessIT Innovations also showed that they had little sympathy for the underlying ideas of the innovation system, but rather saw ProcessIT Innovations as a consortium for need-driven research. Relatively few people in the IT companies knew about the visions and objectives underlying the innovation system. The fact that the system's rhetoric is thus not particularly well established among the actors raises the question of whether the actors' awareness of the ideas underlying cross-sector collaboration is an essential prerequisite for functioning collaboration.

Regarding knowledge development in the innovation system, the universities are the leading actor. There is a role conflict, however, that may have a negative effect on knowledge development because the universities strongly overestimate their own importance in comparison with the importance that the other actors ascribe to them. The reason for this might be that the fact that knowledge development is one of the universities' chief tasks in society. But the different views of the universities' importance may also be explained by "knowledge" meaning different things to different actors and by the universities valuing scientific knowledge over practical knowledge based on experience. This role conflict and the differences it creates may affect the cooperative climate among the actors, since the universities also depreciate the companies' importance when it comes to evaluating optimal solutions based on existing technology or their ability to develop basic knowledge that may result in innovations. In combination with the universities' strong influence on the development of visions and objectives and their control of the operative management of the innovation system, this role conflict might lead to faulty resource allocation and the companies' competence and abilities not optimally utilized. The universities' action in these areas may be understood as an example of actors, when given an opportunity, will try to steer the collaboration in an innovation system in directions primarily beneficial to them.

When focusing on the more commercial activities in the innovation system, our results clearly illustrate the central role that the companies (in particular the IT companies) play in these activities, consistent with Table 9.1. Here the university actors rate themselves low in the key activity of introducing innovations on the market. This attitude, by which the universities' role is restricted to their research efforts, reflects a traditional division of labor between academics and practitioners, where the practitioners take over the responsibility when the academics have "completed their research" and indicates the existence of yet another role conflict that has to be overcome. Commercialization of research can also be viewed as a way of disseminating research results and creating opportunities for feedback, which in turn may lead to improvements of the developed innovation. This reasoning leads to the conclusion that the universities could benefit from more active participation in the introduction of innovations.

There is extensive collaboration in ProcessIT Innovations in project teams involving many actors. In this collaboration, light is shed on actual problems emanating from the process and engineering industries' need to improve their production process, possible solutions to these problems, the estimated research relevance, and the commercial potential of the ideas and aspects of financing. The work of starting a preliminary study is done both individually and in close collaboration with the other participating actors in the projects and may be described as alternative and functional three-party collaboration in which the actors overlap one another and understand one another's roles and motives for collaboration. On the more overarching innovation system level, this type of three-party collaboration does not work equally well, since at this level the IT companies, which often are small, are not regarded as fully adequate members by the other actors. Instead actors from the public sector function here as a third party in the cooperative constellation.

In summary, through the empirical example of ProcessIT Innovations we found conditions and actor behaviors that are in line with what has been postulated in the literature as well as conditions and behaviors questioning the same literature. We also found various types of role conflict. What the example of ProcessIT Innovations indicates is that actors involved in cross-sector collaboration not only have different roles and expectations during different *phases* of innovative development processes, but also play different roles on different *levels* of these processes. Actors from the public sector play a role in the system as a supportive actors or resource facilitators, it is true, but as clearly shown by our data from ProcessIT Innovations, public actors have a very modest role to play in the actual innovative development work. Instead, commercial enterprises are central, the interaction between large and small companies comprises dynamic and innovative opportunities and academic qualifications are valuable in the development of knowledge based innovations. In this respect, parallels may be drawn with Silicon Valley in the bay Area (U.S.) or Route 128 around Boston (U.S.) but also to less well-known examples in Europe (the example of Oulu in Finland) where the interaction among one or several large locomotive enterprises (Hewlett Packard, Digital Equipment/Compaq and NOKIA respectively), small but knowledge-oriented advanced partner companies, and universities with an applied research profile has been important (Saxenian, 1994; Ylinenpää & Lundgren, 1998).

An important implication for higher education is that other actors expect more from universities than the universities envision their role to be. In particular, other actors ascribe importance to the university role in launching innovations while the universities tend to think that their work is over once the basic knowledge has been developed. It would be wise for universities to become more aware of the fact that other actors expect more of universities than the universities' self-view includes.

Academics should also be aware that other actors do not believe that universities are the only source of basic knowledge. Other actors feel they have important responsibilities for development of knowledge because they have the practical experience that universities lack. Universities should not over estimate their importance in this regard. A final implication is that since other actors often view the universities as the most important actor it becomes crucial that the university also take the leadership role associated with the position that the other actors are ascribing them.

To conclude this discussion, we may state that all actors involved in cross-sector collaboration have their own motives for their participation, which leads to collaboration being competition, but in a different form, where actors are trying to maximize their outcomes. For this reason there are always role conflicts among actors in an innovation system, which may be seen as a sign of commitment, but this tug-of-war nevertheless has to be controlled by the participating actors in order to be able to attain the joint objectives of the collaboration in the innovation system.

Notes

[1] Data from Leander (1991).

[2] This section is mainly based on Nilsson et al. (2006).

[3] See http://www. ltu. se/samverkan?l = en (Aug. 2008).

[4] In a comment to the annual report 2007, the CEO of ProcessIT Innovations reports that Process IT Innovations during 2007 has handled close to 5.2 million USD.

[5] Classical "utilitarian theory" and "exchange theory" (authors such as Blau, 1964; Homans, 1961) have long shown that collaboration in order to satisfy different utilities or values often leads to compromises where actors use social attraction and power to satisfy their motives, but where actors also consider their efforts in terms of their skills and possible value gains.

[6] "Interactionist theories" (examples of authors are Mead, 1934; Schutz, 1932) have claimed for a long time that self-images and core attitudes are important aspects for understanding that sustainable relations are often formed through a common world view and that actors can create meaning and understanding together. Research on relations has lent strong support to the relevance of this theory, and the problem with differences is tangible in cross-sector constellations. For this reason we think that such a background provides strong support for formulating a potential conflict that many researchers will recognise.

PUBLIC UNIVERSITIES AND REGIONAL DEVELOPMENT IN AUSTRALIA: THE CASE OF MONASH UNIVERSITY

Felicity Wray and John Tomaney
Monash University, Australia

Introduction

Regional development has emerged as a concern in the reassessment of the role of universities in the global knowledge economy. The capacity and ability of universities to meet this challenge, however, is shaped by the context in which universities work, including the evolving politics of national systems of regulation, intellectual and academic cultures, institutional histories and uneven economic geographies.

This chapter examines these challenges in the Australian context through a case study of Monash University. From its origins in 1958, Monash has grown to be Australia's largest university with almost 60,000 student enrollments, equivalent to 42,000 full-time students. At the same time, Monash has developed into one of the foremost universities in the country, signified by its membership of the Group of Eight research intensive universities. In the process, Monash has evolved from a single campus in suburban Melbourne into a complex, highly internationalized institution, a structure which presents particular challenges and opportunities in managing its contribution to regional development.

This chapter outlines how Monash leaders have articulated their regional development mission and strategies and how they have managed the relationship between the broad goals of the university and the objective of regional development. Ultimately, the case study of Monash is concerned with illuminating the issues and challenges confronting research intensive universities in Australia. The chapter draws on 25 interviews, conducted in October and November 2008, with senior managers at Monash and local and regional stakeholders in the state of Victoria.

We begin by describing the Australian context for regional development and the understandings that inform these interactions, focusing particularly on the state of Victoria, which contains the bulk of Monash's operations. We identify a central dilemma—funding for higher education is determined by the federal government, whereas the framework for local and regional development is dominated by the states. We then describe the evolution of Monash's regional engagement before assessing the contemporary scene. We conclude by setting our findings in the context of wider debates about the role of public universities in regional development.

Concepts

Many observers believe that we are witnessing the emergence of a global knowledge economy (see Carnoy & Castells, 2001 for an influential contribution). The notion that the shift to a knowledge economy informs the activities of a range of international organizations and national governments, including the Organisation for Economic Co-operation and Development, the World Bank and the European Union (through its Lisbon Agenda). Similar thinking can be found in the Australian government's Review of the National Innovation System completed in 2008 (Cutler & Company, 2008).[1] The idea that the production, distribution and exchange of knowledge is the new driving force of the economy, although powerful, is not uncontested. Nevertheless, it provides an organizing heuristic for this chapter. In the past, universities were the central sites in society for the production of knowledge, but now they find themselves only one of many potential contributors of knowledge (Harloe & Perry, 2004; Yelland & Pukka, 2007). At the same time, universities have the potential to strengthen their position in society and contribute to development through interactions with other public and private actors.

The region presents one sphere for university engagement in the knowledge economy. Indeed, for some commentators, regions are becoming the crucial nodes in the production, distribution and exchange of knowledge and learning in the new age of global, knowledge-intensive capitalism (Florida, 1995; Morgan, 1997). The evidence for these claims typically is offered in the form of the consolidation of global city regions in financial networks (New York, London, Tokyo) and those regions which were the sites for the new digital sectors such as Silicon Valley in California, Route 128 in Massachusetts and Cambridge in England associated respectively with Stanford University, MIT and the University of Cambridge (Cooke, 2001; Florida, 1995; Scott & Storper, 2003).

Beyond these well known cases from the "leading edge" of change, European research has pointed to the reinvention of traditional industrial regions around strategies of innovation involving universities in places such as Tampere in Finland and Twente in the Netherlands (Boucher et al., 2003; Morgan, 1997). Endogenous growth theories assert the value of investments in knowledge and education as a source of growth (Barr & Sala-I-Martin, 2004; Romer, 1986), while the new economic geography sees growth as essentially localized with strong agglomeration effects associated with technology spillovers (Baldwin & Martin, 2004). But universities are not merely economic actors. Universities can also be conceived of as primarily cultural institutions, with their origins in nation-building and elite formation. The local and regional cultural impacts of universities represent another facet of their regional engagement (Chatterton, 2000) and potentially play a role in "advancing civil literacy and participation" in an era of political disengagement in western societies (Winter et al., 2006, 223).

As national governments respond to the perceived exigencies of the knowledge economy and restructure modes of governance to support more regionalized forms of growth, universities across the globe have been urged to become more engaged with regional development. Underpinning this claim is the suggestion that universities both contribute to and benefit from regional development; successful regions in the knowledge economy require close connections with universities, while successful local economies stimulate the growth of universities (e.g. Goddard & Chatterton, 1999; Chatterton & Goddard, 2000). However, as Harloe and Perry note,

> Not all universities are the same, with the result that different approaches will evolve to allow universities to seize opportunities and manage threats in the current environment. Consequently, more empirical case studies are needed involving different types of higher education institutions, in different regional and national systems and circumstances. The links between contemporary social and economic transitions and changes in higher education and its institutions will only become clearer and better defined after such work is done. (2004, 220)

Contexts

Australia provides an interesting context to examine the role of universities and regional development. Two features of the Australian scene are necessary to an understanding of the context for this study. First, Australia is a federally governed post-colonial society. Secondly, the term "region" carries a particular meaning in Australia.

The Politics of Higher Education in Australia

Australia's formation as a federation was long and difficult. It concluded in 1901 when the Commonwealth of Australia was formed from self-governing colonies as "dominions" of the British Empire. The country gradually loosened its ties with the UK during the 20th century although Queen Elizabeth II remains the head of state. The 1901 constitution essentially defined the powers of the federal government in such areas as foreign affairs, defense and citizenship and immigration, while the responsibilities of the states included education, transport and support for industry. Among other things, the constitution allowed the states to refer powers to the Commonwealth and for the Commonwealth to make grants to the states. These powers have underpinned the growing strength of the Commonwealth over time.

The university system in Australia is overwhelmingly a public one. The oldest ("sandstone") universities were established during the colonial and immediate post-colonial period: Sydney (1850), Melbourne (1853), Adelaide (1874), Tasmania (1890), Queensland (1909), and Western Australia (1912). These were established by acts of state parliaments and contributed to elite formation in the colonies and professional education in fields such as law and medicine. These institutions were funded by fee income and remained largely autonomous with little state interference. The early universities were inspired by the British model, while the later ones drew on the American land grant model. However, by 1939 only 14,000 students attended university in a nation with a population of about 7 million.

After the Second World War, higher education expanded significantly. The Commonwealth began to make grants to existing universities and began to provide student scholarships. Four new universities were created: Australian National University (1946), University of New South Wales (1949), University of New England (1953) and Monash (1958). By 1960 there were 60,000 students in higher education as a result of nation-building efforts and the expansion of the welfare state.

Successive national reviews in the 1950s and 1960s sought to rationalize the structure of higher education which was still formally regulated by the states. In common with many other countries, postsecondary education was divided into higher and further education. Under this binary system, universities issued degrees and undertook research while Colleges of Advanced Education (CAEs) offered more vocationally oriented training. However, there were significant differences among the states with only one CAE in Western Australia and 19 in Victoria.

The expansion of higher education continued in the 1960s and 1970s while the Commonwealth extended its control over the system. In 1974 the federal government undertook full responsibility for funding universities and CAEs, abolished student fees and committed to the provision of universal higher education. By the 1980s, however, this system was under strain. Student numbers were increasing but funding remained static, while some CAEs were moving into postgraduate education and research. Over time public funding per student declined in real terms and the government share of total university income fell from 91% in 1983 to 44% in 2003 (Marginson, 2007b). Some states responded to this by converting some CAEs into universities in an effort to create larger institutions and to achieve efficiencies.

In this context, the government undertook a restructuring of higher education, known as the Dawkins reforms after the minister who oversaw it (Dawkins, 1987). The reforms led to the abolition of the binary system in favor of a "national unified system." The federal government offered incentives to create fewer, larger institutions, with the result that a system of 18 universities and 47 CAEs in 1985 was transformed into 35 universities by 1994. The number of students increased from 420,000 in 1988 to 730,000 in 2001. Research was now funded by competitive grants rather than block funding and student fees were reintroduced.

A striking development in Australia in the 1990s was the massive growth in international student numbers, the fees from which acted to mitigate the effects of declining government support per student (Marginson, 2007a, b). Between 1951 and 1982 Australia participated in the Colombo Plan, an instrument of international aid, which provided support for students in Asian countries to study in Australia. The University of New South Wales and Monash University were important destinations for students arriving under this program. While internationalization was limited in the 1980s, by the end of the decade universities were freed to recruit unlimited numbers of students and to raise international student fees. Within ten years international students comprised 14% of the total student body, as Australia's global share of international students rose from 1% to 9%. Asia was the main source for this growth including Hong Kong, Singapore, Malaysia, India and Indonesia, and later China.

Australian universities also became pioneers in opening offshore campuses. Overall, higher education emerged as a vital export industry, earning US$4 billion by 2004 and characterized, according to Marginson, as an "unambiguously commercial" approach with a "marked growth in business functions and non-academic student servicing rather than in academic capacity" (2007b, 19, 21). However, the country's international research performance lagged behind its success in commercial teaching, reflecting the fact that "Australia made a major commitment to basic research infrastructure between the 1960s and 1980s but then focused one-sidedly on commercialization" (Marginson, 2007b, 21). The Group of Eight universities criticized this situation and there were signs that incoming Labour government in 2008 would address the matter.

The restructuring of higher education coincided with the end of the "Australian Settlement" (Kelly, 1992), a model of national economic development marked by centralized wage bargaining and tariff control which produced a notably egalitarian social structure. During the 1980s the Labour government removed tariff barriers and promoted financial liberalization in an effort to stimulate the restructuring of domestic industry and integrate Australia more directly in the world economy. Prefiguring ideas of the knowledge economy, a more efficient university system was viewed as an essential component of this new model. Dawkins was explicit that higher education could be both an important earner of foreign exchange in the global economy and a means of integrating itself geopolitically in the Asia-Pacific, and that larger universities were a necessary precursor. Subsequently, the Howard government saw fees from international students as relieving some the burden of public funding (Marginson, 2007b).

In summary, Australian higher education has its origins in the ambitions of the colonies and states. By the end of the 1990s, however, the Commonwealth was the key actor in the sector. In 1951 the states provided half of university funding but by 2000 the states had almost disappeared as important funders. By contrast, the Commonwealth provided 50% of direct funding for universities in 2000 (see Commonwealth of Australia, 2002), although there were signs of change in the mid-2000s.

Regional Development in Australia

Regional development as a field of public policy has a complex history in Australia. First, the term "regional" carries a particular meaning in Australia. Beer et al. note that "To a very large degree debates about regional issues in Australia has focused on the nation's non-metropolitan parts. 'Regional Australia' has become a synonym for non-metropolitan Australia and 'RaRa' (Rural and Regional Australia) has dominated policy development and the attention of senior politicians" (2003, xi). Indeed, one of our informants defined the term region as "anything that is not metropolitan." Moreover, the term "region" can carry a pejorative meaning in Australia, suggesting marginalization or a lower level of development. Indeed, many regional communities experienced economic decline and population loss from the 1980s, reinforcing this widely held attitude.

This understanding contrasts markedly with North American and European ones, where regions can be either metropolitan or rural, or can contain both urban and rural settlements. Looked at from a European perspective, New South Wales or Tasmania might be viewed as regions akin to Toscana or Rhône Alpes (see Tomaney, 2009, for a discussion of the concept of the region). Alternatively, given the very large size of the metropolitan areas of Australia, Beer et al. suggest that they should be conceived as a series of distinct regions with particular economic development challenges.

Federal Labour governments of the 1970s and 1980s sought to define a role for the Commonwealth in regional policy. The Howard (conservative) Liberal government (1996-2007) maintained that local and regional development was a state responsibility, although this did not prevent it from funding some regional development, albeit in controversial ways (Prasser & Cockfield, 2007). Although the structure of local government varies among the states, in general local autonomy is very limited in Australia and the states remain the most important actor in local and regional development through the provision of infrastructure, incentives to industry and funding for training and skills development.

Since Federation, the Commonwealth and the states have existed in uneasy tension. Recently these tensions have been manifest in disputes over the management of water in the southeastern states and over plans for carbon emissions trading, both of which have major implications for regions. This presents perhaps the central paradox for the role of the university in Australia: funding for higher education is determined by the federal government, whereas the framework for local and regional development is dominated by the states.

A number of universities have strongly prioritized regional engagement (Garlick, 2000; Winter et al., 2006). For instance, the University of Ballarat in Victoria describes itself as "regional university" while the University of the Sunshine Coast in Queensland states that "the University's mission is to be the major catalyst for the sustainable advancement of the region."[2] Duke maintains, perhaps harshly, that in the realm of higher education "'regional' is seen as a weak, low-status identifier, to be embraced only where there is clear financial advantage" (2004, 303). Nevertheless, it remains the case that research intensive universities have traditionally placed a lesser priority on regional engagement, preferring to emphasise the importance of internationalization and "research excellence." A study of three Australian universities found that they had reactive rather strategic approaches to regional engagement (Gunasekara, 2006b; see also Gunasekara, 2000a).

The State of Victoria

Although many federal policies have had an impact on regions and the newly elected Federal Labour government has committed itself to extending regional policy, the states remain crucial jurisdictions in the promotion of regional development with significant differences in styles and structures of governance and patterns of economic development.

The state of Victoria has a distinctive political economy which provides the main context for Monash University's regional interactions. Traditionally the state was marked by a high degree of government control of the economy, a policy which lasted until the 1980s. F. W. Eggleston (1932) claimed that by the end of the 1920s, the scale of state intervention in Victoria was exceeded only by that of Soviet Russia. In the early 1990s, the Kennett Liberal government in Victoria pursued a program of cutbacks in public services and privatization of state-owned industries; local government reform led to a wave of mergers and a radical reduction in the number of councils. As a result, the state experienced markedly uneven sectoral and regional effects. Generally the reforms favored the urban core of Melbourne, which benefited from policies that accelerated the growth of tourism, leisure and financial sectors. By contrast, manufacturing towns and rural regions suffered. For instance, the privatization of the power industry (the State Electricity Commission of Victoria-SECV) had a major impact on the Latrobe Valley region where it was manifested in large scale job losses in power stations and the brown coal industry.

The growth of regional inequalities was the backdrop to election in 1999 of a new Labour state government which resulted in a more interventionist development strategy. Firstly, the state adopted an innovation-led economic development policy, exemplified by the strategy of attracting investment in the Australian Synchrotron to Melbourne (DPC, 2002; DIIRD, 2008), which offered new opportunities for university research. Secondly, Victoria strongly emphasized international migration and population growth. Finally, a new emphasis was placed on regional development (DPC, 2005).

In summary, by the turn of the 21st century the Victorian government and its stakeholders were seeking to reconcile several strategies including promoting Melbourne as the "Knowledge Capital" of Australia and addressing the fate of lagging metropolitan regions such as the outer southeastern suburbs. In addition, Victoria had to deal with problems of restructuring elsewhere, notably in regions like the Latrobe Valley which not only was dealing with the fallout of previous privatization but confronting a backlash against the environmental consequences of burning brown coal. Thus Monash University's ability to make an impact on regional development is conditioned by the interplay of the political economy of higher education, local understandings of regional development and the strategies of Victorian government.

The Case of Monash

Monash University was created in 1958 (Blackwood, 1968; Davison, 2008; Kent & Cuthbert, 1986; Marginson, 2000). It was named after Sir John Monash, engineer, fabled Australian general in the First World War and prominent Victorian state builder, notably through his role in establishing the SECV which supplies the state with most of its electricity (Serle, 1986; 2003). The State of Victoria established a new university at Clayton, a suburban community 20 *km* from the central business district (CBD) of Melbourne with the financial support of the Commonwealth government. Established as part of the new wave of post-war universities, Monash was intended to contribute to technologically driven national development, although there were few clues as to how this might be achieved.

According to Marginson, the ethos of the university was "nationalist and modernist" (2000, 13; see also Davison, 2008). Unlike the traditional sandstone universities, Monash developed a campus marked by native flora and a collection of contemporary Australian art. However, little thought appeared to have been given to the likely local impact of the Clayton campus: "If Clayton the suburb was expected to develop its own cosmopolitan ambience and institutions, at the end of the 20th century, 40 years after the foundation of Monash, there was no sign of this happening as yet" (Marginson, 2000, 12). In 2008 there was still no direct public transport connection between Clayton and the CBD.

Student numbers grew rapidly, reaching 13,000 by 1976. During the early years, modest but important forms of local engagement emerged. For example, staff and students from Monash operated a number of legal advice centers in Oakleigh and Springvale, relatively disadvantaged southeastern suburbs with large immigrant communities (Burnheim, 2005; Marginson, 2000). Also, a modest internationalization occurred as Monash hosted a number of foreign students under the Colombo Plan. However, during this period the emphasis was on the expansion of teaching and research and building the Clayton campus.

A major transformation occurred in the 1990s, led by an ambitious and enterprising Vice-Chancellor, Mal Logan (1987-1996) who saw the Dawkins reforms as an opportunity for Monash. Unlike New South Wales, where the state government planned a series of mergers, the Victorian government adopted a less directive approach. Logan responded with alacrity and sought the transformation of Monash into a new university committed to engagement, innovation and internationalization. He vigorously pursued mergers with smaller institutions.

Figure 10.1 *Location of Monash campuses (2007)*

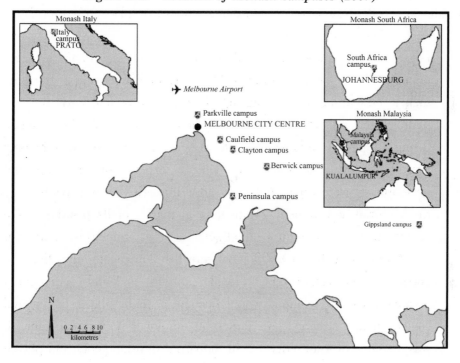

The manifestations of this strategy included the establishment of the Monash Science and Technology Park adjacent to the Clayton campus. The major development, however, was a series of mergers between Monash and other institutions, namely Chisholm Institute of Technology at Caulfield, Gippsland Institute of Advanced Education and the Victorian College of Pharmacy at Parkville just outside the CBD. The College of Pharmacy brought medical activities located in Melbourne's main medical precinct. Chisholm Institute, with a history older than Monash, brought a significant addition to existing offerings in business and economics.

Another campus on the Mornington Peninsula, 40 *km* from the CBD, brought an important nursing school. According to Marginson (2000), Gippsland was the most difficult merger. The Gippsland Institute had its origins in the Yallourn Technical College, which provided training for the SECV in the Latrobe Valley, serendipitously invoking a link with Sir John Monash. The incumbent director of the Institute saw the broadening of horizons at the institution and the region, where no major research took place. However,

> Logan did not want Gippsland to lose its regional character. He understood the local importance of the Churchill campus, the only higher education institution in a region characterised by low participation rates. It had an even more crucial role in a region facing the partial collapse of the local economy. When the University first took on Gippsland in 1998, expectation for regional development were high, but soon after the SECV was privatised by the Victorian government. More than a quarter of its positions were vanished: there were flow-on effects in other industries, and over five years more than 10,000 jobs were lost. Logan thought that, in concert with employers, local authorities and community organisations, the campus would become a major player in regional socioeconomic strategy. An important employer in its own right, it was a source of knowledge-based industrial development, and played a role in the arts and community services... [But] ... it would never be a major money maker. As Logan saw it, maintaining and developing Gippsland was part of Monash's public duty. He also knew that not everyone at Clayton agreed. (Marginson, 2000, 113-114)

A further campus was added at Berwick, a suburb in the outer southeast. As result of these mergers Monash doubled in size. Dealing with the legacies of these mergers in cultural, financial and administrative terms has absorbed much management time and energy into the 21st century. Among the tasks were achieving cohesion of purpose and ensuring that Monash maintained its position as a member of the Group of Eight universities, while absorbing campuses with little tradition of research and an emphasis on providing access to disadvantaged students.

International students have had a presence at Monash from the outset but international concerns remained at the margins. Logan sought to make Monash a player in Australia's growing geopolitical engagement in the Asia-Pacific. Through a mix of academic, political and financial motives Monash became the leading destination for international students coming to Australia. At the same time it opened a new campus in Kuala Lumpur and, later Johannesburg. In 2004 more than 17,000 international students (some 30.6% of all students) studied at Monash, the largest number at any Australian university. International students contributed 17.7% of total revenue (Marginson, 2007b).[3]

By 2007 Monash had 58,300 students in eight diverse campuses, making it the largest in the country. After 1990 Monash was transformed into "an international university and a Victorian state university" with a presence in the inner eastern region where it competed with Melbourne as a university for the privileged and the middle classes; at the same time it provided access to higher education in the Mornington Peninsula, the outer east and Gippsland, regions where participation rates were amongst the lowest in the state (Marginson, 2000).

Superficially, it would seem that a multi-campus structure would lend itself easily to the promotion of regional development but in practice a series of obstacles need to be confronted. A central challenge is to ensure that regional engagement is widely understood and accepted as a key mission of the university at all levels and across all campuses. A related challenge is to ensure that regional engagement is not considered a task reserved only for "regional" campuses. In practice this means gaining acceptance for the idea that the fate of the university and the fate of its regions are closely linked in a knowledge economy. This requires a sophisticated understanding of the meanings of concepts like region, development and engagement that go beyond simple notions of commercialization that have dominated many aspects of Australian higher education policy. At the very least this would mean that the mission of regional engagement should figure prominently in strategy documents and operational plans, and that key performance indicators should measure the impacts. However, Monash, along with most other Australian universities, faces some dilemmas, notably its dependence on revenue from international student fees. Reconciling these regional and international missions is particularly tricky. Many of these issues are beyond the capacity of a single university to address, even one as large and influential as Monash.

The potential for Monash to become an actor in regional development, widely conceived as an economic, social and cultural process, requires close links with other actors in governance systems. Identifying stakeholders in the regional development process is one important task, but so too is developing shared agendas. Key interlocutors include the state and local government as well as business and non-governmental organizations (NGOs). This again points to the need to develop explicit regional strategies. Although institutional histories, structures of funding, and cultural attitudes all present obstacles, there are a number of opportunities for Monash.

The Clayton campus lies at the heart of a major concentration of high technology industry and research and development activities, which form a key component of the southeast Melbourne growth corridor. The Clayton Innovation precinct is intended to stimulate some of this development and also to contribute to the ambition of state and local authorities to ensure Melbourne as the Knowledge Capital of Australia. A key enhancement of the technology cluster was the decision strongly supported by the Victorian government to locate the Australian Synchrotron adjacent to Monash's

Clayton campus. The location of a major entity at Clayton might also be expected to generate research synergies, but it requires thinking beyond facilities to pay more attention to the synergies between existing actors and potential actors; how relationships might move beyond a narrow commercialization agenda and how academic incentives for researchers might encourage them to engage these processes. This rethinking could include the role of the Clayton campus as a wider cultural resource (including theater and art) for the southeastern suburbs and as a contributor to a more spatially balanced development of the metropolitan region. All this would require closer relationships between the university and public and private actors.

The "regional" campuses can point to efforts to embed themselves in their communities through the creation of community advisory councils and close connections with local employers. The Gippsland Education Precinct, funded by state and federal governments, seeks to address the low educational and poor employment outcomes of young people in the Gippsland, with particular emphasis on the Latrobe Valley. However, the central concern with student equity programs raises questions about the esteem of these campuses in a research intensive university.

The original ambition set out for the Gippsland campus was to become an actor in transforming the socioeconomic status of the region. Despite earlier restructuring, the Latrobe Valley remains the center of the coal and power industries. As debates about climate change intensify, the future of the region is uncertain, especially as the region produces energy from brown coal. While engineering solutions such as carbon sequestration—in Monash has research strengths—are important, there is a larger question about the future that speaks to many facets of the debate about sustainable development, including its social and cultural dimensions that Monash is uniquely placed to lead.

The state government's innovation policy provides opportunities for Monash. The Australian Regenerative Medicine Institute was established at Monash, while the Melbourne Centre for Nanofabrication was located at Clayton both with combined state and federal funding. The state was re-emerging as an important funder of university activity. In 2003-2005 Monash's federal sources of income outweighed state sources by 19:1, by 2007 the ratio was reduced to 8:1. These developments raise the possibility of matching research and regional developments more closely.

Drawing on a study of community engagement by universities in Victoria, Winter et al. argue that, "older universities such as Melbourne and Monash universities tended to be more state, national and, increasingly, internationally focused. [The post-Dawkins] Victoria University, Swinburne University and RMIT report that benefit to community is part of their statutory Acts, which specify local community in regional terms, and responsibility in practical terms (meeting higher education needs, liaising with industry)... While Monash and Melbourne universities regard themselves as part of the international community, the University of Ballarat strives to attain a regionalism that is internationally excellent" (2006, 220; see also Winter et al., 2005), although region here is clearly understood in the non-metropolitan sense.

In a study by Burnheim of external engagement at the University of Western Australia (UWA), University of Queensland (UQ) and Monash, Burnheim found an uneven pattern of involvement. She suggests that Monash's external engagement was dominated by two factors: "the history of Monash as Melbourne's 'second' university and its broad spread of campuses, which give it distinctive relationships at each geographic site, and also create internal tensions and difficulties in coherent action" (2007, 10). According to Burnheim, external engagement is a "nascent" activity across Australia; her case study universities show that external engagement was "strongly associated with their regional and outer urban campuses and with their student equity programs...However, the regional campuses are expensive to run, have little research profile and do not attract high-scoring students" (2007, 17, 18).

Conclusion

The ability of universities to contribute to regional development is shaped by the evolving politics of national systems of regulation, intellectual and academic cultures, institutional histories, and uneven economic geographies. The case of Monash University demonstrates this clearly. The Australian context provides many obstacles to an internationalized research intensive university making a sustained contribution to regional development. Recognizing these constraints is not the same as announcing that the task is impossible. On the contrary there are reasons to believe Monash is well placed to overcome these obstacles.

Monash has evolved into an international multi-campus university with competing and contradictory missions. The conventional wisdom in Australia suggests that Monash University must choose between engagement and excellence. Many structural imperatives, not the least of which is finance, appear to compel that choice. However, Monash may well possess the capacity to transcend this dichotomy. Its multi-campus structure means that it can contribute to regional development at a range of scales: Victoria, Melbourne (as a Knowledge Capital), southeastern Melbourne as region in order to ensure balanced metropolitan development, and Gippsland and the Latrobe Valley as lagging regions facing economic restructuring. Kuala Lumpur and Johannesburg provide an international dimension to this conception. As Victoria grapples with the task of finding routes to sustainable development, it becomes apparent that these scales are not mutually exclusive but constitutive of the problems and solutions (Flannery, 2008). Similarly, the mission of teaching, research and engagement need not be mutually exclusive, but can all contribute to regional development in the widest sense. For this positive-sum scenario to be achieved, however, Monash will need new understandings about regions, development and engagement in their widest sense. Monash may be uniquely placed to develop these new visions and become the regionally engaged Group of Eight university.

Acknowledgements

   This chapter draws on research supported by the Office of the Deputy Vice-Chancellor (International), Monash University. We are grateful to those people who agreed to be interviewed as part of this study. We are especially grateful to Michael Simmonds and Benjamin Leske for their assistance in the organization of the interviews. We are also indebted to the senior managers and local and regional stakeholders who discussed the results of the study at a seminar on November 2008. Phil Scamp drew the map in the School of Geography and Environmental Science at Monash University. We are especially grateful to Kathryn Mohrman, Andy Gillespie, Michael Simmons, Ben Leske and Graeme Davison for comments on earlier draft. The content of this chapter is the responsibility of the authors alone.

Notes

[1]   For more details of the review see: http://www.innovation.gov.au/innovationreview/Documents/NIS_review_Web3.pdf.

[2]   See http://www.usc.ed.au/Community/RegionalEngagement/Philosophy.

[3]   Although Monash attracted the largest number of international students of any Australian university in 2003/4, several other universities derived a higher proportion of their revenue from international fees, the highest being the University of Central Queensland, which derived 38.2% from this source. At a number of Australian universities more than 40 of international enrollments are offshore.

NANJING UNIVERSITY
AND THE DEVELOPMENT OF JIANGSU PROVINCE

Zhehua Dai

Nanjing University, China

Introduction

Higher education brings about economic and social benefits, both to the individual and the public, produces qualified human capital, generates and distributes knowledge, promotes international cooperation and improves competitiveness in the global knowledge based economy (NASULGC, n.d.) Universities worldwide, especially public institutions, must develop an interactive and mutually beneficial relationship with society to exist and prosper. As is the case nowadays, universities have moved from the marginal position to a more central position in social and economic development. In addition to the widely recognized three basic tasks of teaching, research and social service, or expressed as talent training, science development and service to the society (Hu et al., 2005), university engagement in social development is becoming a high priority dimension of higher education's responsibilities. National leaders and policy makers have also realized that research universities, public and private, are important for national development (Altbach, 2007).

Presently, however, there exists a big gap between the development of universities and the development of society. First, with an emphasis on academic freedom and autonomous operation, universities strive to maintain exploration and inquiry, whereas applicability and competitiveness of research is more cherished by the society with a much clearer market orientation. Secondly, universities seek to train students with comprehensive knowledge is pursued by universities, while businesses want students with capabilities to apply knowledge. Those problems must be probed and resolved.

Nanjing University, a prestigious institution of higher learning, is located in Jiangsu Province, one of the leading areas of China in economic, cultural and educational development. Jiangsu Province, working closely with China's Ministry of Education, provides significant funding to Nanjing University under Project 985 to facilitate its development into a world class university. Realizing the important role the government can play in economic planning and resources allocation, Nanjing University has changed its interactions with local governments and industry for regional development, from the traditional "combination of teaching, research and industry" style to the "combination of teaching, research, industry and government." Believing collective strengths are more helpful in serving diversified needs, Nanjing University's social engagement and service models have also changed from "point-to-point cooperation" to "point-to-area cooperation" and from spontaneous service by individual professors to organized service by the university.

So far, Nanjing University has signed cooperation agreements with quite a few cities in Jiangsu Province, including Nanjing, Changzhou, Yangzhou, Wuxi, Suzhou, Taizhou, Yixing and Jiangyin. The partnerships have diversified the areas of cooperation and the models of interaction based upon consideration of each partner city's industrial structure and development strategy. The university has provided support for R&D and human resources for both core technologies and common technologies in the local industry chain. The different forms of cooperation are aimed to solve specific problems in industry and business to speed up the economic growth and gain support in return for the university's research advancement and faculty development.

The partnerships have also expanded from human resources and science and technology to cooperation in all dimensions and at different levels. The Senior Forum on Jiangsu Development, which was first launched in 1997 by Nanjing University, is indeed a case in point.

The Origin and Objectives of the Forum

Ten years ago, then Vice President of Nanjing University Hong Yinxing was concerned about the fact that theory was hardly being connected with practice. He sought a way to build a bridge between scholars and the government so that more scholars would be encouraged to care about and study the practical issues in Jiangsu's economic development, more communications would be carried out between theorists and government agencies and departments, and scholars could provide consultation and references to the government. Hong and Chen Huanyou, then Secretary of the CPC Jiangsu Provincial Committee, jointly initiated the Senior Forum on Jiangsu Development, a policy forum to discuss major issues about Jiangsu's development and problems faced by the Yangtze River Delta area. These leaders created the forum in order to boost Jiangsu's social sciences and soft science research, to promote reform and opening up and various social and economic activities of Jiangsu Province, to provide up-to-date research findings in social science to the government and enterprises for reference and thus to help turn the research findings into practical productivity.

Chen is now honorary chairman of the Forum and Hong, now Secretary of the CPC Nanjing University Committee, chairs the academic committee. Hu Fuming, who authored the article "Practice Is the Sole Criterion for Testing Truth," is an advisor to the Forum, among others. Scholars from Nanjing University and other higher education institutions and leaders from major provincial government agencies are academic commissioners.

Ever since 1997, despite leadership changes in both government and university, the Forum has continued to be held. Professor Zhang Erzhen of the Nanjing University Business School and Secretary of the Forum analyzed that the Forum has indeed served as an important interface for decision makers, scholars and experts. Li Yuanchao, former Secretary of the CPC Jiangsu Provincial Committee said, "This is indeed a reflection of scientific decision-making. It is a fine tradition of several successive leaders of CPC Jiangsu Provincial Committee and it should be carried on in the years to come" (Wang, 2008).

To date, 25 sessions of the Forum have been held, with participation of more than 400 scholars and leaders from Jiangsu Provincial Committee of the Communist Party of China (CPC) and Jiangsu Provincial Government. It has been recognized as the highest level platform of policy consultancy for Jiangsu Provincial Government. Providing a large number of proposals for the government decision makers, this Forum has contributed to local economic development and social advancement and is giving full play to the universities' function as a government think tank.

The organizational committee of the forum is situated in Nanjing University, and its routine work is being undertaken by the Research Center for the Social and Economic Development of the Yangtze River Delta, which is a national key research base of humanities and social sciences at Nanjing University approved by China's Ministry of Education.

The objectives of the Forum are articulated as follows: Focused on the theme of Jiangsu Development, pooling the outstanding research strength in theories and policies for Jiangsu Province's development, releasing the recent research findings in theories and policies, the Forum provides consultancy to the CPC Jiangsu Provincial Committee and Provincial Government to help them with democratic and scientific decision making (Research Center, n.d.).

In the past 10 years, the forum has become one of the most important platforms in providing consulting service to local Party committees and governments to help them make decisions in ways that are more scientific and democratic. The forum has gathered hundreds of scholars, government officers and entrepreneurs, focusing on the strategic and practical issues in Jiangsu's economic and social development.

For example, to find ways of coordinated and collective development of the southern part, the middle part and the northern part of Jiangsu Province, the 12th session in March 2001 focused on Jiangsu regional economic co-development strategies and measures. In August 2007, the Forum looks at opportunities, challenges and responses for Jiangsu to develop international outsourcing businesses, in order to promote the transfer of international service industries.

Focused on strategic thinking for economic development, hundreds of outstanding scholars, government officials and entrepreneurs have attended the Forum. Between 1997 and October 2008, 25 sessions have been held in total, and more than 400 experts, scholars and government officials have submitted consultation reports and research papers to the sessions of the Forum. Chen Huanyou, Hui Liangyu, Li Yuanchao and Liang Baohua, four consecutive secretaries of CPC Jiangsu Provincial Committee, have presented themselves at all those sessions. Each time the Forum serves at the highest platform for policy consultancy to Jiangsu provincial party committee and government.

The Operational Mechanism of the Forum

While academic conferences are usually held to share newly developed knowledge, inform colleagues of new research findings and encourage communication among academics, the Senior Forum on Jiangsu Development is mainly held to tackle the strategic and practical issues encountered and predicted by the government, industry and business. It is an opportunity for academics to sit face-to-face with senior government officers and a chance for outstanding entrepreneurs to find the best possible solutions to problems and issues in economic development and social advancement. While being different from academic conferences, the Forum is usually operated in the following way:

1) The academic committee of the Forum and some related departments of Jiangsu provincial party committee and government propose three to five topics to the provincial party committee. The secretary of the Party Committee chooses one topic after discussion with colleagues. He may also suggest a topic for the session directly. All topics are related to the major issues or problems faced by Jiangsu's economic and social development.

2) After the topic is finalized, the forum organizers issue a call for papers and then collect the papers and consultation reports from the well known universities and philosophy and social science research institutes in Nanjing, Jiangsu, and other areas both inside and outside the province. Specialists and scholars are urged to conduct in-depth research and come up with consultation reports on the session topic. The forum organizers publish these papers as the forum proceedings. Usually the notice of soliciting articles is sent out one month before a particular session is held.

3) The speakers are selected accordingly to the quality of papers and consultation reports. Some well known domestic and foreign experts are often invited to give keynote speeches. Generally the speaking time allocated is 20 minutes for the keynote speaker, 10 minutes for the session designated speaker and 5 minutes for open speaking. Every one is free and equal to speak or discuss at the forum, no matter whether he/she is young or senior, high ranking or otherwise. The sessions of the forum last for three and half hours, with no break in between. The total number of speakers at each session is generally about 20 persons. The secretary of the Jiangsu Provincial Party Committee takes part in discussion as an ordinary scholar, and then gives a 15-minute talk before the session concludes.

4) The outcome of every session of the Forum is published in a book, with main points of view to be written in the forum briefings for the

government and provincial party committee to take as reference when they make decisions.

5) The Jiangsu Provincial Finance Department covers the expenses to hold the forum, while the conference room has always remained at Nanjing University.

Effects and Significance of the Forum

As a relatively developed area in economy, culture and education, Jiangsu Province takes a lead in each major restructuring of national development. To ensure democratic and scientific decision making at the top level, the CPC Jiangsu provincial committee and the provincial government consult with experts and scholars on major strategies of the economic and social development at each session. Major issues are usually reflected at the Forum.

Again, as a leading province in economic development and social advancement, Jiangsu Province provides a good demonstration site for studying China's reform, opening-up, transition and other related issues. Many thoughts on Jiangsu's development are based on extensive investigations and in-depth studies and finally consolidated at the Forum.

Since China started to reform and open up to the outside world in late 1970s, Jiangsu has seized two development opportunities. The first one was the development of township enterprises. [1] The second was the opening-up of Pudong New District in Shanghai and the rapid development of export-oriented economy.[2]

What would be Jiangsu's next step? In May 1997, after the second session of the forum focused on structural adjustment and the third opportunity for Jiangsu's economic development, Chen Huanyou concluded with other participants that strategic economic structural adjustment would be Jiangsu's next chance in sustainable development. He then included the research results of the Forum in his working paper and brought it to that year's National People's Congress meeting. Again,

Jiangsu went ahead of other provinces and cities in the country, raising the idea of economic structural adjustment after the CPC's 17th National Congress held in October 1997 (Wu & Zeng, 2008).

In April 2003, after the 15th session on the transfer of world manufacturing centers and the development of the areas along the Yangtze River in Jiangsu, the provincial government officially proposed the strategy of cross-Yangtze River development. In October 2003, after the 16th session on development issues of the eastern Jiangsu area on the Longhai Railway (between Liangyuangang Seaport in Jiangsu Province and Lanzhou City in Gansu Province), the Jiangsu Provincial Party Committee mapped out plans about the development of Xuzhou and Liangyungang economic zones.

In January 2007, after the 22nd session studying scientific outlook on development and the new southern Jiangsu development model, the provinice held the largest scale Southern Jiangsu Working Meeting in Suzhou. The 24th session was held in April 2008 with the theme of the transformation of Jiangsu's economic development mode, the theme inspired by central government leaders. Jiangsu is one of the pilot provinces in the practice of the scientific outlook on development. In that year's National People's Congress sessions and CPC's national congress, President Hu Jintao expressed his wish that Jiangsu should take the lead in the transformation of economic development, as well as in scientific development, comprehensive development and coordinated development. Therefore, Jiangsu Party Secretary Liang Baohua decided that the theme of 2008 session would be the transformation of the province's economic development mode.

On October 21, 2008, the 25th session was held with the theme three-dimensional rural issues concerning agriculture, countryside and farmers in Jiangsu. The session proposed concrete measures for reform of the urban-rural structure to improve rural productivity, expediting the development of modern agriculture and improving infrastructure for farmers' living.

China's Vice Premier Hui Liangyu, when he was Secretary of the Jiangsu Provincial CPC Committee, summarized the roles of the Forum as "outside brain," "integration of knowledge and practice, macro and micro, concrete matters of work and principles," "think-tank and general staff," and "bridge and linkage" (Institute for Jiangsu Development, 2008). Li Yuanchao once commented on the high-level forum, "We have gradually developed a system that before making any major decisions, we should fully listen to experts' different opinions and views and then analyze these propositions from different perspectives. Only in this way can we ensure that we make our major decisions scientifically" (Wang, 2008).

The high-level forum improves the predictability of major decisions on modernization. Many years ago, southern Jiangsu developed relatively fast while the middle and the northern parts were growing slowly. Different people had different opinions on how to coordinate the development in different regions. Some said that the provincial government just supported the southern part and did not support the northern part, and suggested accelerating the development in northern Jiangsu. Some other argued that if the southern Jiangsu did not expedite the development, how could they support the development in northern Jiangsu. Later, the ideas and measures of common and collective development of regional economy were put forward. Regional co-development strategy became acceptable to all and then played a guiding role in the practice (Wu & Zeng, 2008).

The forum raises the enthusiasm of experts and scholars in offering advice and suggestions. Most participants of the Forum are outstanding experts and scholars, some are entrepreneurs, but only a small number are political leaders and government officials. At the Forum, every one speaks freely without any worries. In this relaxed and liberal environment, all good suggestions can be conveyed through this platform.

This environment can ensure experts' participation and also benefits the sustainable development of the Forum.

The lively form and democratic style is a major feature of the Forum. If someone is late, he can only take a seat in the back row. As Zhang Erzhen, Secretary of the Forum, described, "Leaders and scholars sit at a round table to exchange ideas face to face. We do not have seat cards in front of us, and there is no hierarchy distinction." Hui Liangyu, then Secretary of Jiangsu Provincial CPC committee, once said while attending the meeting, "Today 20 scholars have already spoken, I am then the 21st one." Evidently, at this forum, the provincial party committee secretary just attended this forum as a scholar. Chen Huanyou also commented, "Everybody is equal in the forum. This strengthens the forum's constructive nature"(Wu & Zeng, 2008).

Conclusion

The Senior Forum on Jiangsu Development has existed for ten years, with 25 sessions held so far. Why is it so attractive and gaining support from the government, business and industry and academia? The major reason is, first of all, it ensures the combination of theory and practice. It provides consultation to government and industry as they need to make decisions on the issues and problems facing economic, industrial and social advancement. Secondly, it sets up a platform for the government, industry and business, research and academia to share and exchange views on social and economic issues. Thirdly, the Forum expands the sphere of academics to serve the society at large and thus sets an example for other provinces in China and even organizations in foreign countries in their efforts and initiatives getting help with regional development.

To ensure sustainable development of the Forum itself, some conditions should be considered and guaranteed. First of all, the government should trust but not interfere into university's academic research. University's academic freedom and independent thinking provide different but objective voices on the issues facing government officials dealing with economic development and social advancement. Secondly, the government should ensure financial support to the Forum. The Forum itself does not generate direct economic returns. Who finances the Forum is a critical question. Enterprises and individuals would unavoidably ask for tangible returns if they sponsored the Forum. If the government pays for "consultation service" using taxpayers' money before they make decisions concerning people's living, they should also be held accountable to the public and let the taxpayers believe the Forum is worth its salt. Thirdly, the actual organization work of the Forum should ensure high quality consultation and suggestions. The screening and selection of keynote speeches and other remarks must focus on the balance of academic and practical natures, concrete matters and principles.

Nanjing University's fame as a fine social science research base has been sustaining all these years especially since the article "Practice Is the Sole Criterion for Testing Truth" was published in 1978, which helped launch China's opening-up. The Senior Forum on Jiangsu Development has become another brand name in university's engagement with society. Scholars' research abilities are improved through participation in the Forum and their keen insights are encouraged and advocated. The university leadership should give full support to the development of key programs in social sciences as well as faculty development, with a stronger team of researchers engaged in social sciences studies.

Of course, the Forum is not the only way to get engaged with the society at large, including the government and industry. When providing diagnoses, technology transfer, collaborative R&D to industry, and helping with neighboring regions' comprehensive development strategies and optimization of their priority industry sectors, Nanjing University must ensure favorable conditions for academic research and faculty improvement. The university will also need to keep arms length from the society so as to produce objective and well grounded views in order to propose effective thoughts on the harmonious development of society.

Notes

[1] Township enterprises in China are usually referred to as businesses and factories run by farmers in the countryside. They are usually involved in industry, agricultural products processing, transportation and communications, construction, commerce and catering. Now township enterprises have become a main source of farmers' income and rural economic development.

see http://www. china. org. cn/english/features/38203. htm

[2] Export-oriented economy is a kind of economy in which economic interactions with an export-driven industry and business structure are open to international markets, extensively using international resources and taking part in international work division and exchanges.

see http://wiki. mbalib. com/wiki/Export-oriented economy

Appendix

Themes of all sessions of Senior Forum
on Jiangsu development (as of October 2008)

The Competitive Edge of Products Made in Jiangsu
Structural Readjustment and the Third Opportunity for Jiangsu's Economic Development
Capital Operation and Enterprise Re-organization
The Financial Crisis of Southeast Asia and Jiangsu's Countermeasures for the Crisis
The Methods for Accelerating Jiangsu's Economics Growth
The International and Domestic Economic Development Trends in 1999 and Jiangsu's Countermeasures
The Development of Jiangsu's New and High Technology Facing the New Century
Entry of China's Economy into a New Growing Stage and Jiangsu's Countermeasures
The New Drives for Jiangsu's Economic Development Facing the 21st Century
Urbanization of Jiangsu
The Social and Economic Development Strategies of Jiangsu during the Tenth Five-year Plan Period
Collaborative Development of Jiangsu's Local Economies: Concepts and Measures

How to Utilize the Capital Market Effectively in the New Situation
Jiangsu's Countermeasures After Its Entry into WTO
The Shift of World Manufacturing Centers and the Development of Regions Along the Yangtze River in Jiangsu
The Development of the East Regions Along the Longhai Railway in Jiangsu
Economic Globalization and the Construction of International Manufacturing Bases in Jiangsu
Construction of "Jiangsu under Rule of Law"
Construction of Harmonious Society in Jiangsu
Modern Service Industry Development in Jiangsu
Independent Innovation and Technological Entrepreneurship
Scientific Thinking on Development and New Development Mode for Southern Jiangsu
Opportunities, Challenges and Responses for Jiangsu to Develop International Outsourcing Businesses
The Transformation of Jiangsu's Economic Development Patterns
Three-dimensional Rural Issues Concerning Agriculture, Countryside and Farmers in Jiangsu

Modified by the Research Center for the Social and Economic Development of the Yangtze River Delta of Nanjing University, *Subject Matters of All Previous High-level Forums for Jiangsu's Development*, see http://www. ccjsjz. cn/newslist. aspx?lan = en&classid = 33.

NEWCASTLE UNIVERSITY: HIGHER EDUCATION WITH A PURPOSE

John Goddard and Paul Vallance
Newcastle University, United Kingdom

Introduction

This case study traces the journey of one institution, Newcastle University in the North East of England, in rediscovering its roots as a locally engaged university. Originally founded in the 19th century to help support emerging industries in the city, the university became detached from this original vocation during the 20th century as it concentrated on developing into a strong academic institution in the context of a national system of higher education. However, over the past two decades the university's role in supporting regional development has grown again, driven by changes in the external environment for higher education institutions in the UK. These "third strand" activities are now codified, alongside more traditional academic concerns, in the university's mission statement: "To be a world-class research-intensive university, to deliver teaching of the highest quality and to play a leading role in the economic, social and cultural development of the North East of England."

This region, the North East of England[1], with an economic heritage based primarily on heavy industries such as shipbuilding, manufacturing, steel and coal mining, suffered acutely through deindustrialization in the 1970s and 1980s, leaving it with considerable economic and social problems as it struggled to adjust to a knowledge based economy. The city of Newcastle upon Tyne is the largest city in the region with a local population of a quarter of a million, and has retained a relative level of prosperity as a service center for a regional economy of 4.5 million. Newcastle is the largest city between Leeds to the south and Edinburgh to the north (and in Scotland). In short it is England's most northerly city.

Newcastle University is one of two universities in the city, alongside the University of Northumbria (formerly Newcastle Polytechnic), and one of two research intensive universities in the region, alongside nearby Durham University. It has more than 18,000 students and more than 4,500 staff in total, making it the third biggest employer in the city. Newcastle is part of the Russell Group of the 20 strongest research universities in the UK, each with a' medical school linked to a university hospital.

This chapter has two main parts. In the first we provide background for the case study by outlining the UK context in which higher education participation in regional development occurs. We will identify, in turn, the main regional drivers and higher education drivers behind engagement, following the general framework set out in Goddard and Pukka (2008). This framework was developed as part of an Organisation for Economic Co-operation and Development (OECD) Review of the Contribution of Higher Education Institutions to Regional Development (OECD, 2007). The review revealed that across the OECD, universities and regions were discovering each other through a growing appreciation of shared interests. More specifically, universities were discovering how their cities and regions could support their global aspirations in terms of teaching and research, and provide an arena in which they could demonstrate their contribution to civil society. Likewise cities and regions were discovering the importance of universities, not just as major employers, but also as contributors to business innovation, workforce development, social and cultural cohesion and last but not least, place making and global positioning. Our focus in this first part of the chapter is on the effect of these drivers on a strong research intensive university located in a peripheral economic region, and we make frequent reference to specific features of the North East region.

In the second part we detail the institutional development of Newcastle University in this changing context for regional engagement. We highlight a series of regional development initiatives that the university has been involved in with key external partners, in order to show the different ways in which universities can become locally engaged through both research and teaching activities. This discussion draws on the experience of one of the co-authors as founding director of the University's Centre for Urban and Regional Development Studies and subsequently Deputy Vice Chancellor with a specific responsibility for regional engagement. In a short conclusion we discuss some of the general issues and lessons for higher education policy and practice that arise from this case study.

University and Regional Engagement in UK Context

Regional Development Drivers

The economy of the UK is dominated by London and its surrounding Southeast region, creating high and persistent levels of uneven development with more peripheral regions such as the North East suffering relatively high levels of unemployment. Government policy to address this problem has entered into a new phase during the past 10 to 15 years. During the post-World War II period the nation-state intervened directly to reduce regional economic and social disparities through demand-side industrial policies that aimed to support established firms and divert mobile investment to regions with high unemployment. Following the breakdown of this international Keynesian consensus in the mid-1970s there was a period of less state assistance to struggling regions in the UK, especially with the market-led policies favored by the Conservative government of Margaret Thatcher.

The revival of the Labour Party in the mid-1990s returned regional issues to the UK policy agenda (Jones, 2001). In the new context of a post-industrialized knowledge economy (DTI, 1998), however, the belief guiding UK regional economic policy changed: the experience of regions such as the North East meant the Keynesian demand-side policies of the post-war era had come to be regarded as helping to create *branch-plant* regional economies overly dependent on external investment in manufacturing to exploit lower costs of production (land and labor) and without the endogenous capacity to generate growth themselves (Phelps et al., 2003). As a result, the focus of regional economic policy has shifted to strengthening supply-side factors, and particularly the non-firm institutional base of a region that supports the development of knowledge based industries (Amin, 1999). The model for old industrial regions with a low developmental capacity is to emulate globally competitive *learning regions* that are characterized by a culture of collaborative innovation in networks of local public and private actors (Morgan, 1997).

Whereas higher education was not a part of the earlier demand-side regional economic policies, the recognition of universities as potential sources of specialized knowledge, advanced research and higher level skills has brought these hitherto separated domains of higher education and regional industrial development together in today's innovation-focused supply-side policies. This is particularly true of peripheral regions, such as the North East, that suffer from a deficit of private and public sector investment in research and development, but may have a healthy representation of research intensive universities that policy makers hope can be tapped to fill the gap in their regional innovation system (Benneworth & Charles, 2005). Based on previously successful cases such as the agglomeration of high technology firms around the University of Cambridge (Keeble et al., 1999), higher education institutions have also entered into UK cluster policy discourse as potentially forming important linkages with local small and medium enterprises (SMEs) through their technology transfer, commercialization and spin-off activities (DTI, 2005). Consequently many universities have been linked with property-led science parks often at a distance from the main university campus. No such park was developed in Newcastle.

The rediscovery of the region as a unit of economic organization and competitiveness (Storper, 1995) has been paralleled by changes in the economic governance structure of the UK. Developments on a European rather than national level prompted the changes, with the organization of English regions as political entities so that they may access European Union Structural Fund assistance (Musson et al., 2005). In the mid-1990s European regional policy expanded from mainly funding large infrastructure projects to also supporting research and development activity in peripheral regions (Morgan, 1997). Many of these innovation based programs in the UK involved an integral role for higher education institutions (Potts, 2002).

Since the election of a Labour government in 1997 there has also been a significant restructuring of the UK governance system that affects how economic development policies are delivered. This has, to a degree, reduced the traditionally highly centralized nature of the British state, and left the UK with an asymmetrical governance structure. The biggest changes have occurred through the establishment of a devolved parliament in Scotland and elected assemblies in Wales and Northern Ireland, all of which have inherited powers for coordinating a range of economic development functions in their territories (Goodwin et al., 2005). In England no such equivalent level of national government has been introduced, but there has been an expansion in institutions operating at the regional level (Musson et al., 2005).

Most prominent amongst these are Regional Development Agencies (RDAs), non-departmental public bodies located in each of the nine English regions, with responsibilities for supporting business competitiveness through setting regional strategic priorities and limited financial powers to deliver economic development initiatives through partnerships with local bodies (Deas & Ward, 2000). Under the sponsorship of the Department for Business Enterprise and Regulatory Reform (formerly the Department of Trade and Industry), the RDAs are funded by a combination of central government departments out of a *single pot* which is allocated according to a formula based system that gives more money per capita to those regions with the greatest economic development needs. For 2008-2009 the North East had the highest relative budget of any region, more than five times the per capita figure for the South East RDA (BERR, 2008). Hence, RDAs have emerged as particularly important institutions in peripheral regions, where the relative lack of other private and public investment in research and development means that universities become a key point of engagement in their efforts to develop a knowledge based regional economy (Goddard & Chatterton, 1999). At the same time, RDAs stimulated many local authorities (which had hitherto ignored or taken universities in their area for granted and only engaged with them through land use planning controls) to wake up to the importance of universities as major employers and potential actors in local economic development.

Higher Education Drivers

Higher education in the UK has undergone two major expansions during the past 50 years that have fundamentally reshaped the sector. First, prompted by the Robbins Report (1963), there was a wave of university creation during the 1960s, comprising new institutions mainly located outside of large cities, and the upgrading of what were Colleges of Advanced Technology. Second, in 1992 the government ended the two-tier system of higher education, so that the former polytechnics, which had previously been under local authority control, became new universities (Mayhew et al., 2004). These changes helped participation rates grow from around 5% of 19- and 20-year-olds in higher education in the early 1960s to around 33% in the late 1990s (Greenaway & Haynes, 2000, 7- 8). However, this move from an elite to a mass system has not been matched by increases in government expenditure on higher education, with the consequence that the level of public funding per student in higher education almost halved in real terms between 1980 and 2000 (Greenaway & Haynes, 2000, 13). This squeezing of their core funding has forced universities to be more entrepreneurial in seeking to maximize other potential sources of income (Clark, 1998). As autonomous institutions, UK universities are free to compete for students and research contracts, to market their services and to buy and sell land in support of their activities. For many universities the core public funding for teaching and research amounts to only a third of their income.

In the context of this higher education marketplace, government policy for higher education in the UK does not have a formal spatial dimension. Higher education funding was (and still is) related to student numbers and research outputs with no explicit concern for where those students are taught or the graduates employed, where the research is undertaken or the economic impacts occur, be this international, national or regional. Nevertheless the competition for funding tends to have uneven geographical effects through heavily favoring institutions in London and the South East of England. Universities located in peripheral regions like the North East of England have tighter budgets and have to work harder to create the financial headroom to engage in city and regional development. However, the establishment of the Regional Development Agencies created some opportunities for universities in less advantaged regions to access new sources of funding to support their engagement in economic development.

On the teaching side, the increase in the number of universities in the UK has heightened competition for students between institutions. Basic government funding for teaching is allocated by the Higher

Education Funding Council for England (HEFCE) and equivalent bodies in Scotland, Wales and Northern Ireland according to a formula system based on the number of students enrolled in different subject areas. Since 2006, following lengthy political debate, universities in England have been able to supplement this by increasing the amount they charge domestic students for tuition fees to a maximum of £3,000 (US $4,590) per year. However, as a concession to those who feared that this move would discriminate against students from disadvantaged backgrounds, the right for universities to introduce these capped top-up fees was linked to also meeting widening participation targets, regulated by the newly established Office for Fair Access (OFFA). Because institutions are more likely to recruit low income students from local areas, where they do not have to move away from home to attend university, this has introduced an implicit regional dimension into what is a national, and increasingly international, marketplace for students. For example the government introduced a scheme to encourage students from schools in disadvantaged areas and with a poor track recording of getting their pupils into university to aspire to higher education. The *Aim Higher* scheme was implemented through regional associations of universities working in partnership with selected schools.

On the output side of higher education as reflected in graduates with skills required by the employers, universities had been seen as supplying graduates to a national labor market. Bodies with an explicit charge to support local labor markets, such as local Learning and Skills Councils, were only responsible for basic skills at a level of training below higher education. However, following recognition that higher level skills are crucial to the UK's future economic competitiveness (Leitch, 2006), the RDAs have become interested in working with higher education institutions and local employer associations to increase the supply of skilled workers. The UK ranks poorly in international league tables in terms of the proportion of those in employment with university level qualifications; the government has been encouraging employers to spend more on upskilling their workforce through investment in programs developed in partnership with universities. Again this has been a national focus with an implicit spatial dimension given that employees can most conveniently participate in updating programs run in their local university.

While "knowledge transfer on legs" from research to business via teaching and learning may be a key mechanism, the funding and organization of research in UK universities has gone down a completely separate track from teaching. The UK government provides for a dual system of research funding. HEFCE allocates block funding to institutions on the basis of the Research Assessment Exercise (RAE), a peer review of research quality carried out roughly every three to five years that rates the strength of institutions in different subject areas. Funding for individual research projects primarily occurs through research councils in seven different fields (e.g. medical research, economic and social research), which run themed programs of research as well as open competitions for other applications. The underlying aim of this system is to achieve world class research excellence in the UK, and is therefore oriented towards providing the highest levels of support to institutions that already have strong research capabilities. The geographical expression of this system is a continued funding imbalance in favor of an area labelled *the golden triangle* in the Greater South East of England: just four institutions from within this region (Oxford and Cambridge Universities, University College London and Imperial College London) account for 28.4% of total research funding from HEFCE for academic year 2006-2007 (Figure calculated by authors from Table 1 in HEFCE, 2006).

However, recent policy developments have seen the emergence of a sub-national level of science governance, in the form of multiple regional initiatives that are based on partnerships between higher education institutions and other local public and private bodies. For example, every English region now has an advisory Science and Industry Council with membership from across these sectors (Perry, 2007). Notable amongst these sub-national developments has been the recent designation of six English cities in different regions outside the South East as Science Cities, including Newcastle. Although this program was initiated by central government, it is not heavily supported by national funding; instead it is an attempt to support economic development through mobilizing local actors around building place-based science-business linkages (OECD, 2008). A common enabling factor in these associations has been the interest of regional governance bodies (particularly RDAs) in the potential value of academic research to economic development. So whilst these developments do not constitute a loosening of central government's control over the allocation of core research funding (Perry, 2007), they do create new avenues for entrepreneurial universities outside of the golden triangle to access external funds through tying their research activities into the regional economic development agenda.

HEFCE also runs additional schemes that directly encourage university third mission activity through knowledge transfer to local business and community, such as the Higher Education Innovation Fund (HEIF). The UK is unusual in having a national higher education funding scheme specifically to support external engagement. While HEIF seldom represents more than 1% of the income of a research intensive university and is national rather regionally specific, it has supported many projects that entail collaboration between universities in a region. This reflects an increasing move towards the institutionalization of formal relations between regional universities. For instance, all the English regions now have an association of their universities which involve a mix of institutional types (both research and teaching oriented universities). The first such organization was formed in the North East in 1983, and is now called Universities for the North East (unis4ne). These associations provide a basis for collaboration between the universities and a forum for them to collectively dialogue with other regional bodies such as RDAs.

The Newcastle University Journey

How has Newcastle University fitted into this evolving and complex UK landscape connecting universities and their localities? In many respects the university has been on a journey in which it has re-discovered its roots as a quintessentially *civic university*. Thus the university was born out of the need to support the newly emerging industries of the 19th century and to sustain a healthy population to work in those industries. What was to become King's College, University of Durham was based around departments focusing on various areas of engineering—marine, electrical, civil and chemical, together with agriculture and medicine. The more academic parts of the university remained in the cathedral city of Durham where the university had strong links to the church. By contrast the 19th century manufacturing city of Newcastle had a flourishing secular life that embraced science, engineering and the arts, with places like the Literary and Philosophical Institute and the Mining Institute providing locations where the world of thought and action came together.

The establishment of the independent University of Newcastle upon Tyne in 1963 was followed by a significant expansion of higher education in the UK. This expansion coincided with a major program of urban redevelopment in Newcastle which in turn was part of a national attempt to revive the flagging economy of the North East. An alliance between the then Deputy Vice Chancellor, a landed aristocrat who chaired the governing body of the polytechnic, and the charismatic civic leader, T. Dan Smith, resulted in the consolidation of the present campus as part of Smith's vision of "Education upon Tyne," a vision which anticipated later notions of the knowledge or service based city. In physical terms, this embraced the polytechnic, Civic Centre, university and Royal Victoria Infirmary sites. As a result, unlike many other civic universities, Newcastle was able to expand in situ and develop a single site city center campus.

With the fall of Dan Smith through a corruption scandal and the growing influence of the University Grants Committee in London, the university turned its back on the city during most of the 1970s and 1980s and developed a traditional academic heartland in the arts and sciences. Equally the region ignored its universities and polytechnics. Quite simply, the universities followed the money. Local and regional agencies had no charge or funding to engage with or support higher education.

It was therefore not surprising that new sources of funding from the European structural funds in the 1990s brought about some change. Influenced by the growing body of evidence, some of it produced by the University's Centre for Urban and Regional Development Studies, European regional development programs were increasingly being given an innovation signature, particularly focussing on SMEs. Most importantly, universities were made eligible beneficiaries. In addition, a group of three regional civil servants (the regional directors for the Departments of Trade and Industry, Employment, and Environment) worked together to change UK government thinking in relation to support for business innovation. Partly to exploit these opportunities, the then Newcastle University Pro Vice Chancellor led the establishment of a network of North East universities (Higher Education Support for Industry in the North East—HESIN) and its gateway for SMEs, Knowledge House. HESIN developed into the current association of Universities for the North East as the widening role of higher education in regional development became apparent. Capacity for engagement was built up in the universities and the association through a series of short term projects funded via a variety of European and national time limited programs. However, this endeavor was never embedded into the mainstream funding of higher education.

Two national developments in the 1990s moved regional engagement on: the establishment of a small higher education funding stream to support engagement with business and the community (the forerunner of HEIF) and the creation of the RDAs. The establishment of the North East agency (ONE North East) fundamentally changed the points in terms of engagement by the region's universities. Its first Regional Economic Strategy (RES) recognised the need to rebuild the economy around knowledge based industries, and consequently "placed universities at the heart of the regional economy" (ONE NorthEast, 1999). This exhortation was translated into a "Strategy for Success" hubbed around five "centers of excellence" designated to operate between business and the research base in the universities. These were spread around the region. The RES also recognized the advantage that the region had in terms of a diverse set of universities, some with strong local roots and others with global reach.

Further point-changing developments for Newcastle University and the city were the creation of the Millennium Lottery-funded International Centre for Life, the Newcastle/Gateshead bid to be recognized as a European Capital of Culture and the designation of Newcastle as a Science City. These developments were paralleled by a restructuring of the university initiated by a new Vice Chancellor, appointed in 2001, which enabled the institution to adopt a more corporate response to opportunities in its external environment. Through restructuring, the university rediscovered its roots of "excellence with a purpose." All three developments illustrate the importance of leadership inside and outside of the university.

The creation of the International Centre for Life, led by a former civil servant with a background in urban regeneration (and also vice chair of the university governing body) and the university's Professor of Human Genetics, made it possible to bring together on a single site the university's dispersed strengths in the rapidly emerging scientific field of human genetics. The Centre created space for collaboration with the National Health Service in tackling problems of infertility; space was also set aside for the incubation of new business, a visitor attraction to enhance public understanding of science and an institute to engage with ethical issues. The Centre for Life is a place where all of these activities come together. ONE North East has played a key role in the development of the Centre as one of the key pillars in its "Strategy for Success" program.

A similar place-based strategy emerged in connection with the European Capital of Culture bid. The university created a new post of Dean of Cultural Affairs and decided to contribute to the bid by the development of a Cultural Quarter, re-evaluating the use of its theatre, museums and art gallery, working in partnership with the City Council and various arts organizations. The outcome has taken the form of the remodelled Northern Stage, the relocation onto the campus of the creative writing support agency New Writing North, the £26 million (approximately US$40 million) Great North Museum and the redevelopment of the Old Assembly Rooms as a digital media laboratory. What were once regarded by the university's estate department as financial liabilities are now university and community assets that contribute to the creative buzz of the city and which symbolize both the intrinsic value of the arts and heritage to the university's academic heartland, but also their instrumental role in civil society. For example, the School of English Literature and Language combines academic excellence and community engagement through creative writing and theatre in mutually re-enforcing ways.

Both of these programs provided the experience and confidence in the university and its partners to respond positively to the designation in 2004 of Newcastle as a Science City. Each of the three partners—Newcastle City Council, ONE NorthEast and the university—have distinct but nevertheless overlapping objectives as described in Figure 12.1, such as urban renewal, attracting inward investment and international recognition. For the university the latter has involved the identification of scientific areas where it had research strength and visionary leaders with a strong commitment to the community and where there are prospects of transforming the economy of the city and region by mobilizing its intellectual capital. The areas are: Stem Cells and Regenerative Medicine based on the human genetics area at the International Centre for Life; Aging and Vitality based at the former General Hospital site; and Energy and Environment and Molecular Engineering, both on the main campus.

Figure 12.1 *Newcastle University Businesses and Science City*

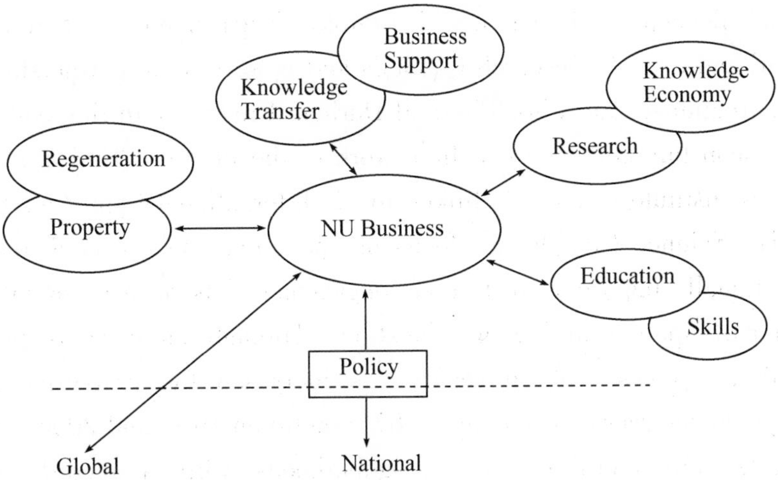

The locations have been referenced because underpinning the Science City strategy has been the principle of bringing science, business and the community together to facilitate the exchange of knowledge through personal interaction. And because the main campus was in effect full, the partnership made the bold decision to purchase the former Newcastle Brewery site in the city center when it came onto the market. The university subsequently decided to provide a new home for the university business school on the site with the express intention of building a bridge between its expertise and that of leading edge scientists.

A further key dimension to the Science City vision has been the ambition to ensure that the university's intellectual capital is mobilized to the benefit of the people of the city and region, not just in terms of more employment opportunities, but also contributing to health and well being and to an environmentally sustainable city. A key part of the program led by the Pro Vice Chancellor for Teaching and Learning involves education—encouraging young people to engage with science and pursue it as a career. The university is also seeking to mobilize business and community knowledge to inform science itself, as it accepts that knowledge creation is a two-way street. It has been designated as a national Beacon of Excellence in Public Engagement in Science by HEFCE and the UK Research Councils and is working in partnership with the International Centre for Life and Durham University in this endeavor. The Beacon builds on the excellent work of the Politics, Ethics and Life Sciences Institute which was linked to the International Centre for Life.

The Science City themes focus on the university's science research base. Equally important to its civic engagement has been an ambition to widen participation in higher education. Through its Partners program with local schools, the university has increased the proportion of its undergraduates recruited locally by 87% between 1999 and 2006. Nearly a quarter are recruited from neighborhoods with a record of low participation in higher education. More and more of its students are taking modules in business enterprise or community volunteering activity. On graduation, many wish to remain in the city by establishing their own businesses or working with local employers. For example, the number of locally recruited graduates taking up employment in the region increased by nearly 200 between 2004 and 2006, bringing the total to 800. Equally significant, 470 graduates from homes outside the region took up employment locally in 2006, representing 37% of the university's non-local recruits.

While the emphasis so far has been on the city and regional links of the university's teaching and research, it goes without saying that both have a strong international dimension. One in eight of its students comes from outside the European Union and 27% of its academic staff are from outside the UK. It attracts many overseas academic and business visitors and participates in international inward investment missions with ONE

North East. Academic conferences fill many hotel beds in the city, helped by the city marketing agency (the Newcastle/Gateshead Initiative) Ambassadors Program. The graduation ceremonies are used to encourage many parents to visit the region as tourists and, in some instances, as business investors. Through a national program on Routes into Modern Languages, the university's School of Modern Languages is working with local schools to turn around the declining interest of young people in languages. The university is also working with the Chinese Government, the City Council, Northumbria University and the local Chinese community to establish a Confucius Institute to strengthen the city's links with China. It is also in dialogue with various faith groups through the Council of Faiths to support overseas students and harmonious living in the city. In short, the university plays a key role in the city's international, multicultural and multi-faith life through its staff, students and alumni.

From these examples it should be apparent that the university's engagement with the city and region embraces virtually all aspects of its core business of teaching and research. Many of the big challenges facing the city, such as aging and health, environmental sustainability and social and community cohesion, do not fit into the traditional disciplinary boxes. Equally important, engagement with civil society is not simply a "third task" but requires mobilizing both teaching and research. For example, the city and region need graduates who can transfer research based knowledge into practice in the workplace and the community and who possess the necessary skills to utilize ever advancing technologies or work with disadvantaged groups.

Such a broad agenda clearly poses challenges of institutional leadership and management. As already mentioned, restructuring of Newcastle University initiated by a new Vice Chancellor in 2001 was necessary in order to create an institution more able to respond to external opportunities in terms of teaching, research and engagement with business and the community.

The strengthening of the academic based management hierarchy by the formation of three large faculties and 27 schools largely followed disciplinary lines, and focused on the first two tasks. It has laid the foundation for a future emphasis, highlighted by a new Vice Chancellor who took up office in 2007, of integration across the hierarchy, not least through the appointment of Pro Vice Chancellors for Research and Innovation and for Engagement, both with cross-cutting roles and responsibilities. These responsibilities also extend into the academic services which support these areas. For example the university estate must accommodate outside parties from both the public and private sectors and play a role in creating a strong *sense of place* for the city. And the communications and marketing function must contribute to positioning both the university and the city.

Realizing the full mutual benefit of engagement with the city and the region not only requires building on the university's own capacity to act in new ways, it also requires a similar capacity building on the part of its external stakeholders. Underpinning Science City and the wide ranging relationships between the university, ONE North East and the City Council are a series of Memoranda of Understanding (MoUs). The partners recognize that delivering on the obligations set out in the MoUs require conjoint planning and the development of people who have boundary spanning roles and who understand the drivers on each side. Building these bridges between the university and the locality undoubtedly needs strong pillars on both sides.

Conclusion

This common understanding between a university and its wider society can most readily come about if the university is strongly rooted in a particular place. Within England there is not a strong sense of regional identity. While this may not be the case in the North East, it certainly does apply elsewhere in England. On the other hand, cities do have an identity. Newcastle, Leeds, Manchester, Liverpool, Sheffield, Birmingham, Nottingham and Bristol are really strong brands nationally and even internationally. University staff and students work, shop, engage in sport, culture and community activity in the place. Each has a strong university hospital. The success of the city, its universities, business, hospitals and public services are inextricably linked. This goes way beyond the simple economic impact of the university as a major employer. These cities are all partners nationally in the Core Cities Network, lobbying government to pay greater regard to the role of the major cities in national development. However, there is not a network of Core City universities.

Our future work will endeavor to continue bridging the gap between theory and practice by working on an academic book on the *University and the City*, which will bring together literatures on universities and on city development, sharing learning about the practice of building city and university partnerships across the UK and worldwide. In a recent speech, the Secretary of State for Innovation, University and Skills has set out a list of five objectives for the British higher education system for the next 15 years, and this has given a new impetus to the task. One of these objectives is "maximising the regional and cultural role of universities." The Secretary of State went on to say, "I wish universities to play to their strengths because I believe all organizations do best when they focus on what they are good at and the (higher education) system's overall strength will increase if we get to a stage where every institution values the work of its peers." Contributing to building a network of great civic universities, striving to learn from each other is a major challenge for the future.

Notes

[1] A more detailed profile of the North East region and higher education sector can be found in Peer Review and Case Study reports for the UK section of the OECD project *Supporting the Contribution of Higher Education Institutions to Regional Development* (part of the Programme on Institutional Management in Higher Education). Both of these publications are available on the OECD website (accessed November 2008).

CAMPUS PARTNERS:
STRATEGIC COLLABORATIONS
FOR URBAN NEIGHBORHOOD REVITALIZATION

Stephen A. Sterrett
Ohio State University, USA

Disinvestment and deterioration afflict many of the nation's urban neighborhoods. Universities, hospitals and other institutions often are place-bound in these neighborhoods. These institutions have discovered that they can choose to wall themselves off from their neighborhoods or seek creative engagement with neighborhood and community stakeholders. Although these institutions are usually the most economically powerful entities in their neighborhoods, they don't have the resources to engage alone in regional development and revitalization. Challenges of poverty, unemployment, education, housing, crime and economic development are complex and interrelated and do not lend themselves to a single solution.

The Ohio State University has engaged with the City of Columbus and other public, private and non-profit stakeholders since 1995 in an extraordinary series of partnerships to revitalize the distressed urban neighborhoods around its main campus. Ohio State and community stakeholders have employed a comprehensive and collaborative approach to regional development involving highly participatory community-based planning; multiple city, university and neighborhood partnerships; and the implementation of strategic projects of sufficient scale to change perceptions of neighborhood disinvestment and to stimulate market-based revitalization.

While this approach is complex, the challenge of neighborhood vitality can be stated simply. If people choose to live, work, and invest in a neighborhood, then businesses will thrive, property values will rise, and the population will grow (or at least remain stable). When a neighborhood is in decline, its private market is not functioning well. People are choosing not to live or invest there. To revitalize a neighborhood, institutions and citizens must restore the private market by taking advantage of the neighborhood's assets and by removing the barriers (crime, blighted properties, poor schools, etc.) which keep people from choosing to live or invest in the neighborhood. Ohio State's market-based strategy is based on the premise that public commitment precedes private investment. The city and the major institutions in a neighborhood—often universities or hospitals—must commit to cooperation with the neighborhood and to using their political and fiscal resources to removing the barriers. The expectation is that the public commitment will spark renewed confidence by the private sector.

The Setting

Ohio State's main campus is bounded on the north, south and east by older urban neighborhoods, which collectively are known as the University District and comprise about 300 square blocks. (The west side of the campus, with athletic fields and agricultural uses, abuts an affluent suburb.) Based on the 2000 Census, Columbus had a population of 711,000 and the University District had a population of 43,700. Ohio State enrolls more than 52,000 students on its main campus. Approximately 10,000 students live in residence halls on the campus, more than 13,000 live in privately-owned housing in the University District, and the remainder commute from outside the University District. University students are concentrated in the neighborhood closest to the campus, while the other neighborhoods of the University District are more diverse, including Weinland Park which is predominantly African

American and low income.

In the decades that followed World War II, Ohio State's enrollment swelled. The Columbus campus became one of the nation's largest single campuses. As permanent residents of the University District moved to the new suburbs in the 1950s and 1960s, apartments were built and single family homes converted to rental housing to serve the booming student population, often with insufficient regulatory oversight. Problems with crime, disinvestment, an antiquated public infrastructure, limited parking and inadequate municipal services grew in the 1970s and 1980s. By the early 1990s, the appearance of residential and commercial structures and the quality of life in the area, including public safety, had become a major issue.

In 1995, E. Gordon Gee, then president of Ohio State, with support from the mayor of Columbus, established Campus Partners for Community Urban Revitalization, a non-profit redevelopment corporation to spearhead improvements in the University District. Campus Partners receives ongoing operating funds from Ohio State, and the Campus Partners Board of Directors is chaired by Ohio State's vice president for university outreach. The board's 11 members include university administrators, the city's development director, and representatives of students, permanent residents of the University District and the community. Campus Partners' initial priorities were to develop a comprehensive neighborhood revitalization plan and to actively promote projects and programs which could have an immediate positive impact.

Reasons for Engagement

Ohio State's interest in urban neighborhood revitalization was based in concern with its institutional image, its enlightened self-interest and its heritage of public service. In describing the importance of image, Bromley (2006) wrote:

Colleges, universities, neighborhoods, local governments and metropolitan regions are enormously dependent on their "images". A positive image is an attraction for most people and investors, while a negative one attracts only the desperate, the mal-intentioned and the foolhardy .... A great variety of "rankings" purport to measure institutional standing, but just as important to many potential students, faculty and donors is their perception of the place where the college or university is located. A good place contributes to the standing of a good college or university, and a good college or university contributes to the economic development and cultural vitality of the place in which it is located. (8)

In the early 1990s, Ohio State committed to significantly improving its academic reputation and attracting better-prepared students. Campus Partners' initial planning document (1996) noted, however, that "prospective students and their parents, especially high ability students, are deciding not to attend Ohio State due to a setting that is perceived as disintegrating and unsafe" (11-12). News reports of serious crimes in the University District were carried statewide. Students already enrolled at the university were more and more choosing not to live in the adjacent neighborhood. Based on university generated enrollment data maintained by Campus Partners, the number of students living in the 43201 zip code around the university campus dropped from more than 14,000 in 1986 to about 10,500 in 1995. This weakness in the student housing market led to further disinvestment on the fringes of the neighborhood.

To meet its academic goals and to respond to concerns of students and parents, Ohio State—not unlike many other urban universities—recognized an enlightened self-interest in neighborhood revitalization. Again, Bromley (2006) described the situation more broadly:

Faced with the reality that they cannot move, many colleges and universities have increasingly come to see themselves as "local stakeholders"—institutions which have an enlightened self-interest not only in improving their own campuses, but also in improving the neighborhoods around their campuses and in strengthening the economy and image of their municipalities and regions .... Recognition of stakeholder status thus serves as a rallying call, both to commit resources and to form strategic alliances with other organizations. (11)

Once Ohio State was committed as a stakeholder, then local government, neighborhood civic organizations, and property owners responded positively because they perceived the university as a partner with resources and influence.

Critical to Ohio State's long term engagement in regional development is its heritage as a land grant college. That 19th century land grant mission was to teach agriculture and the mechanical arts, as well the classics, and to benefit society through research and public service. Through much of Ohio State's history, this public service tended to focus on agriculture, but the late 20th century brought increasing attention to society's urban problems. Ohio State President Gee in the mid-1990s chaired the Kellogg Commission on the Future of State and Land Grant Universities. This commission issued a seminal report in 1999 that called for higher education to renew its commitment to the larger society. The report emphasized that "an engaged university must put its critical resources (knowledge and expertise) to work on the problems the communities it serves face" (10) .

Ohio State was determined to be in the forefront of this outreach and engagement movement in higher education, and Campus Partners was one focus of its efforts. Over the past decade, this engagement has resulted in Ohio State's expansion of its image from that of a major public research institution to include a vision as an urban university. In 2000, Ohio State adopted its far-reaching, strategic Academic Plan, which included an emphasis on Ohio State's expanded role as a land grant university and on community engagement. The plan notes: "While strengthening our work in these traditional areas [as represented by Ohio State University Extension's work in agriculture and rural development], we need to bring a similar sense of commitment and leadership to issues that greatly challenge Ohio's urban communities in the 21st century." (7)

Embedding community engagement in the university's Academic Plan has provided a strong platform for Ohio State's involvement in regional development. Equally important to Ohio State long term commitment, however, has been enduring support for Campus Partners and its initiatives from the university president and the Board of Trustees. President Gee created Campus Partners in 1995. He was succeeded by new presidents in 1997 and 2002 and then he returned as president in 2007. Each president has kept Campus Partners as an institutional priority. This support from the university's leadership has been matched by the mayor and City Council as a mutually reinforcing partnership, even with a change in the mayor's office in 2000. Support from the top has fostered cooperation down the line.

Planning and Early Implementation

In 1995 and 1996, Campus Partners led a broad community-based process to develop the *University Neighborhoods Revitalization Plan: Concept Document* (Campus Partners, 1996), a comprehensive plan for improving the University District. The planning process itself was an important trust- and consensus-building exercise for all stakeholders. This was important not only to overcome decades of mistrust of the university by some neighbors, but also to improve cooperation between rental property owners and long time homeowners, who had often clashed in the past. A critical member of the consulting team that prepared the revitalization plan was the Campus Collaborative, an interdisciplinary body formed in 1994 representing Ohio State faculty and graduate students from more than 40 colleges, departments and offices. The Campus Collaborative was seeking opportunities for engaging Ohio State scholars in critical community issues. As a member of the consulting team, the Campus Collaborative conferred widely with the community to prepare recommendations on social services, community health, public education, faculty involvement and student life. Participation by the Campus Collaborative gave the plan faculty support within the university, rather than having the plan perceived only as an initiative by the university administration.

The revitalization plan articulated a common vision for the University District and offered a comprehensive series of some 250 recommendations for action. In 1997, the plan was adopted by neighborhood civic and business organizations, Columbus City Council and Ohio State's Board of Trustees. Campus Partners intentionally sought broad approval of the plan to validate the planning process.

Beginning in 1997, a dozen priority implementation measures were initiated across the neighborhoods of the University District. These implementation measures included a university-sponsored homeownership incentive program which offered $3,000 in down-payment assistance to employees who bought homes in the University District. So far, more than 90 employees have used the incentive. In addition, Campus Partners has coordinated a series of standing committees that have initiated ongoing and incremental improvements in municipal services, including refuse collection, housing code enforcement, street sweeping, public safety and street lighting. These committees, which continue to meet regularly, include representatives of municipal departments, neighborhood civic leaders, business owners, and the university.

Meanwhile, in 1997, the U.S. Department of Housing and Urban Development awarded a three-year Community Outreach Partnership Center grant to the Campus Collaborative to work with residents of the Weinland Park neighborhood of the University District on programs involving health, small business development and schools. These activities provided useful services and helped to build cooperation among university faculty and students, residents and neighborhood agencies, but they couldn't effectively address the fundamental urban challenges of concentrated poverty, disinvestment and crime. For example, academic enrichment efforts implemented in Weinland Park Elementary School had limited success because the mobility rate of children in the school was so high, due at least in part to the transience in the area's highly concentrated and poorly managed subsidized housing. A strategy was needed to deal with underlying conditions in the neighborhood.

Two of Campus Partners' major roles have been as planner and as coordinator of neighborhood committees and partnerships. The third role is developer—directing the strategic, transformational projects which help to implement the planning and for which no other entity has the mission or resources. The community planning and coordination are central to building partnerships, promoting civic engagement, improving basic services and identifying the transformational projects, but they alone often can't remove deeply rooted barriers and restore the private market. Campus Partners has directed three transformational projects, one on the "Main Street" of the University District and two in the Weinland Park neighborhood, which are imperative to sustain long term revitalization.

South Campus Gateway

The revitalization plan (Campus Partners, 1996) had identified a potential redevelopment project along High Street in a blighted three-block area near the university campus. High Street is the "Main Street" of Columbus and the primary commercial corridor through the University District. Urban planners and real estate consultants said that High Street wasn't failing, but it was performing far below its potential. Students, university employees, residents and visitors were spending their money elsewhere. Many retail stores had moved to the suburbs. Bars and fast food restaurant remained, but not a range of other businesses to draw customers. The area lacked convenient parking. Most buildings were too small to accommodate modern retail.

Campus Partners spearheaded a second planning process in 1997 and 1998 to prepare a master plan for High Street (Campus Partners, 2000) and development and design guidelines (Campus Partners, 2002), both of which were adopted by Columbus City Council in 2002. The High Street plan also tested the market feasibility and delineated the size and scope of the redevelopment project which became South Campus Gateway. This $154 million mixed use project along High Street, adjacent to both the university campus and Weinland Park, is rebuilding the University District's commercial vitality.

As developer of Gateway, Campus Partners in 1999 conducted a design competition for Gateway and negotiated an economic development agreement with the city in which the city committed to public infrastructure improvements on the site and use of eminent domain, if needed, to assemble the 7.5-acre site. Site assemblage was completed in 2002, infrastructure improvements done in 2003, and construction of Gateway begun in 2004. Gateway opened in mid-2005 within a series of buildings whose architectural quality exemplifies the best in "Main Street" urban design. The project includes 225,000 square feet of retail, 88,000 square feet of office space, 184 apartments and a 1,200-space parking garage. The retail anchor is a Barnes & Noble university "super-store," and the entertainment anchors are a seven screen arts cinema and an array of 10 restaurants.

Campus Partners formed its own community development entity and received an award of $35 million in federal New Markets Tax Credits in 2003 to construct Gateway's retail buildings. Campus Partners also used $12 million of another allocatee's NMTC award. The complex project financing includes a city investment of $9 million in infrastructure improvements, a state grant of $4.5 million toward the cost of the parking garage, a tax increment financing district to support the parking garage, an investment of $20 million from the university's endowment to acquire the site and $65 million in university tax-exempt bonds for construction of the non-retail portions of the project.

When Gateway opened, Campus Partners held job fairs specifically for neighborhood residents interested in employment at Gateway's retailers. An assessment by Economics Research Associates (2005) concluded that Gateway has improved job opportunities, tax revenues and public safety; generated more than 700 fulltime equivalent jobs; and drawn more than half its employees from qualified low income communities. *Business First* newspaper reported in early 2008 that Gateway has sparked millions of dollars in private investment in renovation and new construction of commercial buildings along High Street and of apartment buildings in the adjacent neighborhood.

In addition to Gateway, the planning efforts identified a business improvement district (BID) as an important initiative for the vitality of High Street. Houstoun (1997) explains that through a BID "properties and/or businesses within a legally constituted district pay a special tax or assessment to cover the cost of providing facilities or services for which the district has a particular need" (8). Often a BID starts with clean and safe services, such as litter pick-up and security teams. These services are managed privately by the BID rather than the local government.

The planning efforts recommended creation of a BID to address the untidy appearance of High Street (outside the Gateway area) with its litter, graffiti, and panhandling. Under Ohio law, the BID is established upon petition by a super-majority of property owners. Beginning in 1999, key property owners established a committee to promote a BID for High Street in the University District. Campus Partners engaged a BID consultant and underwrote the legal expenses of preparing the BID petition. The university and the city agreed to make voluntary contributions to the BID. After several years, however, the BID effort stalled despite support from a majority of property owners. A few property owners simply opposed the idea of contributing to a BID, while others saw no need to contribute because they argued that they already maintain their properties.

The failure to establish the BID is most likely the biggest setback in the efforts to improve High Street's vitality. One lesson may be that careful planning and strong partnerships in regional development can't guarantee that democratic processes and private rights won't block some of the planners' and community's good ideas.

Community Properties of Ohio

The revitalization plan (Campus Partners, 1996) recognized the challenges of concentrated poverty, deteriorated housing, instability and crime in the Weinland Park neighborhood of the University District, but it offered general goals rather than a specific strategy. The crime and disinvestment in Weinland Park bled into the predominantly student neighborhood immediately to the north. By 2000, Campus Partners clearly recognized that these challenges in Weinland Park had to be addressed more comprehensively and more boldly if revitalization were to succeed.

Weinland Park is a predominantly African-American neighborhood with 4,800 residents, based on the 2000 Census. Few of the residents are university students. More than half of the population is below the poverty level. The annual median household income in Weinland Park in 1999 was $15,831, compared with $37,897 for Columbus as whole (City of Columbus, 2006). Weinland Park also has the highest concentration of project-based, Section 8 government subsidized housing in the city. Most of these subsidized, privately owned housing units were badly managed and poorly maintained. The high turn over rate of 50% annually in the subsidized housing contributed to neighborhood instability and a mobility rate of more than 85% among the students in Weinland Park Elementary

School. This mobility undermined any efforts at educational enrichment. Clearly, further public and private investment in Weinland Park would have little or no impact until the subsidized housing was turned around.

The breakthrough in Weinland Park came in 2001 when Campus Partners negotiated a purchase agreement for a complex Section 8 portfolio which was the nation's largest scattered-site housing portfolio entering the federally mandated "mark-to-market" restructuring program. The majority of the portfolio, now known as Community Properties of Ohio (CPO), consisted of 1,300 units in 250 buildings in seven urban Columbus neighborhoods ("Housing credit to help fund renovation," 2003). Campus Partners sought control of the portfolio because 550 of the CPO units are in Weinland Park, representing a significant portion of the neighborhood housing stock. Neither the city nor local non-profit housing developers had the capacity to deal with this distressed housing portfolio, which had a reputation of "housing of last resort." The CPO residents, of whom 89% were single females between the ages of 19 and 24 with children, earned a median annual income of between $5,000 and $7,000 (Community Properties of Ohio Management Services, 2004).

Campus Partners convened a broad group of stakeholders, including neighborhood leaders, affordable housing advocates, local, state and federal offices, social service agencies and the university, to fashion an innovative "mark-to-market" restructuring plan. This plan proposed massive renovation of the housing, improved management, supportive services for the residents, and a limited but significant de-concentration of this Section 8 housing by spreading a portion of the portfolio more widely in the county.

To implement the restructuring plan, Campus Partners assigned its purchase agreement to Ohio Capital Corporation for Housing (OCCH), which finances affordable housing projects throughout Ohio. OCCH acquired the portfolio in 2003, installed new management and began extensive renovation of the properties in 2004. The units remain low income housing, but OCCH is investing $100 million in interior and exterior improvements with more than a third of that investment in Weinland Park. OCCH also has implemented a public safety program associated with the housing that has cut the crime reports in Weinland Park by 25%. As a result, CPO's occupancy rate has risen, children are staying in school and the neighborhood is stabilizing.

The acquisition of the CPO portfolio was a daunting challenge that neither the city nor other housing providers were prepared to take on. Campus Partners and Ohio State provided the credibility needed to address the challenge. Campus Partners, however, did not possess the staffing and experience to implement the restructuring plan, but it was able to bring OCCH to the table as the development partner. Although not involved in the day-to-day management of the CPO properties, Campus Partners and Ohio State have continued to work with the management company on a number of initiatives, including federal grants for "gap financing" for the housing renovation and for CPO's public safety program.

More Planning and More Redevelopment

With the substantial progress made with the CPO housing, public and private interest in Weinland Park began to grow. In 2004, the city joined with the Weinland Park Community Civic Association and other neighborhood stakeholders to prepare the *Weinland Park Neighborhood Plan*, adopted by City Council in 2006. Campus Partners secured funding to employ consultants to work with neighbors and the city planning staff to give greater depth to the market research and urban design incorporated in the plan. Like the previous planning efforts, the Weinland Park planning involved a large steering committee and six subcommittees composed of neighborhood residents, staff from social service agencies, university faculty and graduate students and other stakeholders. Numerous public meetings were held, including two planning workshops.

The Weinland Park plan envisions the neighborhood evolving into a true, mixed income community through revitalization without displacement of existing residents. The plan supports a supply of well managed subsidized housing, as well as opportunities for renovation and new construction of market rate housing. As Weinland Park attracts greater private and public investment, the plan will guide development to protect the neighborhood character and assure benefits for the whole community.

Throughout the 18-month planning process, many residents were skeptical of the value of a neighborhood plan and were uncertain who would take responsibility for implementing the plan's recommendations. The skepticism is common in low income neighborhoods where residents often feel powerless and ignored by city government. The planning effort gained credibility, however, when Campus Partners and the city tackled a major "brownfield" site in Weinland Park.

Campus Partners became involved in a second transformational project in Weinland Park when an old industrial plant, Columbus Coated Fabrics, closed its doors in the neighborhood in 2001. The firm filed for bankruptcy a year later. The 20-acre "brownfield" property soon became a major visual blight and public safety hazard in the neighborhood due to arson, illegal salvaging and building deterioration.

After extensive negotiations, Campus Partners in 2006 was finally able to reach a purchase agreement for the property through the bankruptcy court. In partnership with the city, Campus Partners performed detailed environmental assessments of the site, led the successful effort on behalf of the city to obtain a $3 million state grant for environmental remediation, and under contract with the city oversaw demolition of the existing buildings in 2007.

Campus Partners engaged a private developer, Wagenbrenner Development Company, to prepare a redevelopment proposal for the site consistent with the *Weinland Park Neighborhood Plan*. In March 2008, Columbus City Council approved terms of an economic development agreement with Wagenbrenner under which the city will contribute $14 million in infrastructure improvements on and adjacent to the site. Campus Partners will assign its rights to acquire the site to Wagenbrenner, which in turn plans to invest $80 million in construction of more than 500 units of market rate housing on the site. Wagenbrenner will oversee remediation on the site in 2009 with the possibility of new construction in 2010. This will help to meet the Weinland Park plan's goal of creating a mixed income neighborhood.

The city, the university and other stakeholders are making other significant investments in Weinland Park. These include:

Public safety. The city and the university are jointly constructing a "neighborhood policing center" at a total cost of $4.4 million. The policing center will open in late 2008 in a central location in the University District on the border of both Weinland Park and the predominantly student neighborhood.

Education. With the neighborhood stabilizing, Ohio State's College of Education and Human Ecology developed a nationally significant partnership with Columbus City Schools and the city's Recreation and Parks Department. The new Weinland Park Elementary School opened in early 2007. Co-located with the elementary school, Ohio State built the Schoenbaum Family Center, which opened in mid-2007 as the nation's first early childhood education laboratory in a low income neighborhood. More than half of the 88 children served by the center are drawn from Weinland Park. Scholars representing a variety of disciplines are using this laboratory to study child development among diverse populations and to engage the elementary school and the neighborhood in a variety of urban issues. The city has upgraded the adjacent recreation park to serve the family center, school and neighborhood.

Grocery expansion. In the fall of 2008, the Kroger Company began a major renovation and expansion of its 30-year-old grocery on High Street in Weinland Park. As the only grocery store in the University District, it has been criticized for its outmoded facility and limited selection. The renovated store will meet the High Street development and design guidelines with an urban building that extends to the street and places its parking behind the store.

Employment and skill-building. The university has engaged neighborhood residents in a number of programs. For example, an OSU Extension educator assigned to the University District has worked diligently to create an "employment pipeline" for neighborhood residents to compete more successfully for entry level staff positions at the university.

Despite the progress made in removing barriers to private investment in Weinland Park, a new and unanticipated challenge in 2008 has been the mortgage foreclosure crisis. Wagenbrenner Development Company estimates that more than 200 properties in Weinland Park are going through or likely will go through mortgage foreclosure in the coming months. A large number of vacant or abandoned properties in Weinland Park will continue to lower property values and depress the market for new and renovated homes.

With support from a foundation grant, Campus Partners prepared a business plan in the fall of 2008 for the next stage of revitalization in Weinland Park. The business plan investigates the possibility of a bulk purchase of properties before they go through foreclosure and the creation of a pool of capital to renovate the properties to a specific standard and then make them available for homeownership and well managed rental housing. The plan also will outline specific needs in workforce development, public safety, education and social services.

Lessons Learned

In evaluating the outcomes of Ohio State's engagement in regional development through its Campus Partners initiative, two interrelated measures are paramount: the public perception of the university and of the University District neighborhoods and the ability to attract private investment in the University District.

The public perception of the university and the University District appears to have improved, according to student indicators. Ohio State has been very successful in recruiting high ability students over the past decade. The average ACT composite score for first-year students who entered in 1995 was 22.8 and in 2007 had increased markedly to 27.0(The Ohio State University, 2007). The reasons for this successful recruiting are many. The improved perception of the University District may have played only a small and difficult-to-quantify role, but the perception is not hindering recruitment. The number of students choosing to live in the University District had dropped significantly by 1995 when Campus Partners was formed. That decline leveled off after 1995 at about 10,500 students. The number began to rise again early in this decade as private rental property owners, reassured by the engagement of Ohio State and the city, made significant investments to improve their units. The opening in 2005 of Gateway and a new recreation center on campus also played a role. A student housing survey in spring 2008 estimated that more than 13,000 students now live in the University District.

Another measure of the perception of the University District is the greatly improved housing stability rate in the more than 500 units of subsidized housing in the CPO portfolio in Weinland Park. When CPO took control of the housing in 2003, the annual turnover among its residents was 50%, but in 2007 and 2008 the turnover averaged 19% to 22% (Community Properties of Ohio, 2008). This reflects both the renovation of the properties and the improved conditions in the neighborhood.

The Campus Partners initiative has been successful in attracting private investment to the University District. South Campus Gateway is an important anchor that has enhanced the commercial vitality of High Street and greatly strengthened the surrounding student housing market. Since

1995, private and public investment in and commitments to projects along High Street and in the neighborhoods have totaled more than half a billion dollars.

Over the past 13 years, the Campus Partners staff has found that the structure and function of university-community partnerships around the nation are quite diverse. This is due to the great variety of local conditions which affect the expectations and needs of all parties, the constraints of the existing built environment, and the resources available. Thus, the composition of these university-community partnerships will vary, but the experience of Ohio State suggests a model for the strategies to be employed if these partnerships are to be successful. These strategies include:

Community-based planning. This first step is critical for articulating a shared vision for the neighborhood, identifying the neighborhood's market strengths and barriers to revitalization, and building a consensus for specific actions. The planning cannot be rushed because it also serves as a trust-building exercise among stakeholders with different interests and who may have little history of cooperation. If the stakeholders can't agree on a common plan and develop mutual trust, then it is unlikely in a time of scarce resources that revitalization will move forward. Agreement on a shared vision and a plan also allows the parties to move much more quickly when market opportunities arise.

Comprehensive approach. Urban decline is due to many factors, so no one solution or one project is likely to work. From the planning effort should come multiple partnerships to address employment, housing, public safety, education and other issues. These partnerships need to be targeted to reinforce each other. As an example, the well managed CPO housing is helping to stabilize neighborhood residents and reduce the mobility rate in Weinland Park Elementary School. In turn, efforts at educational enrichment in the school will be more effective.

Market-based. Programs and projects must be focused on removing barriers to private investment. Ultimately, the public dollars and university commitment are limited and must support efforts which over time will validate people's choices to live, work and invest in the neighborhood.

Transformational projects. Through the planning process and in light of market conditions, the revitalization effort must identify strategic projects of sufficient scale and potential to positively alter the underlying market conditions and shift the public and private perception of the neighborhood. South Campus Gateway has brought new uses, a cleaner streetscape and additional parking to rejuvenate the High Street market. Millions of dollars in private investment up and down the street have followed.

University engagement. To maintain university commitment over the long term, the university-community partnership must have support from both the university administration and the faculty. If the partnership is viewed as only an administrative initiative, then the pressures for additional resources for the university's core academic mission over time may erode support for the partnership, particularly if there is a change in administration. In the same vein, the strongest university-community partnerships will align the mission of the academic unit with the neighborhood's goals. For example, Ohio State's College of Education and Human Ecology built its child development laboratory in Weinland Park precisely because the college believed its teaching and research would be enhanced in a neighborhood setting.

Focus on the long term. Urban neighborhoods declined over decades, and most won't be revitalized in a few years. For Ohio State, its neighborhood involvement is not a project with a specific timeline, but this engagement represents a new and ongoing relationship with its neighbors. Even as revitalization moves forward, new challenges and opportunities will arise. The University District revitalization plan (Campus Partners, 1996) did not anticipate the potential to acquire a large portfolio of subsidized housing, but the vision in the plan certainly propelled Campus Partners to take advantage of this opportunity.

Apart from the strategies in Ohio State's model is Campus Partners itself. The redevelopment corporation has functioned well as a separate entity, but affiliated with Ohio State. With a relatively small board and staff, Campus Partners can respond quickly to market opportunities, buy and develop properties without going through the more cumbersome university processes, and serve at times in the capacity of "honest broker" among the divergent interests of the university and neighborhood stakeholders. With its Ohio State backing, however, Campus Partners also has the credibility to undertake the complex issues of government subsidized housing and "brownfield" redevelopment.

A strong university-community partnership can be enormously beneficial for both the university and its neighbors. Through an authentic partnership, the university stakeholders can enrich their teaching, research and service through observation and participation as an agent of change. For neighbors, the hard work in building trust and a partnership with a large, often confusing, Hydra-like university can be worth it. As an ally, the university—with its status and political power in the community—can be instrumental in building credibility for the partnership and in bringing other stakeholders—government, businesses, institutions, foundations—to the table to help address the issues of regional development and urban revitalization.

SICHUAN UNIVERSITY'S POVERTY REDUCTION STRATEGY FOR PROMOTING REGIONAL DEVELOPMENT

Shijing Yan and Yu Zhang
Sichuan University, China

As the premier university in western China, Sichuan University (SCU) has a record of more than 110 years of service record in providing quality education and knowledge advancement, as well as delivery of professional services to both the nation and the region. Under the direct supervision of the Ministry of Education, SCU and its faculties have earned a national reputation in education quality assurance, cutting edge research in various disciplines and interdisciplinary areas, and commitment to addressing critical national and social issues. It is with this commitment that SCU has taken various initiatives, directly or indirectly, to solving serious policy problems with nationwide impact. Poverty reduction, crucial to regional development, is one of these initiatives. This chapter presents the SCU experience in promoting regional development through mitigating the problem of poverty in five strategic areas: technology, talent development, medical support, financial aid for students and think tank contributions.

Western China as the Central Battlefield of Anti-poverty

Poverty in China

Eradication of poverty has been a major policy goal of the Chinese governmentin the past decades with great success: the number of poor people was reduced from 250 million in 1978 to 21.5 million in 2006 and around 14.8 million in 2007 (http: // gov. people. com. cn/46728/53739/ 53747/3751/678.html). Notwithstanding, poverty in China is still a serious problem. The following figures are revealing: first, 148 million poor people in 2007 earned an annual income below 785 yuan or US $115 (approximately US $0. 32 per day); second, around 57 million people hover just above the 785 yuan poverty line and are rather poverty elastic, that is, they are more susceptible to falling into poverty when their income falls (Jensen, 2003); and third, when the one US dollar per day standard of the United Nations is applied, 90 million people (6.9% of the population) are classified as poor.[1] The poverty problem is further complicated by increasing inequality between rich and poor, and other constraints, such as having 73% of the poor living in remote mountain areas (http: // gov. people. com. cn/GB/46728/53739/53747/3751678. html).

Considering the prospects for eradicating poverty in the near future, the trends in poverty reduction over the last few years could be a good guide for making forecast, because the reduction in poverty in recent years has occurred in the context of China's rapid modernization. In brief, the Chinese economy is becoming more value-added, knowledge-based, technology-driven and creativity-induced, leaving little room for the poor, who tend to be illiterate, unproductive, and/or undetermined to maneuver. It is therefore not surprising to learn that between 1978-1988 the number of poor people was reduced by 13.7 million per year, while the number decreased merely by 6.2 million per year between 1989-1999, dropping further to 1.5 million in the past few years (http://gov. people. com. cn/GB/46728/53739/53747/3751678html).

China is primarily producing low-tech, low-value-added, and inexpensive goods and products with decreasing comparative advantage. The future prospects for poverty reduction in China are dependent upon world stability and the condition of the global economy: that is, the political economy at the world scene may alter the course and pace of

China's economic development, thus severely affecting the wellbeing of low income groups. Given that the poverty elasticity in China is rather high, an abrupt halt of economic development may push many poor people and low income farmers into the "bitter sea," not to mention the fact that many of those 90-135 million people who hover above the UN poverty line are likely to become poor when they get ill.

Even when economic development prospects are good, the competition for jobs is still keen, making the young, knowledgeable, educated or committed the winners, and the aging, low killed or uneducated the losers. Poor people in cities and villages may continue their struggle for survival, but sadly they find that they can be easily excluded from the labor market when more young and determined workers compete for the limited number of jobs. In addition, the poor farmers in villages keep producing low price crops and products that do not increase their income substantially. In short, poverty is still and will remain a serious critical national problem. More important, poverty has been and will continue to be serious in western China. It is thus the central battlefield of anti-poverty.

Poverty in Western China

China can be conceptualized in various ways. The most typical is to geographically divide China into three regions—eastern, central and western. According to the classification of regions in 2000 by the National Bureau of Statistics (NBS) of China, western China covers Chongqing, Gansu, Guizhou, Ningxia, Qinghai, Shaanxi, Sichuan, Tibet, Xinjiang and Yunnan (10 entities). On January 1, 2001, the State Council issued a document on the policy measures for developing western China, in which the classification was modified, adding Guangxi and Inner Mongolia to the region, while three minority ethnic group autonomous regions in Jilin, Hunan and Hubei were classified by the State Council as special regions entitled to the policy benefits earmarked for administrative entities in the region (Chow & Luo, 2007). National Bureau of Statistics of China (NBS) statistics (http://www.stats.gov.cn) indicate that, in 2000, western China represented 71.5% of the total land area but 22% of the population and only 14.6% of the nation's Gross Domestic Product (GDP). In addition, the average disposal income of urban dwellers and farmers in western China is much lower than that of people in central and eastern sections of the country. In short, these figures reflect that, while western China is vast in territory, it is relatively underdeveloped economically.

Related to economic backwardness is the pattern of social mobility; talented persons in western China tend to migrate to metropolitan areas in the eastern region for better jobs, prospects, career development and/or relatively modern lifestyles. Such a cross-region brain drain has adversely affected the capacity of the region to develop socially, economically and even politically. Another form of cross-region brain drain is the migration of more capable farmers to work in urban areas, leaving behind the women, children, untrained or uneducated adults and the elderly, and thus making contemporary villages in western China stagnant, similar to the situation in the mountain areas in central China.

More than 40% of the poverty-stricken counties of the nation and 55% of the people in poverty are in western China. NBS statistics show that, by the end of 2007, the average education level in the region is only 6.7 years, 1.3 years lower than the national average; the percentage of the population completing junior middle school and thus basic literacy is only 77% in the region, comparing with the national average of 91%. The percentage of illiterates at age 15 and above in the region amounts to 9.02%, compared with the national average of 6.72%. At the same time, research indicates that the average life expectancy and the health level of women and children are also lower than in the eastern region (Gong, 2007). From these data, it can be seen that the western region presents a great challenge in China's campaign against poverty.

Sichuan University's Strategies for Poverty Reduction

Amartya Sen (1982), winner of the Nobel Memorial Prize in Economic Sciences in 1998, suggests that poverty can be classified into three categories. The first is poverty caused by low income, resulting in the incapability of maintaining even a basic life. The second is human poverty, which refers to problems of basic capacity such as illiteracy, malnutrition, short life expectancy, poor maternal and child health and affliction by preventable diseases. The third is knowledge poverty, which refers to not only low education level but also the lack of ability to obtain, absorb and exchange knowledge and the lack of channels in this regard. The last two types of poverty are mostly found in developing countries (World Bank, 2001), even though the same can be observed in such well-off countries as the United States (U.S. Census Bureau, http://www. census.gov).

While SCU is committed to reducing poverty, formulation of strategies and tactics to accomplishing the goal has been difficult, as all three categories of poverty can be found in western China, while available resources are limited. The SCU leadership has had organized many expert panels in the past decade to assess the difficulties and to entertain the most effective approaches. Basing on collective wisdom, the key decision made is that SCU must accept that, as the premier university in western China, she has a special and irreplaceable role to play in the reduction of regional poverty. To voluntarily accept the self-assigned historic mission means that SCU must also have a long term view and some institutionalized efforts, rather than ad hoc, piecemeal and temporary actions. To produce stable and longer term efforts, SCU must make the anti-poverty campaign sustainable. Optimizing the values of her current resources, particularly her talented faculty and existing knowledge and technology, SCU must also build networks for stable partnerships and new resources. It was with these clarifications and key decisions that created a series of strategies for SCU to accomplish her mission in reducing poverty and promoting regional development.

Poverty Alleviation through Technology Development

According to human capital theory, one of the social benefits of investment in higher education is the promotion of economic growth. Adams (2003) uses new data from 50 developing countries and 101 intervals to examine the impact of economic growth on poverty and inequality. He finds that growth represents an important means for reducing poverty in the developing world. When economic growth is measured by mean income, there is a strong statistical link between growth and poverty reduction. In his analysis of the data set, he finds that the gap between rich and poor does not change rapidly; income inequality on average increases less than 1.0% a year. Since income distributions are relatively stable over time, economic growth tends to raise incomes for all members of society, including the poor. On average, a 10% point increase in economic growth will produce a 25.9% decrease in the proportion of people living in poverty ($1 a person a day). In other words, to some degree, technological innovation means poverty alleviation.

The achievements of technological innovation by SCU are directly integrated into regional economic development and optimize the industrial structure in the region, thus bringing considerable economic benefits. SCU has taken great efforts to construct university based technological parks and technology transfer centers. In recent years, SCU has concluded joint R&D agreements with a dozen large scale enterprises and public institutions, such as Chang Hong Group, China Nuclear Industry Group and China Three Gorges Project Corporation, as well as more than 50 municipal and county governments. Other partnerships include the Tibet Autonomous Region Government and the State Property Management Commission of Sichuan Province. The networking for stable partnerships has developed a total of 259 projects that integrate industrial production, academic teaching, and technological research.

For example, the application of the "theory and technology integrating multidimensional complicated data and graph information," developed by SCU, has played a significant role in the establishment of China's largest modern R&D base of air-ground intelligent traffic commanding outfits. This R&D base has become a major force in the independent knowledge innovation in fields related to civil aviation, dominating more than 90% of the domestic market and yielding a direct economic return to SCU of more than US$51 million to sustain university research and other efforts to promote social, economic and scholarly developments.

SCU's research achievement of "slurry concentration process-based preparation of solid ammonium phosphate" was awarded the first prize of National Scientific and Technological Progress Award in 1988. Based on this research, the industrial production of ammonium phosphate has been predominantly applied in the domestic production, with five factories constructed in western provinces of Guizhou and Yunnan. Accounting for more than 60% of the national total production of ammonium phosphate, the industries have become new economic growth points and pillar industries in these economically backward provinces, while making the region the most important phosphoric chemical technological center and production base in China.

SCU has also developed a series of ecological environment preservation techniques, such as the "high-efficient vegetation restoration in the decertified alpine grassland" and "rapid restoration of vegetation damaged by human activities" which have become important technologies for the ecological restoration and environmental preservation in western China. The technologies have been used to restore more than 100,000 *mu* of land (6,670 hectares or 16,470 acres) in such poverty stricken areas as Ganzi and Aba in Sichuan. Their application has helped increase the yield of grass by 300% and in turn the income of herdsmen by about 40% realizing significant social and economic benefits.

Poverty Alleviation through Talent Development

According to Schultz (1981), human capital mainly refers to the knowledge and skills of laborers and the labor capacity based on them. His research suggests that human capital is the major factor of economic growth, and those workers who have mastered knowledge and skills are the most important resource among all production resources. Therefore, SCU considers that human capital improvement is the university's most significant contribution to poverty reduction. Up to now, SCU has produced more than 200,000 graduates, 60% of whom are employed in western China and have become a powerful force for local poverty reduction and economic development.

To develop backbone talents required for local economic and social development, SCU has worked actively with local governments, enterprises and public institutions to jointly operate various training schools and colleges that offer much needed pedagogical and professional specialties. For instance, it has worked with Yun Tian Hua Company to launch masters and doctoral degrees in engineering, and has cooperated with China Guangdong Nuclear Power Group and other enterprises to provide students with internships and employment opportunities. In cooperation with Kangding Ethnic Normal College, SCU has also consecutively established Sichuan University Vocational College Kangding Branch and Sichuan Net Institute to provide higher level training in such fields as jurisprudence and public administration.

In recent years, SCU has intensified her efforts to speed up the development of education in areas inhabited by ethnic groups. It has dispatched three vice presidents and three administrative officials to Tibet University and Xinjiang University to provide various forms of support. Generally, they worked there for three to four years, providing strategic contributions in managerial, financial and technological areas. In addition, SCU has dispatched about 40 senior researchers to serve as vice county governors in charge of science and technology in Tibet, Xinjiang, Chongqing and Sichuan, in addition to mobilizing more than 2,000 teachers and technicians to various localities to provide direct support to program development.

Furthermore, SCU has sent more than 15,000 student volunteers to poverty stricken rural areas in western China to teach rural students for one academic year. Since 2003, SCU has institutionalized the "university graduates serving the western region" program. Jointly launched by the Central Committee of the Communist Youth League of China and the Ministry of Education in 2003, it recruits young volunteers to move to the west of the country and to help in development efforts. The graduates go to impoverished rural areas to work for one or two years in such fields as education, health, agricultural science, poverty reduction and youth work management. After their voluntary terms, graduates are free to choose whether to continue to work in the west or seek opportunities in other regions of the country. The volunteer program is widely regarded as having provided a new way to provide intellectual support to the western regions and to serve the western development strategy.

Poverty Alleviation through Medical Support

Given the fact that the poor medical and health conditions have constrained the development in many remote areas in western China, SCU's Huaxi Medical Center, which is the largest and most modernized in the region, has made great efforts to contribute to medical development in western China. A part of SCU, Huaxi Hospital has established a medical health cooperation network covering more than 70 medical institutions in the poor areas of the region to provide such services as resources sharing, two-way medical examination, disciplinary support, long distance medical consultation, long distance lecturing and academic coordination. In the past few years, Huaxi Hospital has dispatched a total of 50 groups (with more than 300 medical workers involved) to 61 poverty-stricken counties and ethnic counties to provide medical operation guidance and technical training.

Huaxi Medical Center has contributed more than US$1. 17 million to help Tibet University to establish its medical college so as to train senior medical professionals urgently needed to upgrade medical services and education in the region. SCU has successfully launched real time two-way satellite teaching programs to provide more than 2,000 lectures in 33 subjects to 114 students in four grades of Tibet University Medical College. At the same time, it has also taken the initiative to offer support to five county hospitals in the Ganzi region and Nanchong Municipality in Sichuan, while hosting more than 1,000 medical workers from poor areas of western China for advanced studies in order to train a large number of grassroots medical professionals. Most of the newly trained medical workers return to their home areas, either continuing staffing the hospitals or opening new clinics by themselves in those poverty areas. In this way, they teach other medical workers what they have learned at SCU and improve the health conditions of local people greatly.

Poverty Alleviation through Student Support

As SCU is located in the less developed region of China, a significant proportion of its students come from poor families. In this regard, SCU has established a comprehensive policy for helping impoverished students that includes:

- State subsidized student loans: Since the creation of new national financial aid programs in 2004, SCU has acquired US$38. 57 million, benefitting approximately 13,000 students.
- Scholarships and grants-in-aid: In 2007, 12,423 SCU students received more than US$500,000 in scholarships and grants from the national scholarship program, while about 35% of SCU

students received university scholarships annually. In recent years, because of increasing reputation and effort, SCU has attracted more and more donations from enterprises, individuals and alumni. The university society financial aid program has increased from 30 in 1999 to about 160 at present. Each qualified student who has the need can gain about US$900 financial support annually.

- Financial difficulties allowance: SCU supports students according to their financial condition. Each year SCU devotes about US $250,000 to the "Financial Support Program of Western Region Development" by exempting or reducing tuition fees each year.
- Work-study program: SCU helps students find part time jobs while studying at the university.
- Medical insurance: Low cost medical premiums for students eliminate all economic problems relating to medical service.

These efforts have helped a large number of students to realize their dreams of a top quality college education to change their poor living conditions. Not only have these efforts changed these excellent young people's fate, but they also helped promote economic and social development in backward areas.

Poverty Alleviation by Building Think Tanks

Reform and development are often preceded by innovative concepts. With a view to bolstering the economic and social development of western China, SCU has established a number of research institutes of distinctive regional characteristics and formulated the corresponding technological strategies and research projects to provide advanced concepts and theoretical guidelines for local economic development. For instance, SCU's Western Development Institute (WDI), which is committed to the research on how to promote the social and economic development in the region and to provide local governments with consultation services, has become a think tank on development of western China.

In order to integrate domestic and international research resources, WDI took the initiative in 2003 to establish the Consortium for Western China Development Studies, involving Columbia University (USA), Chuo University (Japan), and ten Chinese universities. SCU has also undertaken more than 380 research projects in the past five years, including research on western economic development and ecological environment rebuilding and economic and social development in ecologically vulnerable areas. More than 300 poverty reduction reports prepared by SCU have been adopted by all levels of governments, especially by provincial and county governments. And, among these reports, the Ecological Barriers on the Upstream Areas of Yangtze River research series has provided practical solutions for China's regional development.

In addition, WDI has successively worked with all levels of governments and local institutions to jointly convene many international conferences under such themes as "Challenge of Sustainable Development and Globalization: New Perspective on China's Western Development," "South Asia and China's Western Development," "Top Public Research-oriented Universities and Local Economic and Social Development" and "Poverty Elimination and International and Regional Cooperation." These conferences have brought scholars from all over the world to discuss, share ideas and cooperate on issues of western China, and thus have promoted western China research effectively. WDI has also conducted various policy research and theoretical discussions about the issue of rural areas, agriculture and farmers; currently, the institute has 60 researchers working on this issue. These researchers have produced many reports, academic dissertations and books, all providing powerful theoretical frameworks and action guidelines for poverty alleviation practice.

The Cases of Institutionalized Efforts and Self-initiation

Sichuan University-Tibet Medical Program

Tibet Autonomous Region covers an area of 12.284 million square kilometers with a 2007 population of 2.84 million. It is located on the Tibetan Plateau, the highest region on Earth. In northern Tibet, elevations reach an average of 4,572 meters (15,000 ft). Mount Qomolangma(Mount Everest) lies on Tibet's border with Nepal. Sichuan, Qinghai and Xinjiang lie to the east and north of the region. As a result of long historical changes, ethnic Tibetans have settled not only in Tibet but also in Sichuan, Qinghai, Gansu and Yunnan provinces, mostly in rural areas. There are few people in the north part of Qinghai-Xizang Plateau because of harsh climates. In the southeast of Tibet covered by primeval forests, population density is not high because of poor transportation and others unfavorable conditions.

Though the Tibetan economy has developed in recent years, productivity is still very low, with farming and animal husbandry as major activities. As a result, the output of agricultural production is neither high nor stable. Meanwhile, Tibet's people have a relatively lower educational level than that of other provinces or regions, with a large proportion of illiterates and semi-illiterates. The weakness in educational infrastructure and the lack of advanced and intermediate professionals and staff are the major problems in Tibet. The infant mortality rate in Tibet had fallen from 430 per thousand in 1959 to 97 per thousand by the year of 1990, and the current life expectancy has reached 60 years, compared with 35 years in 1959. But there is still a wide gap between urban and rural people in the death rates, with rural people dying at a lower age. In addition, the mortality rate at all ages in Tibet is much higher than the average for China as a whole. The infant mortality rate, while improving, remains high in Tibet with great difference between sexes. To sum up, due to Tibet's harsh natural conditions and its history of social development, the living standards of the people are still lower than the nation's average.

Sichuan is a neighboring province adjacent to Tibet with many ethnic Tibetans living in Sichuan. When chairing International Conference on Anti-Poverty and Regional Cooperation in 2006, SCU President Xie Heping mentioned: "Universities play a unique and important role in anti-poverty efforts. Serving local social economic development is one of the key functions of SCU." Then, where should we start? In the rural areas of western China, especially those remote areas inhabited by ethnic groups, poverty-induced diseases and disease-induced poverty are particularly grave, seriously restricting local economic development and the improvement of the people's living conditions. So, considering Tibet's comprehensive conditions and the medical advantages of SCU, SCU's leaders decide to devote great efforts in Tibet, especially by the way of medical support to alleviate regional poverty.

In recent years, SCU has successfully developed a series of research and reform programs to work with international partners (e.g., China Medical Board of New York Inc. CMB[2]), and has set up Tibet Long-distance Medical Education Program, Tibet Therapist Training Program, Mountain Sickness Research and Laboratory Construction Program, and Tele-consultation Program, among others.

The training of high level medical professionals is the key to breaking the vicious circle of "poverty induces diseases, which in turn induce poverty." In this regard SCU has taken the following measures to institutionalize her anti-poverty efforts. For example, SCU has applied computer technology to establish a hospital network involving 118 county and municipal hospitals in ten provinces in the region. The member hospitals participate in the long distance classes sponsored by SCU's Huaxi Clinical Medical Institute. Up to now, a total of 2,000 classes have been completed, with the number of participants reaching 100,000. These activities also cover remote areas as well as regions inhabited by ethnic groups. More important, SCU has institutionalized a two-way real-time e-learning system to provide bachelor's degree training to the Medical School of Tibet University to develop medical students. By the end of 2007, as part of the China Medical Board Program, the "tour e-learning classroom" had been established. SCU medical faculty members have taught a total of 2,578 classes in 15 subjects for the Clinical Medicine Department of the Medical School of Tibet University, including pathology, pediatrics, anatomy and dissection, obstetrics and gynecology. SCU faculty members have also created 672 classroom teaching disks and 37 experimental teaching disks for the Medical School of Tibet University. Meanwhile, 26 medical faculty members of SCU have been sent to teach in the Tibet University in more than 20 specialties such as preventive medicine and pediatrics. SCU has hosted the further studies of 24 medical professionals in such fields as clinical medicine and pharmacology, as well as 10 persons for one year internships, while providing training to 21 postgraduates and joint training for two doctoral students.

Tibet has spectacular alpine scenery. The distinctive geological conditions, however, nurture a variety of diseases for the residents in the region. In a way, the medical conditions and technological level of a locality determine the health of the local people and affect the quality of its human resources, and in turn its economic development. With these in mind, SCU does not limit her involvement only in medical training. She has also carried wide and intensive cooperation with Tibet in medical research, as shown in the following three aspects.

First, SCU establishes research projects jointly implemented by SCU and Tibet University, including the mountain sickness laboratory international program, involving a fund of about US $1. 6 million, and the pathogeny and epidemiology research of the bacillary dysentery in Zalang County of Tibet, with a grant from the Science and Technology Bureau of Tibet Autonomous Region. Second, SCU has helped Tibet University to establish its public health and pharmacology departments, and has provided the nursing department of Tibet University with demonstration teaching and faculty training, in addition to donating almost 7,000 books to Tibet University. Third, SCU has also institutionalized other supports in medical services. For example, in 2007 the People's Hospital of Tibet Autonomous Region, a teaching hospital under the Medical School of Tibet University, was formally transformed into a joint venture entitled Sichuan University Huaxi Hospital Network Hospital. The new hospital was established under SCU support and its distance medical education and medical consultation are undertaken by Huaxi Hospital. In sum, all those SCU initiatives and institutionalized efforts have helped Tibetan people receive quality medical services.

Self-initiated SCU Efforts for Wenchuan Earthquake Relief

On May 12, 2008, the Wenchuan area of Sichuan Province was hit by an 8 magnitude earthquake. It caused massive destruction in the towns and villages, with millions of houses collapsed, roads cracked and blocked, thousands of people homeless, and many who lost their families. In the wake of the earthquake, the Chinese government and people have joined their hearts and hands to achieve a preliminary success in the nationwide campaign to relieve the disaster.

It is well known that disaster remains a serious constraint to poverty reduction progress in rural areas and an important cause to the return to poverty. Statistics show that about 10% of villages are hit by natural disasters each year, and for the key poor counties entitled to central government support, the ratio rises to over 50%. The main victims in this disaster of earthquake are old revolutionary basis areas, areas inhabited by ethnic minorities, and poor areas. Among the 45 counties identified by the State Council as fatally disastrous areas, the key poor counties entitled to central government support number 13, those counties entitled to provincial government support stand at 24, and the poor villages more than 4,000 and poor population more than 1.4 million. Due to the earthquake, the achievements of poverty reduction over the past 20 years were damaged, reducing many people back to poverty (http://www. hpichina. org/special/index3. htm). A consensus has emerged in the society, as reiterated in many occasions by President Hu Jintao and Premier Wen Jiabao, that poverty reduction should proceed in conjunction with post-disaster reconstruction.

Only 92 kilometers from Wenchuan, the epicenter of the deadly May 12th earthquake, SCU also suffered from damages. The teachers and students as responsible citizens were eager to help the victims of the earthquake and denoted nearly US $3. 08 million in cash and in-kind service. SCU's four hospitals provided intensive medical care to more than 3,000 critically injured persons, with Huaxi Hospital alone caring for 2,655 persons. The university organized 21,342 volunteers in 1,365 groups to go to the quake-stricken areas to provide a wide variety of services, such as medical care, danger removal and psychological consultation.

To provide longer term support, SCU has also introduced a series of measures to give concern to the students of the stricken areas, such as the "Give Support to the College Entrance Examination Takers in the Quake-stricken Area Program," the "Relief Plan for Students in the Quake-stricken Area" and the "Relief Fund for Sichuan University Students from the Quake-stricken Area." SCU has made a solemn commitment to the public that there will be no SCU students dropping out due to the financial hardship of their families in the stricken areas. To materialize the pledge, SCU provided all kinds of financial support, including funds from the national government to all students from the quake-stricken areas who had lost financial resources. For the students whose parents died in the earthquake, the university provided a whole package of support that covered tuition, accommodation fees and basic living allowances.

The Wenchuan earthquake caused heavy casualties and immense losses. The post-quake reconstruction is a pressing long term and arduous task confronted by the Chinese government and society. In this regard, SCU has self-initiated her post-quake restoration and reconstruction action plan in the stricken areas, covering nine fields, including economic reconstruction, medicine and health, and ecological environment. On 21 June 2008, the Relief and Research Center for Post-quake Reconstruction in Sichuan was jointly established by SCU and Hong Kong Polytechnic University (HKPU), the first relief and research center established between a mainland university and a university outside the mainland. The center has brought together interdisciplinary expertise from SCU and HKPU, providing both short term relief and long term support for Sichuan in the areas of rehabilitation and health services, psychological counseling, community building, construction and engineering technologies and economic reconstruction. Through this center, the two universities have not only provided timely post-quake relief and reconstruction services for the victims, but also offered training for more than 3,000 relief workers and volunteers using the "Training-the-Trainers" approach.

Concluding Remarks

All in all, SCU has achieved many important goals in fighting poverty, but anti-poverty is a long term and arduous mission. From the anti-poverty endeavors of SCU, the following useful lessons can be drawn:

First, the anti-poverty strategy should be multidimensional. Income poverty, human poverty and knowledge poverty are interrelated and interactive. The lack of income will cause the lack of nutrition, clean food and proper education; human poverty and knowledge poverty make it difficult for the poor population to break out of income poverty; and those who have temporarily broken out of income poverty may regress into their former poor state due to diseases, disasters or illiteracy. Thus, it is obvious that a singular poverty alleviation strategy will produce very little effect. With this in mind, SCU has concentrated its efforts on constructing a comprehensive system of regional support in five aspects: knowledge and technology, human resources, medicine and health, tuition assistance and concept instillation. The SCU programs in these five aspects are interrelated and mutually supportive and, acting in concert, have powerfully created new conditions that help reduce poverty in western China in the long run.

Second, public universities' efforts to alleviate poverty must be based on strong leadership commitment. The leaders can inspire and motivate faculty, staff and students to participate in both institutionalized and ad hoc anti-poverty programs. Partners, including other universities and colleges, institutions, governments and non-profits also need such a leadership commitment to reinforce their participation. Due to leadership commitment, many competent scholars and staff of SCU were inspired to go to poverty stricken areas to serve as consultants and even civil servants under the SCU "scholar civil servant program." One such SCU staff member acted as the deputy chief of a county government in Aba, Sichuan. With his pioneering work in setting up new programs with technical supported from SCU, new plants and tourism projects were introduced. His contributions were possible only because of his willingness to leave behind the comfortable life in Chengdu, and the willingness was prompted by the leadership commitment to reduce poverty in western China.

After the Wenchuan earthquake, SCU gave a rapid response to immediately undertake various measures to save the lives and property of the stricken people. SCU is actively involved in the post-quake reconstruction to help people from regressing into poverty. All these are feasible and become operational, again due to leadership commitment, which was reflected in various commitment meetings chaired by the senior leaders of the university and reflected by university's allocation of resources to fund the various institutionalized and ad hoc programs.

Third, to achieve anti-poverty goals, cooperation between universities and governments is needed. Though widely recognized for their public service functions, universities have not been able to serve the public at their full capacity. Several issues contribute to the explanation. First, governments, especially government authorities in less developed regions, have not been able to fully understand the tremendous impact of universities on local economic development. They lack a clear understanding regarding the balanced development and coordinated mechanism between universities and regional economy. Second, most corporations, particularly private ones, are more concerned with immediate and short term benefits instead of long term strategic support to the public. Third, universities depend too much on governmental support, especially for those institutions in developing countries. In SCU's practice, great efforts have been devoted to remove these barriers. SCU has worked actively with local governments, enterprises, and public institutions to jointly operate various programs, either training schools or colleges that offer much needed pedagogical and professional specialties, long term medical support which improves the health of local residents, or emergent disaster rehabilitation projects that aim to prevent regressing back to poverty. In all, to realize high efficiency of poverty alleviation projects, universities, governments and enterprises should work collaboratively, and a practical cooperation mechanism is essential.

Notes

1 See http: // gov. people. com. cn/GB/46728/53739/53747/3751678.html. (Retrieved on August 1, 2008). It should be noted, however, that, according to the World Bank's News Release (No: 2006/416/EAP), titled "World Bank's New Partnership Strategy for China Focuses on Economic Integration, Poverty, and Sustainable Development," there are 135 million people living on less than US$1 a day.

2 The China Medical Board (CMB) is an independent US foundation that aims

to advance health in China and neighboring Asian countries through strengthening medical, nursing and public health research and education. It is a highly-focused grant-making foundation targeting its support to carefully selected Asian grantees.

RURAL PROSPERITY AND DISTRIBUTED LEARNING: TEXAS TECH'S COMMITMENT TO RURAL COMMUNITIES

Valerie Osland Paton, Robert Hickerson,
Matt Baker and A. Michelle Demel
Texas Tech University, USA

Introduction

Public universities play an important role in the future of American rural environments and, as this chapter will demonstrate, Texas Tech University has utilized distributed educational interventions to fulfill this role. This chapter will describe the elements required for developing successful partnerships with communities in order to foster rural and community prosperity through access to higher education. Essential elements include institutional commitment to distributed delivery, adaptation of pedagogies to distribute curricula, mutuality and reciprocity between community and educational partners, technology as an enabler of partnerships and the financial infrastructure required for sustainable delivery of distributed academic programs.

Evidence clearly shows that a major contributor to rural prosperity is educational attainment (Isserman, Feser & Warren, 2007). Educational attainment is possible only if it is accessible. In some rural regions of the United States, an educational investment by local community members is viewed with skepticism. Many rural high school youth do not remain in their local communities due to a lack of employment opportunities. When graduates leave their local communities for employment opportunities in urban areas, the community is left without the benefit of an educated work force and the result is a declining tax base (Goetz & Rupasingha, 2005). When public universities partner with communities, however, distributed delivery of educational programs can provide solutions and support for rural economic development.

In spite of rural community restructuring due to a national trend of decline in rural areas within the last century (Green, 2005), West Texas has numerous employment opportunities that are emerging or are at the cusp of emerging, resulting in critical employment shortages in certain industry segments. As a result of its aggressive approach to expanding higher education access in rural West Texas, Texas Tech University and its university system partner institutions are uniquely poised to engage the region in outreach and distributed academic programs for significant workforce development. Such development is the linchpin for rural prosperity.

One industry segment that Texas Tech has sought to support with workforce development is wind energy production. Although issues exist in the transmission of electricity from sparsely populated regions of the state to more densely populated regions (Northcott, 2008), West Texas offers a combination of elevation and consistent wind to capitalize on a rapidly growing industry (Mattei, 2008). In fact, the region's wind energy business is booming (Hollandsworth, 2008). In July 2007, the Texas Higher Education Coordinating Board approved the first doctoral program in Wind Science and Engineering at Texas Tech (Texas Tech University, 2008). Additionally, the Texas Workforce Commission has invested one million dollars for further curriculum development in wind energy at the technical/vocational, baccalaureate and graduate levels, charging both Texas Tech and Texas State Technical College in Sweetwater, Texas, to deliver electronically as much of the content as is possible (Cranford, 2008).

According to Northcott and Hargis (2008), large-scale solar projects are in development in California's Central Valley and Mojave Desert, and it is possible that such projects will soon be initiated in West Texas as well. The boom-and-bust petroleum industry is also in need of workers. The recent oil boom has added literally billions of dollars and 26,000 jobs in the Permian Basin alone (Blaney & Caldwell, 2008). The changing economic landscape of this large region provides the context for this discussion about the use of distributed delivery to meet the emergent workforce and leadership needs of rural communities.

In this chapter, we discuss lessons learned from Texas Tech's engagement with rural communities. We first consider the institutional context and commitment to distributed delivery, as well as the pedagogical adaptation that has permeated Texas Tech's academic culture since inception of the institution. Next we describe Tech's philosophical approach of reciprocity and mutuality in partnerships with communities, an approach that arises from the perspective of appreciative inquiry rather than a deficit model. Finally, we discuss the pragmatic issues of technology as an enabler of distributed delivery and the financial considerations of successful partnerships.

Institutional Commitment to Distributed Delivery

"Texas Tech is the largest comprehensive higher education institution in the western two-thirds of the state, serving a region larger than 46 of the nation's 50 states" (Texas Tech University, 2008).

The map below demonstrates the scope of the region served by Texas Tech and provides the context for the institution's commitment to distributed delivery since its founding in 1923—a commitment that continues today. At the university's opening in 1925, Texas Tech's first president, Paul W. Horn, established a large vision:

Figure 15.1 *Southwestern United States and the location of Texas Tech University*

Everything that is done on these West Texas Plains ought to be on a big scale. It is a country that lends itself to bigness. It is a country that does not harmonize with things little or narrow or mean. Let us make the work of our college fit in with the scope of our country. Let our thoughts be big thoughts and broad thoughts. Let our thinking be in worldwide terms. (Horn, 1925)

Early in the university's history, the concept of taking education to students was supported by the university. The "flying professor program" delivered faculty members to sites throughout West Texas and bordering states to meet the needs of communities, including education and engineering coursework required by communities to support their educational and workforce infrastructures. Faculty members also drove to communities to deliver second language and workforce instruction that was not delivered by the K-12 schools or community colleges in the region. This delivery of higher education curricula was viewed as integral to the institution's identity and essential to the growth and development of communities across a vast area.

Within a decade, Texas Tech had developed a large extension curriculum offering "approximately two hundred and fifty courses to those who cannot attend the regularly scheduled classes" (Bulletin, 1935, 200). As the collegiate curriculum expanded in correspondence format, a parallel effort provided K-12 curriculum through the correspondence format as well. Commitment to distributed delivery is evidenced in the 1966-67 *General Catalog,* which states:

> At the request of a sufficient number of students, extension classes may be organized in convenient centers. The number of students required to justify the organization of such a class increases with the distance from the campus. Both graduate and undergraduate work may be made available. (Bulletin, 1966, 66)

One example is the College of Arts and Sciences' delivery of linguistics courses for teacher education to numerous West Texas and Panhandle schools in the 1970s. This flexible approach to distributing curricular delivery was bolstered in 1971, when the Texas legislature transferred the site now known as the TTU Center at Junction from Texas A&M University to Texas Tech University. Within the decade, the Junction site—270 miles from Texas Tech in Lubbock—offered face-to-face art education and field-based science instruction. In the late 1990s, the College of Education formalized its partnerships with Educational Service Centers across the state to deliver courses to regional independent school districts via video conferencing. In 2001-2002, in response to requests from communities for increased access to higher education, Texas Tech established four more teaching sites in Abilene, Amarillo, Fredericksburg and Marble Falls, Texas (Paton, 2005). In fall 2007, a fifth teaching site opened in El Paso, addressing the region's need for access to the field of architecture; the closest architecture program was more than a six-hour drive from El Paso. In 2005 the American Institute of Architects' reported that less than 2% of its members listed their ethnicity as "Hispanic/Latino" (American Institute of Architects, 2005, 2). Therefore, the El Paso teaching site addressed a unique national need for increased numbers of Hispanic and Latino students trained in the field of architecture. In order to deliver curricula to these teaching sites, Texas Tech leveraged available technological resources and the history of adaptive instructional methodologies.

In the 1960s and 1970s, Texas Tech's College of Engineering began the early adoption of electronically delivered curricula. In 1985, in response to the increasing need for distance delivery, the College of Engineering began delivering the Master of Engineering through videotapes of lectures. Over the years, the College of Engineering engaged its faculty and researchers in developing new delivery solutions and employing existing solutions for delivering course work to students by utilizing film, video, audiotapes, DVDs, video conferencing, streaming video to the Internet (with synchronous audio, live video and audio) and archived video and audio. In 1998, Texas Tech and Texas A&M were approved to jointly offer an Ed.D. in Agricultural Education at a distance, which is the only program of its kind in the nation. Since then, four more Texas Tech doctoral programs have been approved by the Texas Higher Education Coordinating Board for distributed delivery: the Ph.D. in Technical Communication and Rhetoric, the Ed.D. in Educational Leadership, the Ph.D. in Computer Science, and the Ph.D. in Systems Engineering and Management.

Thus, Texas Tech's first 85 years have been marked by a distinctive identity and a commitment to distributed learning. Through every available delivery modality—print-based, electronic media, intensive face-to-face, off-campus, and hybrid—Texas Tech has pursued its original vision of serving one of the largest educationally underserved regions in the United States. This history is a testimony to the institution's commitment to access and its flexibility in adapting to the needs of learners.

Adaptation of Pedagogies to Distribute Curricula

The historical context at Texas Tech provides the setting for a description of its current endeavors to increase access to higher education and partner with educationally underserved communities. Although some of these communities are rural, the lessons learned and models developed can be generalized to metropolitan partnerships as well. The working definition of "distributed learning" applied to the discussion in this chapter is taken from the Institute for Academic Technology at the University of North Carolina, as cited in Bates (1999):

> A distributed learning environment is a learner-centered approach to education, which integrates a number of technologies to enable opportunities for activities and interaction in both asynchronous and real-time modes. The model is based on blending a choice of appropriate technologies with aspects of campus-based delivery, open learning systems and distance education. The approach gives instructors the flexibility to customize learning environments to meet the needs of diverse student populations, while providing both high-quality and cost-effective learning. (27)

Within this context, faculty commitment to distributed learning is paramount. The academic environment that includes numerous distributed degree programs provides a hospitable environment for faculty to explore modalities and pedagogies that best fit their disciplinary interests. Faculty initiative and entrepreneurial behavior have generated distributed delivery of more than 30 baccalaureate, master and doctoral degree programs and certificates at Texas Tech.

A rich distributed learning context provides faculty with many choices to deliver curricula. Figure 15.2 below conceptualizes these choices and the connecting component of "interaction" among them.

Figure 15.2 *Blended/hybrid delivery options*
dependent upon faculty determination of pedagogical approach to subject matter

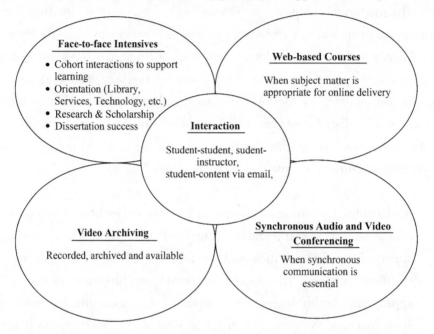

In order to understand how this graphic describes distributed delivery, two doctoral programs serve as examples. First, the Ed.D. in Agricultural Education is distributed to in-state, out-of-state and international students using a combination of web-based instruction, synchronous video conferencing, archived lectures, intensive face-to-face sessions, and various student-to-student, faculty-to-student, and student-to-content interaction environments. Because this degree program is offered by two major research institutions, the best available technology resources from both institutions are utilized for instructional delivery. Most of the courses are delivered via synchronous video conferencing to student end-sites (including home sites, agricultural extension sites, K-12 schools, community colleges and universities). Archived courses are available during specified periods of time, subject to the respective faculty members' determination and institutional policy pertaining to intellectual property and archival protocol.

A second example is found in the Ph.D. in Technical Communication and Rhetoric, which distributes most of its content via web-based delivery to students worldwide. To compliment this web-based instructional delivery and increase the scholarly production of students and graduates, an intensive face-to-face technical writing conference is held each year on the Texas Tech campus in Lubbock. Students participate in workshops conducted by faculty members and attend lectures by nationally recognized scholars. They also receive academic advisement and annual reviews of their performance, attend doctoral defenses and work in the department's usability lab. The conference is an opportunity for faculty and students to build relationships. These two examples of distributed doctoral programs demonstrate the interaction between the various methods of instructional delivery depicted in Figure 15.2.

Technology and policy infrastructures have been developed to support the distributed delivery of course content. In 2007, a new College of Outreach and Distance Education was established to institutionalize the role of distributed learning and to provide enhanced resources and services to faculty and students. In addition, the technology infrastructure includes a Teaching, Learning, and Technology Center that assists faculty with developing curricula in various technology assisted formats. Several course management systems are utilized to deliver online content, including commercial and locally developed solutions. Video conferencing resources are available at on-campus and off-campus sites; curricula can be delivered to students' home end-sites as well. Colleges have developed distributed delivery solutions that best meet their faculty and student needs, including synchronous video to individual student home computers, synchronous chat, asynchronous chat and video capture and archiving. The Texas Tech University Library's focus on digital materials and web-based access enables students to receive library resources through electronic means. Many other educational support services are online; students have access to the ombudsman, career center, student legal services and technology help. Policies and procedures to support faculty and student success, as well as intellectual property and resource stewardship, have been developed and are utilized.

Mutuality and Reciprocity between Texas Tech University and Community and Educational Partners

The nature of partnerships between Texas Tech and local communities is very important. In *Higher Education for the Public Good* (2005), Chambers writes: "In the new social movement to strengthen the public relationship between higher education and society, there needs to be more creative and collaborative efforts to understand the needs of those partners in the relationship." An open dialogue between the representatives of communities and Texas Tech has been an essential component of ensuring that there is mutuality and reciprocity in the understanding of partner needs and that resulting agreements address these needs.

Rural communities prosper when educational opportunities are made available; prosperous counties have lowerun poverty rates, lower unemployment rates, lower high school dropout rates, and lower rates of housing problems than the nation as a whole (Isserman, Feser & Warren, 2007). The National Governors Association encourages state universities to be responsive to the needs of rural communities:

> To meet the needs of cluster businesses for highly skilled workers, states have deployed colleges and universities as training centers. States can ensure that cluster businesses in remote, rural communities have access to the same capital and technical resources as their more advantageously located competitors. (1)

Toward this end, communities have been the initiators of partnerships with Texas Tech University in order to meet specific educational needs that are critical to community growth and development. Each partnership has been unique as areas of common interest and benefits are identified. Paton (2005, 35) describes the "symbiotic benefits" that are derived from these partnerships: 1) expanded access to higher education; 2) increased leadership talent in the region; 3) intersections between economic development activities and faculty research interests; 4) investment in the regional K-12 infrastructure and academic preparation of students; 5) economic impact on the community and region; 6) expansion of broadband access and technology expertise; and 7) infusion of new revenue resources from regional, state, alumni, and donor sources.

Figure 15.3 depicts this mutuality and reciprocity of benefits for communities and Texas Tech. With this focus on mutual and reciprocal benefits, Texas Tech has entered into collaborations as varied as the communities they serve. All such collaborations have been in response to community initiatives and have been built on the foundation of local educational and research needs. In response to community requests to host regional academic delivery sites, Texas Tech has initiated needs assessment activities and convened interested stakeholders, including potential academic partners.

Community partners and stakeholders have included regional community colleges, regional universities, economic development boards, city and county governments, local private foundations, chambers of commerce, local school districts, community-based organizations with an interest in higher education, alumni chapters and private donors. These entities have been encouraged to provide their unique viewpoints during initial planning and during the drafting of memoranda of agreement. The memoranda of agreement guide the collaborative start-up in its initial stages.

Figure 15.3 *Diagram of mutuality and reciprocity of university-community partnerships*

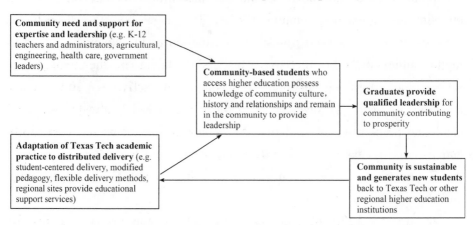

Based upon Texas Tech's experience with numerous community partnerships, the quality of execution of any initiative is tied directly to the quality of the initial written agreement. When memoranda of agreement were vague (or worse yet, unwritten), expectations varied substantially among the various partners. These agreements should make explicit the following elements: the role of all partners, expected accomplishments and timelines for introduction of academic programs, benchmarks for continuing support and operations, and exit strategies when the expectations of the original agreement cannot be met for one or more of the central partners.

Challenges with planning and execution have been ameliorated somewhat through the formation of local advisory boards and committees, when the purpose of the group was clearly stated and the group was ably led. Texas Tech has gained substantial return on investment from the time and energy invested in the formation and support of a regional advisory board associated with multiple teaching sites in the Hill Country region of Central Texas. Because the university was forming a backbone of three teaching sites positioned one hour's driving time apart across a ten-county area, an advisory board was created with the specific purpose of helping local communities commit to a regional educational initiative. This type of cooperation was difficult for most communities to envision, having previously known only competition with their neighbors over economic development opportunities. However, the regional advisory board, with representation carefully selected from each community across the region, has proven very successful in helping community leaders understand the power of several community colleges and universities collaborating—rather than competing—while attempting to meet the educational needs of students.

In every case where Texas Tech has offered undergraduate programs through blended delivery at remote locations, K-12 entities and the community colleges have been important partners in providing degree pathways. Under specific articulation agreements, the community colleges provided the complete lower division curriculum in support of the baccalaureate degree offered by Texas Tech. At El Paso Community College, for example, the community college and Texas Tech collaborated on facilities, academic advisement, admissions processes, student financial aid and other educational support services to provide a successful transfer and an undergraduate degree pathway. In cases where the Texas Tech teaching site was not located at a community college, Texas Tech and the community college partner occupied the same community-provided administrative space in order to visibly promote the partnership and brand the collaboration in the minds of students and supporters.

In the collaboration among three teaching sites in the Hill Country, Texas Tech University developed close working relationships with other institutions in the Texas Tech University System—specifically, the TTU Health Sciences Center and Angelo State University. For instance, at one site the university provided office, telecommunications and clerical support for a Regional Dean from the TTU Health Sciences Center, who coordinated the delivery of upper division B.S. and M.S. in Nursing degree programs throughout Central Texas. Angelo State University collaborated to offer graduate programs at three different teaching sites. In effect—through collaborative agreements—Texas Tech University, TTU Health Sciences Center and Angelo State University developed a system infrastructure to serve a 15,000 square mile region.

Texas Tech's teaching sites and the programs offered through them have been growing slowly since their inception in 2001-2002. Sites located in rural environments without a metropolitan statistical area (population of 50,000 or more) yielded fewer students and necessitated distributed methods to deliver curriculum. Enrollment in cohort-based, distributed-delivery graduate programs (such as the M.Ed. in Education Leadership) has produced sustainable enrollments in rural communities. Undergraduate programs have been more difficult to deliver to students in rural communities due to the impact of these programs at Texas Tech's main campus and inability of faculty to meet the existing demands and support new programs at the same time. In some cases, faculty members in impacted programs have been less responsive to implementing distributed delivery modalities. Rural students have sought programs where there is a nexus between education and employment, as is the case in undergraduate and graduate programs in education. Since school districts and health care providers are major employers in most rural communities, demand for baccalaureate and graduate education and nursing programs has been strong in more developed rural areas.

As Texas Tech's teaching sites approach eight years of operation, there is evidence that graduates are making a difference on their communities. In spring 2009, Texas Tech will celebrate its 100th graduate from the M.Ed. in Educational Leadership program delivered in the Hill Country. Because these graduates were afforded access to a graduate degree and K-12 principal certification preparation, they were qualified to assume positions of leadership throughout the region. Rural school district boards and superintendents have found that they can provide for leadership succession of educational administrators, promoting candidates from their teaching ranks who have extensive knowledge and understanding of rural educational environments. In a similar manner, through Texas Tech's partnerships with regional community colleges, nurses have progressed from licensed vocation status to a doctorate in nursing without leaving the region or their jobs. Many of Texas Tech's nursing graduates have gone on to positions of great responsibility, leading programs and divisions at large regional health centers, while some have become qualified to fill faculty roles at area community colleges.

While the communities that have partnered with Texas Tech have hoped for significant economic development impact as a result of providing higher education opportunities, in reality those benefits are realized slowly over many years. The immediate gains are associated with growing future leaders and retaining young talent in the region—a constant challenge in rural communities. Because many of Tech's collaborating communities have started building general purpose higher education facilities, some immediate economic advantage has been realized by engineers, architects and construction firms. However, some of these communities expect their efforts to flower into a branch campus of a general purpose university, with the promise of students from outside the region moving to their communities to access education opportunities. The probability of such an outcome for the community is dependent on demographic changes that are often not on the near horizon.

The Texas Tech experience has been that few of our collaborating communities were realistic in estimating the length of time required to build high quality academic programs and delivery infrastructure. Rapid advances in technology and the pressure on state resources have each contributed to the changing nature of higher education delivery, making it unlikely that complex general academic institutions will be developed in the rural areas. This environment suggests that the utilization of distributed educational delivery systems and off-campus teaching sites such as those implemented by Texas Tech may be an economical and high quality method of addressing the needs of rural students and communities.

Technology as an Enabler of Partnerships

Technology services have been an integral part of the infrastructure needed to expand access to rural students through regional collaborations. Unfortunately, although the technology that supports distributed education has improved substantially in recent years (as has innovation in the pedagogy needed to capitalize on these technological capabilities), many barriers still exist to the use of technology as a solution for educational delivery.

First, community leaders who seek educational partnerships have been generally unfamiliar with the use of technology as a means of delivering content. Because they were more familiar with the classic face-to-face delivery model, they believed (at least in the beginning of collaboration) that distributed, electronic delivery (electronic-to-group and electronic-to-individual) was a lesser form of education. When thinking about educational partnerships for their community, they normally defaulted to the classic model and resisted any mode that did not fit with their paradigm. Community members were eager to have their students enjoy the face-to-face "campus experience" and this desire sometimes included unrealistic expectations about the availability of the kinds of co-curricular activities found at a large, general academic institution.

In Texas Tech's experience, the barrier to community acceptance of electronic delivery has been overcome by providing information about the development of technology use in education. Community leaders were informed about the changing nature of higher education in general (namely the vastly increased use of blended or hybrid instruction) and about the research which indicates that high quality blended/hybrid instruction increases access and can be more effective than face-to-face instruction in many fields of study. Texas Tech representatives invested time to assist partners in understanding that many of today's students are inclined to be comfortable with the technology used in distance education and that students are quite capable of developing meaningful relationships with classmates and professors via electronic communication. One of the most effective means of conveying this information has been to provide community leaders with the opportunity to participate in sessions that demonstrate the capabilities of electronic instruction (interactive video, web-based instruction, and podcasts).

Secondly, although rural access to modern telecommunications access has expanded significantly, many rural areas still lack access to broadband internet services at a reasonable price. In delivering its distributed programs to the Central Texas Hill Country region, Texas Tech has discovered that a large percentage of students lack broadband service at their homes. Those students who do enjoy such access pay at least twice as much for the service as students in a metropolitan area do. In July 2008, a Pew Research Center Publication stated: "38% of those living in rural American now have broadband at home.... By comparison, 57% of urban residents have high-speed connections at home now and 60% of suburban residents have such connections .... " (Horrigan, 2008). For this reason, Texas Tech has provided access to computer labs for students taking online courses and conducting research. In spite of the rapid pace of technological change in our society in general, rural access to broadband internet services has grown slowly due to relatively small market demand.

Another issue impacting the use of technology to deliver distributed programs has been the quality of connectivity. For some coursework, Texas Tech utilized interactive video conferencing to deliver instruction to groups and individuals, particularly for graduate professional programs in which peer interaction has been viewed as a vital component. Cohorts of our students participating in graduate programs in Educational Leadership repeatedly stressed the importance of group instruction and eagerly expounded on the value of the lifelong relationships developed among members of the cohort. However, when delivering instruction through video conferencing to rural areas, connection quality has been identified as a significant challenge. An estimated 10-15% of interactive electronic time has been lost due to dropped connections and audio/video quality degradation from heavily stressed transmission lines. For these reasons, Texas Tech has developed a process of certifying all synchronous delivery end-sites, and provides information technology specialists as support at the end- and send-sites for all classes, including night and weekend sessions.

Pedagogy and technology are inextricably linked when considering the design of academic programs delivered in distributed modalities. Texas Tech's teaching sites have provided for the addition of cohort-based and intensive instructional options to be added to electronic and other distance delivery modalities. For this reason, when designing programs for delivery to teaching sites, Texas Tech faculty have adopted blended/ hybrid delivery options that are the most effective for the specific subject matter of the course or program. This approach capitalizes on varied opportunities for student-to-student and faculty-to-student interaction, as those cited in the center circle of Figure 15.2. Faculty selecting this blended/hybrid approach report that it has increased retention of students over asynchronous options. This combination—of web-based instruction, interactive video, and intermittent, intensive face-to-face instruction by faculty at the teaching sites—has yielded retention and graduation rates that match or exceed those on the main campus in Lubbock.

Financial Infrastructure Required for Sustainable Delivery of Distributed Academic Programs

In initiating regional partnerships and creating distributed degree programs and teaching sites, careful attention has been paid to financial projections. Funding for the expansion of programs has been limited. Furthermore, allocation systems have not always returned proportionate funding to the revenue centers. Therefore, in Texas Tech's partnerships, contributions from communities for dedicated start-up funding have been essential. For that reason, the development of business plans with accurate cash flow projections has been viewed as essential, and plans have been updated annually.

Texas Tech's experience in starting teaching sites has shown that sources of start-up funding vary greatly but have generally drawn on both institutional and external funding. Collaborating partners in the regional start-up efforts have included various combinations of local government agencies (city and county), local economic development corporations, private foundations and K-12 school districts. Community-based non-profits have been created specifically to fund the needs of the off-campus sites and those of community college partners who provide lower division course work supporting articulated undergraduate degrees. In all but one case, the community college partner was operating outside of its taxing district in remote service area locations. As a consequence, there was limited funding for community college offerings and partnerships with non-profits were necessary for start-up and sustainability of the academic programs.

All Texas Tech start-up operations have received resources from the university, usually in the form of personnel and operational costs. Often these institutional allocations were characterized as "matching funds" to community contributions, and this expectation was included in the memoranda of agreement discussed earlier. In one example, the university required special legislative support to be secured, and although the university included that item in its biennial appropriations request, the community led the effort of informing the local legislative delegation about the need. In that regard, the regional advisory board comprised of influential leaders from local government, business and the retired community was instrumental in obtaining required funding.

In almost every start-up, resources were obtained from local economic development boards in addition to other funding. In Texas and in rural communities in general, the ability of community economic development corporations to support regional teaching sites has been limited. For that reason, initial academic programming was expanded to include a research component that could be funded. In some cases, a partnership was created with a cognizant community college in order to provide a much desired workforce development program. For one teaching site start up, Texas Tech and a hosting community provided access to state-funded technology infrastructure grants in order to finance a regional telecommunications hub. The hub provided connectivity to three classroom and administrative facilities as well as computer labs and interactive video conferencing classrooms. In another example, a community eager to tap into the Hill Country initiative raised private donations for the operational expenses associated with the first two years of an academic site. In another case, community partners that were unable to provide cash donations provided 5,000 square feet of administrative space at no cost, while the local school district provided classrooms, office space, and maintenance and cleaning services free of charge.

Institutional and community partner commitment to the financial infrastructure for new teaching sites must consider both the start-up needs and the long term requirements for site operations and distributed program delivery. Although state and institutional revenues eventually return to the teaching site, ultimately the sustainability of these partnerships has been dependent upon the institution and the community. The success of these partnerships has been predicated on the understanding that long term commitment is required to generate the intended benefits of higher education that contribute to the prosperity of the community.

Conclusion

This chapter has illustrated the successful partnerships that have utilized distributed learning solutions to provide mutually beneficial and reciprocal relationships between Texas Tech University and communities. The conditions required for these relationships include the following: institutional commitment to distributed delivery, adaptation of pedagogies to distributed curricula, mutuality and reciprocity between communities and Texas Tech, technology as an enabler of partnerships, and the financial infrastructure required for sustainable delivery of distributed academic programs.

As the population of the United States continues to concentrate in metropolitan areas, the needs of rural communities become more obvious. Historically, the U.S. population has migrated from one coast to another, with the regional population in the central U.S. supporting the population of the coasts and metropolitan regions through agricultural, transportation and energy infrastructures. Today, West Texas and rural communities of the United States provide the food, transportation connections and energy sources of the nation. Within this context, sustaining and growing rural communities through access to higher education is an important investment in the prosperity of those communities and the nation. As exemplified in this chapter, public universities like Texas Tech that have a demonstrable and historical commitment to engagement with communities provide a critical connection between higher education and the future of American rural communities.

BRIDGING UNIVERSITY AND COMMUNITY: THE POWER OF COLLABORATIVE PARTNERSHIPS FOR SOCIAL CHANGE

Rosemarie Hunter, Sarah Munro, Linda Dunn and Katie Olson
University of Utah, USA

Introduction

There is renewed interest today in redefining the responsibilities that public universities have toward their surrounding communities and in developing new strategies for university-community collaborations. At their core, these efforts are based on the twin premises that an integral part of public education is the experience of community engagement, and that through engagement, public universities can and should be powerful engines of social change in their surrounding communities. While initially these relationships focus on the issues of local communities, they ultimately seek to define the role of higher education in understanding and addressing societal problems. Furthermore, there are widely held societal expectations that institutions of higher education will develop responsible citizens, prepare the workforce and pursue knowledge that informs best practices and social policies (Jay, 2000).

Perhaps the most intriguing aspect of university-community partnerships is the potentially transformative power they have not just for universities but for entire communities and regions. This potential for transformation is not a given. Rather, it lies entirely in the *process* through which educators and community partners engage with each other and the extent to which the definition, analysis and solutions to social priorities are collaboratively developed and executed. University-community partnerships do this in three ways: 1) by *leveraging existing resources* in the community and at the university to achieve more with fewer resources; 2) by creating a *process of communication and a culture of capacity-building* among institutions and individuals that normally do not interact with one another; and 3) by creating a *shared space to develop specific joint actions focused on structural and social change.*

This chapter provides an overview of the community engagement model at the University of Utah, with specific partnership examples for those interested in recreating similar programs at other institutions. At the University of Utah, the *community engagement continuum* is defined by tying community involvement to the academic triad of research, teaching and service, for which faculty are evaluated. By utilizing service learning curricula, university-community partnerships and community-based research, faculty, staff, students, community organizations and residents currently engaged in community development efforts with one another have found that their discussions and activities can lead to mutually beneficial partnerships that are enriching institutions of higher education and fostering communities of greater social and economic justice.

Highlighted in this chapter are four examples of complex university-community partnerships focused on regional development and social change. They include:

- Westside Studio, a service learning course and community partnership focused on re-development of blighted urban areas;
- Education First Mentoring Partnership, a student-led initiative focused on creating greater access to higher education for historically underrepresented youth;
- Hartland Partnership Center, where teams of professors, students, community organizations and residents work together to address community-identified needs and build the capacity of social

service systems and schools to better address the needs of newly resettled populations; and the

- Westside Leadership Institute which supports the development of local resident leaders as catalysts for positive change in their communities.

In the context of the role of public universities in regional development, the authors will examine issues of reciprocity, sustainability and institutional structures instrumental in involving public universities in successful social development.

Building Institutional Capacity and a Culture of Engagement

The University of Utah, as the state's flagship university and a research intensive institution, has developed a unique approach to community engagement at the intersection of its own goals and the broader interests of the community it serves. The University of Utah is educating the scientists, educators, and policy makers of tomorrow, so it is vitally important to infuse students with an understanding of their communities and their responsibilities as citizens. In addition, the university has a deep stake in increasing access to higher education for the state's rapidly growing minority populations, who are markedly absent in the lists of graduating high school seniors and entering college students at state universities. As such, the institution must facilitate the entrance of increasing numbers of underrepresented students in order to remain competitive and retain its standing as a relevant and engaged public university. Nevertheless, increasing access to higher education over the long term requires a broad social development vision that addresses the systemic obstacles that prevent economic and educational success, from employment and affordable housing to effective organizations that can win the attention of local government to address community needs. This chapter focuses on the extensive social development vision of the University of Utah's campus—community partnerships, a vision that provides the broadest terrain for faculty and students to engage with community partners around issues of mutual substantive interest.

For two decades the University of Utah has focused on building institutional capacity and defining innovative approaches to community engagement. As the level of university involvement in the community has grown, so has the need to develop additional support structures on and off campus. By creating two complementary entities for community engagement and scholarship, the university has been able to maximize its resources and relationships both on campus and in the community to focus its efforts on regional development and social change. These two community engagement centers work in tandem to enhance and support the goals of the four campus-community partnerships described in this chapter.

On Campus—The Lowell Bennion Community Service Center

In 1988 the Lowell Bennion Community Service Center began as a center for student-led community service and has developed into a national model for diffusing service learning throughout the university curriculum. Located on campus and administratively under University Student Services, the Bennion Center offers students a range of opportunities including self-directed work, curricular service learning, post graduate initiatives and community-based fellowships. The student-directed programs are designed to engage students in long term, sustainable relationships with non-profit organizations. All activities of the Bennion Center are reciprocal relationships that encourage students and faculty to learn leadership and citizenship skills while building the capacity of non-profit organizations. Such programs as Alternative Spring Break and Saturday Service Projects invite students to take part in one-time service programs, while programs like America Reads, a federal government funded work-study program, allows students to earn a portion of their financial aid while tutoring children in low-income neighborhoods.

Through the service learning programs at the Bennion Center, faculty are provided with support for developing courses that connect their curriculum and research to the community. Institutional support through the Bennion Center includes:

- workshops and web-based materials providing faculty with technical assistance for developing service learning syllabi;
- funding to hire students who act as service learning coordinators in classes; and
- seed grants to develop community based research projects and community engaged teaching

In the Community-University Neighborhood Partners

In 2001, resulting from a direct move by the President's office, the University of Utah intensified its commitment to community engagement and scholarship by initiating University Neighborhood Partners (UNP), a university-community partnership program located off campus and focused on building long term collaborations among university faculty, staff, students, local non-profits, city government and social service systems of all kinds. With 18 partnerships in 17 locations, UNP has forged strong relationships with community organizations, small businesses, financial institutions, schools and residents.

UNP has approached the assessment of community needs from a grassroots, asset-based philosophy in which neighborhood and university participants are partners engaged in mutually beneficial relationships. The critical issues on which UNP focuses its work emerged through nine months of extensive personal interviews with more than 250 local residents, representatives of community organizations, faith-based organizations, university faculty, students and staff. This research yielded the following four priority areas for social development:

1) increasing access to educational opportunity for youth;
2) promoting the development of resident leadership;

3) building the capacity of neighborhood organizations to address health, housing, employment, safety and environment; and

4) overcoming the multiple social divisions in the community related to politics, religion, ethnicity, and class.

All of these factors have been challenged in new ways by the recent rapid influx of immigrants, populations in resettlement (refugees) and newcomers to the state.

The university's two-pronged approach (Bennion Center and UNP) for community engagement and scholarship creates a structure for maximizing resources, while providing a reciprocal process for mobilizing diverse stakeholders. Nevertheless, there are ongoing challenges associated with creating an institutional culture of engagement. While many faculties are passionate about social change agendas, the research environment and institutional restraints immediately surface as significant factors in determining the level of faculty participation in community engagement. Faculty often express that they view their primary institutional responsibilities as research and teaching, and that successful community engagement requires strong leadership and commitment from the university administration, system rewards, and substantial changes in the culture of the academy.

With this feedback in mind, the University of Utah has created several mechanisms that support the institution's academic mission and connect community involvement to teaching and research. Specifically, the Bennion Center supports student-led initiatives and faculty in the development of service learning classes and UNP connects faculty and students to resident identified projects which can be funded through the Bennion Center's Community-Based Research grants. The Community Scholar in Residence, Faculty Fellows and the Public Service Professoriate are additional examples of structures that provide funding (course buy out) and recognition (teaching and research awards) for engaged scholars. Together UNP and the Bennion Center provide a broad range of institutional structures to strengthen faculty involvement in community scholarship by tying their involvement to the academic triad of research, teaching and service.

Social Change in Action

Similar to other major cities in the country, Salt Lake City is a large metropolitan area that is experiencing urban decline, particularly in its west side neighborhoods. While there are significant challenges, there is rich diversity and great strength within neighborhoods experiencing rapid change. Recent findings on crime prevention and community revitalization around the U. S. emphasize the importance of community-building in laying the groundwork for positive social change (Hurley, 2004). This chapter gives four examples of university partnerships with Salt Lake City communities experiencing the greatest challenges.

Westside Studio: A Service Learning Course and University-Community Partnership Focused on Neighborhood Revitalization

The west side neighborhoods of Salt Lake City are long-standing residential areas bordered by heavy industrial zones and the international airport. Residents refer to a glass wall that separates the west side from the east side of the city, due to historical divisions created by the transcontinental railways and exacerbated by a freeway that cuts the city in half. Frequent press coverage of gang activity and crime in west side neighborhoods accentuates the feeling of isolation.

In 2005, the College of Architecture and Planning worked with UNP to transform its on-campus graduate urban planning studio into a community-based studio, called the Westside Studio, where students interact with local residents to create new designs for the surrounding neighborhoods—for businesses, public space, transportation, residential and recreational designs. Partnering with UNP and NeighborWorks, a non-profit community organization focused on affordable housing and neighborhood revitalization, the group secured a storefront space that serves as a classroom and a community dialogue space to develop new approaches to neighborhood development. The Westside Studio is guided by a steering committee of local business owners, developers, city officials, non-profits, west side residents and university faculty. At the Westside Studio, graduate planning students gain valuable hands-on experience while providing the community with planning services that would otherwise be unavailable to them, and residents have an accessible place to offer an active voice in shaping the future of their neighborhoods. This credit-bearing course meets twice a week, combining lecture and workshop formats. The capstone project involves presentations of the resulting visions, maps, plans and designs to local planners and decision makers. Its unique contribution lies in the ability of students and residents to offer "out-of-the-box" visions that professional planners may not deem practical, but the ideas open up public debate in important new ways.

One such example is the North Temple Corridor Community Project. The North Temple corridor, though it was once the gateway to the city, has suffered particular decline. The construction of highway overpasses has left this previously thriving area abandoned of most commercial activity. Hotels and businesses are closing, yet it remains the central corridor between the downtown business center and the airport. It has been identified as one of the biggest potential redevelopment areas of Salt Lake City.

Westside Studio students have presented plans for reviving green space along the corridor, public use of abandoned lots and new plans for state fairgrounds that lie empty most of the year, among other ideas, to the Salt Lake City Council, Planning Department, and Chamber of Commerce. Through collaboration with local residents and agencies, they have created the design for two community gardens, for a new building for a youth oriented non-profit, and are currently working with another non-profit to convert a hidden and little known river corridor into an active public space. Perhaps most importantly, in 2006 students worked with the main community partner (NeighborWorks® Salt Lake) to develop visions for a then only hypothetical light rail (TRAX) line that had been proposed along the North Temple Corridor. In 2007 and 2008, residents connected with NeighborWorks® Salt Lake spearheaded a year long mobilization of other local residents to have the light rail line built along the route they wanted, and in 2008 successfully lobbied the City Council to adopt their plan, contrary to the desires of a powerful local developer.

Education First Mentoring Program: A Student-Directed Initiative Focused on Access to Higher Education for Underrepresented Populations

The west side communities are complex and multi-layered with a long history of immigrant and new arriving populations in the city. These target neighborhoods are home to close to 60,000 of the city's 180,000 residents (2000 U.S. Census). Additionally, these neighborhoods are sites of rapid change—the Hispanic population has more than doubled in 10 years to 40% of the area population. Eighty percent of Salt Lake City's refugee population also resides there. Local schools have not been able to meet the language and cultural differences of students and families, and there is a high degree of mistrust between immigrant and long term Anglo residents. One new resident shares his experience and its effect on his future.

As a young person of color who had been in some deep trouble and living on the west side, a college education was a distant dream. However, getting involved in the community and showing other people the ambition and compassion I had to make a difference for marginalized youth was all I really wanted. I longed for the day when someone would just listen (UNP Success Stories, 2007).

The Education First Mentoring Program (EFMP) was developed by a group of University of Utah students interested in promoting higher education to Utah's Pacific Islander high school students. The brainchild of Anita Ahoia Kiteau, EFMP was developed as Anita's capstone project of the Service-Learning Scholars program.

The Service-Learning Scholars program at the Bennion Center is designed for students who want to actively integrate their education and their community service work. Students complete 400 hours of community service, 10 credit hours of service learning coursework and an Integrative Service Project (ISP). This capstone project, combining academic interests and service, is carried out in consultation with and final approval of a supervisory committee selected by the scholar. Graduates from the program receive Service-Learning Scholar distinction on their transcripts and certificates of achievement at graduation.

For her ISP, Anita built a mentoring program at a local high school to encourage students of Pacific Islander descent to attend college. She began by researching this target group and conducting interviews with students, school counselors and administrators to determine their needs. She then organized a committee of eleven individuals to design tutoring and mentoring programs tailored to freshmen, sophomores, juniors and seniors, with each year emphasizing different aspects of college preparation. In its pilot year, EFMP exceeded expectation with more than 50 youth participating and it has been established as a permanent mentoring program at the high school. While a formal evaluation of the program's impact has yet to be implemented, consistent attendance into the second year of the program is a testament to the value of a peer support system for Pacific Islander high school students as they set goals for their future in higher education. To ensure institutional sustainability of this program, Anita successfully applied for the EFMP to become a student-directed program at the Bennion Center for 2008-2009 in partnership with the Pacific-Islander Student Association (PISA) located in the Center for Ethnic Student Affairs.

The UNP/Hartland Partnership Center:
A Community-Capacity Building Model Working
with Residents Where They Live

The Hartland community is a 300-unit apartment complex (until recently federally subsidized) and home to more than 1,500 residents from all over the world—Somalia, Sudan, Peru, Cuba, Mexico, Russia, Bosnia, Afghanistan and the United States. More than 75% of the residents are non-native English speakers, reflecting a rich tapestry of cultural, ethnic and religious diversity. The UNP/Hartland Partnerships Center brings together teams of professors, students, community organizations and residents to address the need for English competency, family financial literacy, early childhood education, youth programs, legal education, health education and screenings, life skills training, counseling and community capacity building.

> Cuban refugees Luisa, Jose and their teenaged son Pedro fled their homeland for a life filled with richer opportunities. Their journey led them over 2,000 miles north to Salt Lake City, Utah, where they arrived in February 2005. The family of three spent their first three months in the United States supported by International Rescue Committee, but soon needed to find a place to live on their own. A serendipitous meeting with a Peruvian immigrant led them to learn about a refugee resettlement site at the Hartland Apartment Complex and a unique campus-community center located there (UNP Success Stories, 2007).

The Center embodies the philosophy that active collaboration among university and community groups and residents enhances learning, teaching and research, benefiting the entire community. Establishing trusting relationships is at the core of co-creating knowledge. As students and university faculty partner with community organizations and residents tackle institutional and societal barriers, a shared reality emerges.

Guided by a resident committee, faculty and students work with resident leaders from seven countries to understand differences in cultural practices, particularly those associated with education, health care, parenting and the roles of family members. Through partnership team meetings, training workshops and reports, this information is documented and shared with local social service agencies, health care providers and schools. Faculty and students at the Center utilize this information to inform providers about the historical context of migration, appropriate cultural approaches, gaps in services and system barriers.

Tapping into the knowledge base of the resident community at the Hartland apartments is fundamental to building the capacity of all stakeholders. In its third year, the interdisciplinary cluster seminar is one of the formal mechanisms for co-creating knowledge. Faculty representing eight academic departments and the resident committee members co-teach the seminar, exploring the complexity of social and cultural issues within the community, and examining social, political and economic topics from different disciplinary perspectives. Faculty and residents come together in weekly meetings to plan the curriculum and form "teaching pairs" that lead seminar discussions. Resident narratives reflecting stories of migration, cultural perspectives of childhood, family, education, health and mental health are incorporated as class readings for the seminar. In this way, resident knowledge becomes part of the curriculum. The interdisciplinary cluster seminar represents an important step in validating the knowledge of residents and bringing that knowledge to the university (UNP Annual Report, 2007).

Luisa, Jose, and Pedro followed through on the suggestion of their new friend and moved into Hartland Apartments in July 2005. Immediately, they enrolled in many of the different programs offered by Hartland Partnership Center—including ESL, financial literacy, and soccer for their son. Through the information and networks they were able to tap into, this family of three learned how to budget and save for a home of their own, qualifying them for assistance through Neighborhood Housing Services to purchase a home. Fifteen months later, they moved into a two-story, newly built home located in west Salt Lake (UNP Success Stories, 2007).

Westside Leadership Institute: Developing New Curricula to
Support Local Leaders as an Engine for Social Development

Another of the social development challenges facing the west side community is the isolation and relative lack of political voice of the neighborhoods within city and state government. This led to an accumulated lack of investment in infrastructure (quality schools and services, community centers, and attention to safety, crime, and street repair) and economic development strategies (small and large business development). One strategy for improving this situation, identified by key stakeholders, was to increase the voice and efficacy of west side residents and community leaders in getting these problems on the public agenda. Supporting the development of local leaders as an engine for social development was essential to this plan.

While stuck in a dead-end job, Kyle heard a radio commercial for Westside Leadership Institute (WLI) one day in 2004, and decided a leadership class might provide a way to get ahead at his job. Instead, he says, what he got was a belief in his ability to create change in the world (UNP Success Stories, 2007).

The Westside Leadership Institute (WLI) is a campus-community partnership that was created by UNP to support the development of west side resident leaders as catalysts for positive change in their communities.

The WLI offers leadership workshops taught by university faculty and community leaders to west Salt Lake residents while connecting them to local decision making bodies, funding sources, and further support. The goal of the WLI is to equip ordinary citizens to take civic action in their communities, while providing learning opportunities for university faculty and students. It is an example of the importance of helping university and community partners with shared goals to "find" each other, and how resources can be leveraged to create a powerful new initiative with relatively little new funding.

UNP, in partnership with several community non-profit organizations, created and opened the WLI in spring of 2004, with UNP bringing additional university departments and faculty to the table. Faculty members from the university collaborate with west side community leaders to co-teach a ten-week grassroots, community leadership course once each semester. Participants are registered as non-credit U of U students through Continuing Education. WLI participants apply the skills they learn to plan and implement a project to benefit the community. Each participant can create an opportunity to move a personal interest into community action. In addition, participants can apply for a $400 Community Mini-Grant, provided by the university, to carry out community projects. Examples include neighborhood cleanups, identification and design of a community park, creation of a local farmers' market, a neighborhood conference on domestic violence, group training for Latino soccer coaches, youth documentaries about immigration and racism and others.

Attention to the collaborative process and to leveraging shared resources has led to specific engagement strategies that have made the WLI a viable long-term partnership. The first strategy is *identifying the right partners*. NHS/NWSL and the Center for Public Policy and Administration (CPPA) at the University of Utah are now the lead partners, each of which already had the goal of developing local leadership as part of its existing mission. CPPA and UNP recruit other faculty who share this substantive interest. The second strategy is *collaborative dialogue* among all stakeholders to identify how the program will help each partner achieve its own mission. Third, partners *combine resources* such as physical space, materials, expertise and staff time from the community, and faculty and graduate student involvement from the university. The example below describes how these combined efforts have provided residents with resources to put their ideas into action.

> According to Kyle, the community yard sale project he directed while enrolled in WLI inspired him to envision the People's Market, a weekly farmers' market that provides an opportunity for west Salt Lake residents with large gardens and small farms to sell their surplus produce. By the summer of 2006, Kyle developed partnerships that allowed him to host 14 markets over the summer months. Held at the International Peace Gardens, this venue creates a space where local growers sell good food and other items at bargain prices to consumers from across the city. The first summer was so successful; Kyle secured a three-year contract with the City of Salt Lake to ensure material support for a weekly market during the summer for the next three years. (UNP Success Stories, 2007)

Key Elements of Sustainable Partnerships

Each of the examples described above illustrates diverse mechanisms for regional and social change to fit the specific dynamics of the partnership. This section identifies three key elements of the collaborative process underlying all of the partnerships that are fundamental to their success.

Inclusiveness: Equal Voice and Neutral Space

What distinguishes the University of Utah approach to community engagement and regional development is a commitment to an inclusive process. Importantly, from its position as part of the Office of the President of the university, UNP offers a neutral ground in that it is not part of any department or college—yet it is located in a position (the neighborhood) that identifies community engagement as a priority of the institution. Similarly, the Bennion Center, located under Student Services, gives a strong message that it is the goal of the university to develop active citizens and to provide support for faculty interested in engaged scholarship. The success of both UNP and the Bennion Center lies in understanding their role as conveners—they bring individuals and stakeholder groups together who would not ordinarily interact with each other: university professors, local residents, students, non-profit staff, marginalized populations and majority populations. UNP and the Bennion Center staff members concentrate entirely on bridging and connecting (not "doing"), and they are intensely focused on developing meaningful relationships with people from all backgrounds. They act as catalysts for facilitating equal voice and dialogue among the partners focused on social development issues in terms of both academic questions and community engaged solutions. The consistent inclusion of all stakeholder groups is evident in the makeup of the Advisory Boards for UNP and the Bennion Center. In addition, the Hartland Resident Committee, the Westside Studio dialogue space and the Westside Leadership Institute steering committee are examples of this continuous process of inclusive communication.

A Place of Shared Power

UNP and the Bennion Center work hard to ensure that university needs or interests are not given priority and that community voices and priorities remain at the center of the work. At the core is a philosophy that values community knowledge and university knowledge equally. The mission of the Bennion Center is to "foster lifelong service and civic participation by engaging the university with the greater community in action, change, and learning." This commitment is reaffirmed and extended in the UNP mission to "join University of Utah and west side resources in reciprocal learning, action, and benefit ... a community coming together."

Reciprocal Benefit: How We Want to Work Together in Partnership

Through their different vantage points, UNP and the Bennion Center have a shared role to identify and convene stakeholders at the university and in the community who have common concerns that reflect community identified needs, and to create a space for meaningful participation that involves all as equals. The central challenge is to frame social development issues in a way that allows all partners to achieve their own goals—thus reciprocal benefit through the partnership. These partnerships do not add new elements; instead they identify the core missions or existing goals of stakeholders and convene those who share similar goals, thus achieving objectives more effectively, or with fewer resources, than they could alone. Participation in the partnership must be seen as a vehicle to success for all involved, not an additional burden.

One example may suffice: The Westside Leadership Institute achieves the goals of NeighborWorks® Salt Lake by empowering local residents with tools to change their neighborhoods. Residents benefit by having access to these tools and a connection to funding. The university and faculty benefit by having a means to link their scholarship with action oriented work. This latter bears some explanation, because the link between partnership work and faculty scholarship (as opposed to service) is often the more challenging piece to identify.

Although the WLI began with essentially a "service model" for faculty involvement, with each faculty member agreeing to present one evening's class on his or her own time, UNP has worked to provide resources so that the lead role of the Center for Public Policy and Administration (CPPA) is solidified in the role of one instructor who plays a combined coordinating and teaching role when needed. In addition, UNP developed and funded a "WLI Faculty Fellow" position to engage an additional faculty person to teach the whole course (the position carries funds for a course buy-out). The goal of this change was both to enable one faculty person to engage deeply enough in the work to be able to link the WLI with courses she teaches or the research she does, and also to identify the work in a way that gets the attention and recognition of department chairs and deans. Both of these steps are critical to sustaining faculty involvement in community engagement. A Public Administration graduate student from CPPA has also been linked with the WLI from the beginning, funded in part by UNP, who connects his or her required major research project to WLI.

The importance of mutual, or reciprocal, benefit cannot be overstated. Partners will only engage over the long term if they feel they are achieving their own existing goals in the process. By definition this also carries limitations: even if a great idea, or a great need, emerges, if there are not both university and community partners who already have that goal as part of their missions then it should not be undertaken as a sustainable university-community partnership. In order to guide these relationships, campus-community stakeholders developed a set of working principles, entitled "How We Want to Work Together in Partnership," that are introduced at the start of new partnerships and reviewed annually.

The University of Utah will work to create and sustain campus-community partnerships which:
- Are founded on a shared vision and clearly articulated values.
- Are beneficial to the partnering organizations.
- Build interpersonal relationships based on trust and mutual respect.
- Include the voices of those impacted by community work in the decision making processes of the partnership.
- Recognize conflicts as opportunities for collaborative problem-solving.

- Value short term relationships that meet mutually beneficial purposes, and which may grow into valuable long term partnerships.
- Can, over time, be integrated into the mission and infrastructure of each partnering institution.
- Use a strengths based approach in which all participants are recognized as teachers and learners in mutually beneficial power-sharing partnerships.
- Expect all partners to contribute appropriate resources (e.g., staff time, space, transportation, funds, etc.) to enhance the partnership. (UNP Community Partnership Guidelines)

Impact of University-Community Partnerships on Social Development

A broad outline of the success of the engagement strategies employed by the University of Utah, and of the partnerships described above, can be captured in three broad categories: 1) scope and breadth of partnerships; 2) impact on community residents and institutions; and 3) impact on the university. A few examples from each category taken from UNP and the Bennion Center 2007-2008 annual reports are listed below.

1. Scope and breadth of partnerships
- UNP—18 university-community partnerships in 17 locations on the west side of Salt Lake City
- Bennion Center—45 student-directed programs involving 1,573 students and partners in 18,007 hours of service and learning
- Nationally recognized models (Bennion Center/US News and World Report 2007, Hartland Partnership Center/Mercy Housing Publication, 2006; West side Leadership Institute/ NeighborWorks Report, 2008)
- Over $300,000 raised annually from foundations and corporations to support community engagement

- Third annual Rose Park community festival held to increase participation in local decision making across the neighborhood's diverse groups. Between 2,400 and 2,800 people attended the 2007 Rose Park Festival, a record that included five mayoral candidates for the upcoming elections.
- Five members of Hartland Resident Committee contribute to curriculum of Interdisciplinary Cluster Seminar to integrate resident knowledge into academic work of students.

2. Impact on community residents and institutions

- 11,732 west side residents involved in university-community partnership in the first five years of UNP (2002-2007)
- Six residents in new leadership positions with community councils/ organizations
- New links between existing social service providers increase effectiveness of work (e.g. fewer missed medical appointments, evictions, suspended benefits)
- 15 partnerships established on-site at local elementary, middle and high schools.
- Increased access and graduation of underrepresented student populations (145 higher education graduates from west side neighborhoods in 2008)
- Graduates from Fall 06 WLI organized two conferences on domestic violence for Spanish speakers. Three Spanish graduates have taken positions on local PTAs, and two were hired by a local high school to act as outreach workers to Latina/o families.

3. Impact on the University of Utah

- 130 service learning courses created
- 140 faculty and 3,298 students involved annually
- Seven new faculty/administrative roles created to support engagement
- The College of Architecture and Planning created a new Department of Urban Planning. The Chair of this department was

hired to expand the community-based connections exemplified by the Westside Studio.

- Three colleges are integrating engagement into Retention, Promotion and Tenure (RPT) standards.
- New structures developed to support faculty engagement (Service-learning Grants for Teaching and Research, Public Service Professorships, Community Scholar in Residence, Faculty Fellows)
- Successful recruiting of high quality faculty and new national visibility of engaged departments (Linguistics, Social Work, Education, Occupational Therapy, Metropolitan and City Planning).

Conclusions and Continued Engagement

At the University of Utah, the *community engagement continuum* is defined by tying community involvement to the academic triad of research, teaching and service for which faculty are evaluated. This continuum provides a wide range of ways for higher education to be present in the community while still meeting its primary academic mission. Some examples include direct community service by university students, service learning courses that require students to apply their academic learning to real-world scenarios, and research that identifies priority community issues, framing them as research questions for graduate students and faculty in specific fields of expertise. Researchers are encouraged to collaborate from early on with community partners so that the outcome of the research is actually useful to the community and not just a report that goes on someone's shelf.

The Bennion Center and UNP are the primary vehicles to develop partnerships and programs that meet the university's academic mission and at the same time enable faculty and students to build bridges between the university and the community. These campus-community partnerships put a face on the abstract and complex issues that challenge society.

Furthermore, the model necessitates that higher education and community agencies work directly with residents to create "partnership teams." Finally, these partnerships provide an environment that validates the knowledge base of the community and become the means by which service-learning and community-based research are institutionalized within the academy (Bishop, Taylor & Arragno, 1997). These reciprocal relationships between education and the conditions of the larger society offer a long-term prospect for positive change at both the University of Utah and in the Salt Lake and broader community.

CONCLUSION

Jian Shi and King W. Chow

The release of the report of the Kellogg Commission on the Future of State and Land-Grant Universities, *Returning to Our Roots: The Engaged Institution* (1999), and the publication of the Organisation for Economic Co-operation and Development (OECD) report, *Higher Education and Regions: Globally Competitive, Locally Engaged* (2007), have documented the emergence of a university engagement movement on the world scene. The basic values of the movement were echoed in the "New Covenant" articulated by the former president of the United States, Bill Clinton, to create a new sense of community in an age of irresponsibility, excess and neglect and to provide opportunity for everybody, including access to a college education for all (Fitzsimons, 2006, 153). The values of opportunity, responsibility and community are underscored as well in the quest for social progression by Tony Blair (153), the former prime minister of the United Kingdom. With this university engagement movement, as Sharon E. Feinblatt wrote in the Introduction of this edited volume, "commitment to community is a *global* higher education standard today" and public universities are increasingly engaged in regional development.

Good intentions and rhetoric, however, as well as publicized reports of university accomplishments, could be misleading. For example, intensified outreach could be misconstrued as genuine engagement and greater involvement in urban revitalization as progressive community development. Needed is a review of issues and problems of university engagement in different socio-economic and political environments and, in light of context specific constraints, a reflection on where we came from, where we are now and where we are heading.

To address these needs, the editors compiled 15 cases of public universities in action in Australia, China, Mexico, Portugal, Sweden, UK and USA. This collection of essays sheds light on critical issues of policy formulation, institutional change, action plan execution, continuous monitoring and evaluation and ongoing strategic planning (Denis, Langley & Rouleau, 2007; Jarzabkowski, Balogun & Seidl, 2007) for turning public universities into engaged institutions. More importantly, the cases furnish a basis to address some essential issues, including:

1) How university leaders articulate their regional development vision and strategies

2) What strategic actions university leaders can effectively use to manage the interactive relationships between university goals and regional development

3) How public universities effectively promote, direct and reinforce regional development internally as well as at the local and/or national level through specific regional partnerships

4) What outcomes are important when evaluating public universities' performance in regional development

5) What issues and challenges arise from regional development activities

The Significance of Constitutional and Substantive Metapolicy

The 15 cases show that answers to the five issues above depend very much on the policy context in which a university is located. Engagement is primarily framed and reframed by the metapolicy of the respective national policy system. Metapolicy is policy about making policies (Dror,

1968, 1983). According to Dror (1970), metapolicy deals with the functioning of policy-making systems (structure, process patterns, personnel, inputs and stipulated outputs) and master policies (overall goals, basic assumptions, conceptual frameworks, policy instruments and similar interpolicy directives). Chan and Chow (2007) classified the first type as constitutional metapolicy and the second as substantive metapolicy.

Constitutional metapolicy sets basic institutional rules and principles and confers policy-making power. For example, administrative centralization of higher education policy in China and Portugal is a constitutional metapolicy that allows respective government agencies to monopolize policy-making power and in turn to prescribe substantive metapolicy that defines missions and parameters of actions of the universities.

The democratic constitutionalism based on liberalism in the U.S. prescribes autonomy for universities. Such a constitutional metapolicy of devolution allows American public universities to formulate their own substantive metapolicy, with which university leaders can decide to reactively, proactively or interactively formulate their own mission and vision. In other words, they are empowered to strategize (Campbell-Hunt, 2007; Laine & Vaara, 2007; Stensaker & Falkenberg, 2007), a process of substantively and instrumentally rationalizing the use of available resources as well as capabilities to create new external and internal conditions necessary to define and then achieve their goals (Denis, Langley & Rouleau, 2007; Hoon, 2007; Jarzabkowski, Balogun & Seidl, 2007).

As such, American public universities have the discretionary power to combine teaching, research and service in ways appropriate to the situational needs related to regional development. The cases of Texas Tech and University at Albany are illustrative. Further, under the devolution metapolicy, university leadership plays a critical role in the formation of vision that redefines both fundamental values of public universities and also their desired impact in regional development, as the Arizona State and Ohio State cases demonstrate.

The scope and intensity of university strategic thinking are still constrained by the substantive metapolicy of their respective countries— the basic missions and functions are ascribed while funding is more a policy decision rather than statutory—propelling universities to engage in predetermined trajectories. Some universities, such as Luleå, have to function as an instrument for economic development through serving business needs, while Texas Tech is pushed to be a provider of education to satisfy the increasing demand for human capital.

Different types of substantive policy " spawn different power relationships among individuals and groups, and these relationships can be described and predicted on the basis of policy type" (Smith, 2002, 379). So are substantive metapolicies. Thus, when changes occur in government directives concerning regional development, Luleå and Newcastle, with pour-in funding, could assume or revitalize their roles as knowledge creator and provider in their respective regions to reduce economic and social disparities, while Monash could complete its mergers with other institutions to become a major "local" university with international campuses, playing a transnational role in enhancing human capital for the global village.

It should be noted that, while constitutional metapolicy is relatively stable, substantive metapolicy is adopted within a particular time nexus and is subject to the manipulation of contextualized and historical forces. The constitutional metapolicy in such administratively centralized countries as China and Portugal set the parameters for university operation, making it difficult for universities in these countries to independently articulate their regional development vision and strategies and to manage the interactive relationships between university goals and regional development. The case of Portugal reveals that social progression in the higher education domain is limited by both constitutional and substantive metapolicy. As a result, citizen rights in the form of access to higher education and capability building through education (Robeyns, 2006) are negatively affected.

The cases of Chongqing University, Nanjing University and Sichuan University show that, while these universities are committed to and capable of promoting regional development, their hands are tied, pending mission assignment. Policy-makers at the central level may revise the substantive policy that governs the universities. Indeed, in the past decade, there has been the granting of greater discretionary power to public universities in China for deciding on development strategies. As a result, Chinese university leaders have more room to strategize, but these institutions can only maneuver at the operational level to provide optimal support to regional development. These cases together highlight a critical issue that developing countries face: that is, how can public universities effectively promote, direct and reinforce regional development in the light of policy constraints? Their central governments, of course, need to cope with the challenge of revising their substantive metapolicy to delegate more formal authority and responsibilities to universities in order to maximize university contributions to regional development. Increased autonomy for setting strategic direction is desirable and necessary, particularly because innovation is now primarily based on networked knowledge sharing (Camisón-Zornoza, Lapiedra-Alcamí, Segarra-Ciprés & Boronat-Navarro, 2004; Swan & Scarbrough, 2005).

In short, metapolicy affects public universities by defining their relationship with regional development, and the parameters set by metapolicy determine the ways and means by which public universities can engage as well as their trajectories in regional development. Thus, American experiences and models are peculiar and not readily applicable in even such European countries as the UK and Portugal. By the same token, engagement efforts in such countries as China and Mexico could not be deemed insufficient or inadequate given the contexts in which their universities live. Further research that accounts for metapolicy reformulation and its potential and subsequent impact on university engagement will help yield satisfactory to the aforementioned five essential questions. So will detailed studies of how universities maneuver to effectuate their community engagement and to optimize their contribution to regional development under the prevailing metapolicy.

Critical Factors and Exemplary Practices of Effective Engagement

Given the blessing or curse of metapolicy in different countries, the cases show that various universities undertake different actions to engage. From the 15 cases, some critical factors for effective engagement in regional development can be highlighted. Leadership is one, which is essential to rational, effective educational policymaking and management (Wahlstrom, 2008). Newcastle University's engagement with the city of Newcastle upon Tyne and the North East of England "embraces virtually all aspects of its core business of teaching and research, " thus supporting the university's key role in the city's international, multicultural and multi-faith life through its staff, students and alumni. The authors of the Newcastle case underscore the significance of leadership in regional development by adopting "a more corporate response to opportunities in its external environment" and in promoting internal institutional changes.

Also very important are policy entrepreneurs, as highlighted in the case of the University of Guadalajara. In reversing the problems of pollution in the Ayuquila-Armería river basin in Mexico, policy entrepreneurs of the university play a critical role in mission accomplishment. The authors of the case point out that "policy entrepreneurs are individuals willing to invest their time, resources and reputation in order to advance their ideas and convert them into public policies. " In the anti-pollution case, researchers of the University of

Guadalajara were directly engaged with the communities of the river basin in which they conducted their research. Their persistence generated solutions to the problems of cross-region pollution. The authors, therefore, argue that "universities can get involved in their communities not only through the production of relevant scientific knowledge and technology but also by encouraging researchers to become policy entrepreneurs. "

One building block of entrepreneurship is passion. The Cornell case reveals the significance of participants' passion for addressing community development problems, and an absence of such passion on the part of university leadership may result in the abolition of a valuable engagement program. Passion also plays an important role in ASU's effort in enhancing "social embeddedness" in which "the university becomes part of the community to learn of its needs, and then directs its intellectual strengths to meet those needs. " Passion for engagement, an internal incentive, helps to promote student development and positive changes in the community. Passion can also reinforce university leadership's commitment and participants' persistence. These topics deserve future research attention, as at the moment external incentives to develop and reinforce faculty's commitment to engagement are still limited (OECD, 2007).

By addressing different issues and problems, universities display different engagement patterns—different goals require different means and actions appropriate to effective mission accomplishment. The cases reported here suggest exemplary practices. Consider the University of Utah. In 2001 the university's leadership initiated University Neighborhood Partners (UNP), " a university-community partnership program located off campus and focused on building long term collaborations among university faculty, staff, students, local nonprofits, city government and social service systems of all kinds. " UNP has organized various programs, such as the Westside Leadership Institute (WLI), to promote visible change in the community. WLI formulated strategies that have made the campus-community partnership viable and sustainable. As the authors report, the first strategy is identifying the right partners; the second strategy is collaborative dialogue among all stakeholders to identify how the program will help each partner achieve its own mission; and the third strategy is the combination of partners' resources such as "physical space, materials, expertise and staff time from the community, and faculty and graduate student involvement from the university."

In the case of Sichuan University (SCU), actions are taken in regional development that revolve around eradication of poverty, based on the strengths of the university. For example, SCU has the expertise and know-how to develop a series of ecological environment preservation techniques, including the "high-efficient vegetation restoration in the desertified alpine grassland" and "rapid restoration of vegetation damaged by human activities." These technologies for ecological restoration and environmental preservation are proven effective in changing the landscape in western China and realizing significant social and economic benefits for the poor. Huaxi Medical Center of SCU, one of the top medical schools in China, provides professional and curricular support to Tibet University to train senior medical professionals urgently needed to upgrade medical services and also to provide education to satisfy healthcare demands in the region.

In the case of the Cornell Urban Scholars Program, not only is service learning enhanced, but also a majority of the interns pursue careers in community development work. The program's success calls for the development of trust-based partnerships, an institutionalized practice and a balance between enrichment of student learning and community service.

Finally, the cases presented in this volume suggest that different universities in different contexts pursuing different types of engagement can be classified: 1) some universities are reactive to the opportunities for making contribution to community building and regional development, as in the cases of universities in China and Portugal; 2) some are proactive, as in ASU, Monash, Ohio State, University of Guadalajara and Utah, which undertake systematic efforts to get prepared for triggering community building and regional development; and 3) others, such as Newcastle, Louisiana State and Luleå University of Technology, are interactive in responding to opportunities and developmental needs in the process of community building and regional development. From the cases, the proactive type seems best able to facilitate significant accomplishments by universities.

Issues and Challenges

The 15 cases furnish a basis to address the aforementioned essential questions. We are now more knowledgeable about how university leaders articulate their regional development vision and strategies, what strategic actions university leaders may effectively use to manage the interactive relationships between university goals and regional development; how public universities can effectively promote, direct and reinforce regional development internally as well as at the local and/or national level through specific regional partnerships; and what some of the issues and challenges that arise from regional development activities are.

This knowledge, however, is still insufficient. For example, we could not address the question, "what outcomes are important when evaluating public universities' performance in regional development?" After all, desirability of outcome is context specific. Besides, activities of engagement may or may not result in positive impact. Effectiveness of solutions to problems in the region arising from engagement may merely be temporary. And major university efforts to promote economic and technological developments may eventually proven to be ineffective as development is always orchestrated by various social, political, historical and cultural factors beyond the control of any one entity (Cobb & Rubin, 2006).

The current literature in the field of evaluation suggests that evaluation is a difficult pursuit (Bussmann, 2008; Mark, 2004), as it "is a site for engaging with differences of perspective, experience, value, ideology, power, privilege and possibility" (Schwant, 2003, 356) where theory-based evaluation (Stame, 2004) can only help us better understand (Sanderson, 2008, 434) situated practices that involve "real" decision makers, "real" participants and "real" actions (Schwant, 2003, 359). In view of the complexity of the networked engagement practices that occur in the conjunction of social, economic, political and organizational systems, a holistic approach to evaluating multi-organizational sphere of effectiveness (Uusikylä, & Valovirta, 2007) in engagement should be used.

In addition to the evaluation issue, we still have to address a fundamentally important question: Development for What? While cases in this edited volume present positive active participation by higher education in urban revitalization, one wonders if teaching effectiveness is negatively affected, and resources are diminished for other goals such as improving access to education (Darling-Hammond, 2007; Voigt, 2007), reducing social inequity (Byng, 2008; Coates, 2007), resolving conflicts in society (Ferber, Herrera & Samuels, 2007; Rabrenovic Levin & Oliver, 2007) and enhancing social cohesion (Jaffe & Quark, 2006). When cases report how universities have intensified their efforts in rebuilding local communities, one wonders if, in order to optimize the payoff of engagement, university resources should instead be devoted to macro-level social projects that concentrate on transforming society and its major institutions (Coates & Heitzeg, 2008) and on revitalizing work ethics rather than leaving the prevailing "consumption ethic" (Reith, 2007) intact. By the same token, should reduction of pollution be a prime concern or should sharing of the knowledge of environmental sociology (Rudy & Konefal, 2007) to promote responsible and empowered citizenship (Bruhn, 2006) for pollution avoidance be the engagement goal? In other words, "What is the right thing to do in the new century?" rather than "How can we get the things done right?" remains a critical question for universities and engagement stakeholders to consider.

In *Returning to Our Roots: The Engaged Institution,* the Kellogg Commission (1999) noted that " ... with the resources and superbly qualified professors and staff on our campuses, we can organize our institutions to serve both local and national needs in a more coherent and effective way. We can and must do better." The cases presented in this edited volume reveal that public universities in regional development are indeed doing better than a decade ago, but also that they are facing more complex and serious social, economic, political, national security and even technological problems in the 21st century.

ABOUT THE AUTHORS

Diana Amado

Diana Amado is a full time researcher at CIPES (Center for Higher Education Policy Studies) in Portugal. She holds a Ph.D. in Educational Sciences from the Faculty of Psychology at the University of Porto. Her doctoral thesis, "How to be a student: An enquiry into how to survive the university," examines the topic of academic integration.

Alberto Amaral

Alberto Amaral is Professor at the University of Porto, Portugal, and Director of CIPES (Center for Higher Education Policy Studies). He has served as chair of the board of the Consortium of Higher Education Research and is life member of the International Association of University Presidents. He is editor and co-editor of several books, including *Governing Higher Education: National Perspectives on Institutional Governance, The Higher Education Managerial Revolution, Markets in Higher Education: Rhetoric or Reality?* and *Reform and Change in Higher Education.*

Matt Baker

Matt Baker is Dean for outreach and distance education at Texas Tech

University. He served eight years as a department chair in the College of Agricultural Sciences and Natural Resources at Texas Tech, with previous faculty experience at the University of Florida and California State Polytechnic University. Baker's research interests include the adoption/diffusion process of agricultural innovations by agricultural producers. He is currently co-principal investigator on a $5.2M, eight-year field research project funded by the Texas Water Development Board that is monitoring a community of practice of agricultural producers in relation to their irrigation management practices.

Katharine Briar-Lawson

Katharine Briar-Lawson is Dean and Professor in the School of Social Welfare at the University at Albany. She is an academic administrator and national expert on family-focused practice and child and family policy. She co-authored *Family-Centered Policies & Practices: International Implications* and co-edited *Innovative Practices with Vulnerable Children and Families*. She is the immediate past president of the National Association of Deans and Directors (NADD) of Schools of Social Work. In addition she is co-principal investigator of the National Child Welfare Workforce Institute funded by the U.S. Children's Bureau.

Georgina Caire Martínez

Georgina Caire Martínez is currently a Ph.D. candidate at *Facultad Latinoamericana de Ciencias Sociales* (Latin American Social Sciences Faculty) in Mexico. She has worked in the Integrated Watershed Management Department of the National Institute of Ecology in Mexico. She is interested in public management, local governments, environmental governance and rural development.

King W. Chow

King W. Chow is Chair of the Department of Public Administration and

Principal Expert of the Sino-US Institute for University Design at Sichuan University. He received his BA, MA and PhD degrees from the University of Texas at Austin (USA), and has taught at Texas Tech University, Chinese University of Hong Kong and University of Hong Kong, at which he was tenured in 1990. He was a member of the executive committee of the Policy Studies Organization (USA) and editor and editorial board member of a number of international refereed journals. He is currently a guest editor of *Public Organization Review*.

Marsha R. Cuddeback

A member of American Institute of Architects (AIA), Marsha Cuddeback is Director of the Office of Community Design and Development (OCDD) in the School of Architecture at LSU. She has led community based practice through internships, service learning and interdisciplinary collaborations through the OCDD.

Zhehua Dai

Zhehua Dai is Associate Professor and Deputy Director of the Office for International Cooperation and Exchanges of Nanjing University. He received his BA from the Department of English, Nanjing University, in 1988 and took graduate courses in world history at the same university. He was a visiting scholar at the Department of History of the Grinnell College (USA) in 1995. His research is focused on internationalization, reform and development of higher education and international human resources management.

A. Michelle Demel

A. Michelle Demel is a senior editor of curriculum at Texas Tech University's College of Outreach and Distance Education. Previously she worked for the Texas Tech Honors College as the developer and coordinator of the College's First-Year Experience Program. Her interests include higher education policy, student affairs, the Great Books and art (ceramics and metalwork).

Linda Dunn

Linda Dunn served as Executive Director of Utah Campus Compact for five years, promoting service learning and student participation in civic and community service throughout the state. She is very proud of the accomplishments of the Bennion Center, including being recognized as third in the nation as a leader in student community engagement.

Sharon E. Feinblatt

Sharon Feinblatt's tenure in higher education has focused primarily in the community-university partnership arena, most recently at Ohio State University as the Director of Community Outreach for WOSU Public Media, the public broadcasting entity of OSU. Sharon received her Doctorate in Education and Masters of Science in Higher Education from the University of Pennsylvania. She received her Bachelors of Arts from Pennsylvania State University.

Madalena Fonseca

Madalena Fonseca is Professor at the University of Porto in the areas of Economic Geography and Regional Development and Policy and Planning, and a researcher at CIPES (Center for Higher Education Policy Studies). Currently, her research focuses on higher education and regional development and industrial relocation and human capital. She was an invited researcher at the University of Bayreuth, Germany, and the University of Technology of Chemnitz, Germany.

John Goddard

John Goddard recently retired as Deputy Vice Chancellor and Professor of Regional Development Studies at Newcastle University. As Deputy Vice

Chancellor he was responsible for a major restructuring of the university and its relations with the city and region. As Professor of Regional Development Studies, he founded the Centre for Urban and Regional Development Studies in 1977. CURDS now has 30 research staff engaged in a range of basic and applied research funded by the UK research councils, government departments, the European Commission and private industry.

Robert Hickerson

Robert Hickerson is Chief Operating Officer—Texas Tech University Off-Campus Sites. He previously served as Executive Director of the Texas Commission on Volunteerism and Community Service, a small state agency which managed the Texas AmeriCorps grant program. He also served in the Governor's Office of Volunteerism under Governor George W. Bush. He is active in several community based non-profit organizations and serves on the board of the Texas Non-profit Management Assistance Network.

Rosemarie Hunter

Rosemarie Hunter is Assistant Professor in the College of Social Work at the University of Utah, where she previously served as Director of Bachelors of Social Work (BSW) Field Education and the co-director of the international social work program. Her current areas of scholarship and teaching include higher education-community partnerships, community based research, community organization and practice and international social work. She has experience in community organization and development, school social work, educational administration and clinical social work.

Johan Johansson

Johan Johansson is Assistant Professor in entrepreneurship and industrial organization at Luleå University of Technology, Sweden, where he also received his doctorate in business administration and economics. His research interest is on collaborative processes and entrepreneurial orientation, especially among collaboration constellations including small and medium sized enterprises, universities and policy actors.

Bonita Kline

A graduate of Arizona State University, Bonita Kline is the editor and publisher of VISTA Magazine. She is involved with the Central Arizona Museum Association and is an emeritus board member of the Fountain Hills and Lower Verde Valley Museum and Historical Society.

Hua Li

Hua Li is Associate Professor of Education, master's student supervisor, Director of Development Research Center and Vice Head of the Institute of Higher Education at Chongqing University. He has directed or participated in more than 30 projects on higher education and sustainable development.

Philip McCallion

Philip McCallion, Director of the University at Albany Center for Excellence in Aging Services, is an expert on the Medicare D program. McCallion conducts Medicare D educational programs for seniors in upstate New York in conjunction with state providers and the Elder Network of the Capital Region. His research and program development activities include evaluating the effectiveness of interventions for persons with dementia, the development of outreach strategies and interventions and assisting agencies with direct care workforce development.

Kathryn Mohrman

Director of the University Design Institute and Professor of Public Affairs at Arizona State University, Kathryn Mohrman has served as President of Colorado College, Dean at Brown University and the University of Maryland, Executive Director of the Hopkins-Nanjing Center and guest scholar at the Brookings Institution. Her international experiences include Fulbright scholarships in Hong Kong, Japan and South Korea, teaching at Sichuan University and research on reforms in Chinese higher education.

Elizabeth Mossop

Elizabeth Mossop is Professor and Director of the Robert Reich School of Landscape Architecture at Louisiana State University. She has actively engaged students in her classes in community recovery efforts since Hurricanes Katrina and Rita and has received national recognition for these efforts.

Sarah Munro

Sarah Munro is Associate Director of University Neighborhood Partners and Assistant Professor (Research) in the College of Architecture and Planning at the University of Utah. Her research includes community organization, leadership and gender relations. Current work focuses on partnerships in the areas of resident empowerment and community leadership, capacity building and collaborative community based research.

John Nettleton

John Nettleton is a senior lecturer in City and Regional Planning and currently serves as the Faculty Director of the Cornell Urban Scholars Program. Prior to this appointment, he served as Senior Extension Associate for Community and Economic Development with Cornell University's New York City Extension Program.

Katie Olson

Katie Olson is the Service Learning Manager at the Lowell Bennion Community Service Center at the University of Utah. In this position, she provides assistance to faculty and community partners in developing, integrating and implementing service learning pedagogy into the educational experience. She spent three years as the Director of Ten Thousand Villages, a non-profit, fair trade organization in Utah before joining the team at the Bennion Center.

Valerie Osland Paton

Valerie Osland Paton is Vice Provost of Planning and Assessment in Texas Tech University (TTU); she also serves as a liaison and resource for the Commission on Colleges of the Southern Association of Colleges and Schools (SACS-COC) standards. She supervised several of TTU's off-campus sites during their early development and maturation to the new Division of Off-Campus Sites. In addition to her administrative duties, Paton serves as Assistant Professor in the higher educational program in TTU's College of Education in the areas of policy, law and planning.

John C. Pine

John Pine is Director of the Disaster Science and Management Program at Louisiana State University and serves as Professor-Research with the Department of Environmental Sciences and the Department of Geography and Anthropology. His research and publications focus on community vulnerability and resilience, emergency response and recovery from disasters and the applications of technology in understanding the nature and impact of disasters. His latest book, *Natural Hazards Analysis: Reducing the Impacts from Disaster*, was published in the fall of 2008.

Edgar E. Ramírez de la Cruz

Edgar Ramírez is Assistant Professor in the School of Public Affairs at

Arizona State University. He has a Ph.D. from Florida State University. His research has appeared in *Urban Affairs Review* and various edited books such as the *International Handbook of Practice-Based Management*. His primary focus is urban governance, but he is also interested in growth management, land use regulations, public management and networks.

Kenneth Reardon

Kenneth Reardon is Professor and Chair of the Graduate Program in City and Regional Planning at the University of Memphis. Prior to joining the Memphis faculty, he was Associate Professor and Chair of the Department of City and Regional Planning at Cornell University where he established, with the support of the Heckscher Foundation for Children, the Cornell Urban Scholars Program.

Carla Sá

Carla Sá is Assistant Professor at the Department of Economics, University of Minho, Portugal. She is also a researcher at NIPE (Economic Policies Research Unit) and CIPES (Center for Research in Higher Education Policy Studies). Her research interests include the intersection of economics of education and spatial economics, with particular emphasis on student decision making processes.

Bruce G. Sharky

A fellow of the American Society of Landscape Architects (ASLA), Bruce Sharky is Professor in the Robert Reich School of Landscape Architecture at Louisiana State University. He has engaged his studio classes in community development initiatives in both New Orleans and Lake Charles, Louisiana, following Hurricanes Katrina and Rita in 2005.

Jian Shi

Jian Shi is Professor of English and Vice President for Human Resources and International Exchanges at Sichuan University. He received his Ph.D. from Lehigh University (USA), and his BA and MA degrees from Sichuan University. He is the Deputy Chair of the National English Teaching Association of China, Deputy Chair of the Translators Association of China, and member of the National Examination Committee of CET-4 and CET-6, as well as Deputy Director of the Teaching Reform Project in College English of the Chinese Ministry of Education.

Jan Shoemaker

Jan Shoemaker is the Director of the Louisiana State University Center for Community Engagement, Learning and Leadership. The center promotes community engagement by serving as a clearinghouse for service learning throughout the LSU campus.

Sarah Smith

Sarah Smith is the Administrative Manager of the Cornell Urban Scholars Program. She earned her Bachelor of Arts in Government from Cornell University in 2005 while participating in a number of community-based change efforts in the Ithaca area.

Bruce Stanley

Bruce Stanley recently retired as Senior Vice President of the United Way of the Greater Capital Region (New York) after 25 years of focusing on community impact, development of collaborations program investment and evaluation, in United Way organizations from Boston to Portland, Oregon. He was also involved in regional and statewide health system planning, plan implementation, project review and policy development for more than 20 years. He has regularly taught courses on health and human services topics in the School of Social Welfare at the University at Albany.

Stephen A. Sterrett

Stephen Sterrett has been the community relations director of Campus Partners for Community Urban Redevelopment since its incorporation. He is responsible for Campus Partners' communications and public relations. He has served in many leadership positions in his community from President of the Dennison Place Association to the local food pantry. Central Ohio Crime Stoppers presented Sterrett with its Citizen Crime Stopper of the Year Award for 2001.

Pedro Teixeira

Pedro Teixeira is Associate Professor at the Faculty of Economics—University of Porto and Research Associate at CIPES (Center for Higher Education Policy Studies). His research interests focus on the economics of higher education, notably on markets and privatization, and in the history of economic thought. Recent publications include several articles in economics and higher education journals and his book, *Jacob Mincer—A Founding Father of Modern Labour Economics* (Oxford UP, 2007). He has also co-edited two volumes on *Markets in Higher Education—Reality or Rhetoric?* (Kluwer, 2004) and on *Cost-Sharing and Accessibility in Higher Education—A Fairer Deal?* (Springer, 2006).

John Tomaney

John Tomaney is Professor of Regional Studies at Monash University, Melbourne; Henry Daysh Professor of Regional Development and Executive Director of Centre for Urban and Regional Development Studies, Newcastle University, UK; Associate Director of the UK Spatial Economics Research Centre; and an Academician of the Academy of Social Science (UK). He has published more than 100 books and articles on questions of local and regional development. His most recent book is *Local and Regional Development* (Routledge, 2006).

Paul Vallance

Paul Vallance is a research associate in the Centre for Urban and Regional Development Studies, Newcastle University. His Ph.D., also at Newcastle University, examined knowledge and innovation in the UK videogames development industry. He is currently working on projects related to universities and city or regional development.

Joakim Wincent

Joakim Wincent is Associate Professor in entrepreneurship at Luleå University of Technology, Sweden. His research focuses largely on how to manage difficult exchanges in strategic inter-firm relations, stress management and effective coping of entrepreneurs exposed to challenging conditions and how to set free the human potential (i.e., unleash cognitive foundations and emotional experiences) of entrepreneurs in new venturing for reaching higher performance and goal attainment.

Felicity Wray

Since 2007 Felicity Wray has been a NESTA research fellow in innovation policy based at the Centre for Knowledge, Innovation, Technology and Enterprise at Newcastle University Business School. Her research interests include geographies of money and finance, particularly the venture capital industry, relational economic geography, innovation and uneven regional development. In March 2009 Felicity will be taking up a lectureship in human geography at the University of Western Australia, Perth.

Shijing Yan

Shijing Yan is Professor of Economics, Director of the International Office and Dean of the School of Overseas Education at Sichuan University. He has been a visiting scholar at the Center for South and Southeast Asia Studies, University of California at Berkeley, and the Center for

Economic and Planning Studies, Nehru University in India. His book, *Research and Practice on the Cultivation of Innovative Talents in International Cooperation,* in 2005 won the Second National Teaching Achievements Award from the Ministry of Education, PRC.

Håkan Ylinenpää

Håkan Ylinenpää is Professor (chair) in entrepreneurship and head of the division of Entrepreneurship and Industrial Organization at Luleå University of Technology, Sweden. His research interests are in entrepreneurial innovation activities and strategies, especially in small and medium-sized enterprises, innovation system research and knowledge management. He prefers research that involves close collaboration with practice and/or policy makers in regional, national or international programs and projects.

Yu Zhang

Yu Zhang is Associate Professor of the Sino-US Institute for University Design at Sichuan University. She received her MA from Southwest Normal University and Ph.D. in education from Southwest University. Her main research areas are institutional comparison, management and reform and development of higher education.

Chengping Zhao

Chengping Zhao is Professor, Director of Office of International Cooperation and Exchanges and Dean of College of International Education and Exchanges at Chongqing University. His major interests of study include second language acquisition, language teaching theory and methodology, material development and teaching Chinese to speakers of other languages. He has conducted many national and provincial level research projects on these topics.

REFERENCES

Adams, R. H. (2003). Economic growth, inequality, and poverty: Findings from a new data set. *Policy Research Working Paper Series.* from http://www-wds. worldbank. org/servlet/WDSContentServer/WDSP/IB/2003/03/22/000094946 _03030704153293/ Rendered/PDF/multi0page.pdf

Alter, T. R., & Book, P. A. (2001). The engaged university: Reorganizing to serve the public good. *Metropolitan Universities, 12(3),* 30-40.

Amaral, A., & Teixeira, P. (2000). The rise and fall of the private sector in Portuguese higher education. *Higher Education Policy, 13(3),* 245-266.

American Institute of Architects. (2005, December). *Summary and Review 2005 Demographic Diversity Audit Report.* Washington, DC: Author. Retrieved August 16, 2008, from http://www. aia. org/SiteObjects/files/cmp_2005_ demographic_ data_summary_rpt.pdf

Amin, A. (1999). An institutionalist perspective on regional economic development. *International Journal of Urban and Regional Research, 23(2),* 365-378.

Arbo, P., & Benneworth, P. (2007, July). *Understanding the regional contribution of higher education institutions: A literature review.* Retrieved June 22, 2008, from OECD website: http://www. oecd. org/dataoecd/55/7/37006775. pdf

Arizona Board of Regents. (2008). Planning for Phoenix biomedical campus (PBC). Retrieved August 30, 2008, from http://www. azregents. edu/1_the_regents/ TRIF/brochures/2008/16 - Planning_for_Phoenix_Biomedical. pdf

Arizona State University. (2004a). One university in many places: Overview of the transitional design to 21st century excellence. Retrieved August 17, 2008, from http://president. asu. edu/node/259

Arizona State University. (2004b). Comprehensive Development Plan. Retrieved October 11, 2008, from http://www. asu. edu/cdp/

Arizona State University. (2007, July 1). 2006–2007 *ASU annual report: A state of forward motion.* Retrieved July 23, 2008, from http://president. asu. edu/files/ ASU%20Annual%20Report%200607. pdf

Arizona State University Walter Cronkite School of Journalism and Mass Communications. (2007). A building rises. *The Cronkite Journal, 1(2),* 6.

Austin, S., Briar-Lawson, K., King-Ingham, A., Spicer, J., & Davis, D. (2005). Role changes, learning enhancements and professional development through a university-school partnership. *Professional Development: The International Journal of Continuing Social Work Education, 8(3),* 84–97.

Baldwin, R., & Martin, P. (2004). Agglomeration and regional growth. In V. Henderson & J-F. Thisse (Eds.). *Handbook of regional and urban economics.* 4. Amsterdam, NL: North Holland.

Barreto, A. (1996). *A situação social em Portugal.* [The social situation in Portugal]. Lisboa, PT: ICS.

Barro, R. J., & Sala-I-Martin, X. (2004). *Economic growth* (2nd ed.). Cambridge, MA: MIT Press.

Bates, A. W. (1999). *Managing technological change: Strategies for college and university leaders.* San Francisco, CA: Jossey-Bass.

Beer, A., Maude, A., & Pritchard, A. (2003). *Developing Australia's regions: Theory and practice.* Sydney, AU: UNSW Press.

Benneworth, P., & Charles, D. (2005). University spin-off policies and economic development in less successful regions: Learning from two decades of policy practice. *European Planning Studies, 13(4),* 537–557.

Benson, L., Harcavy, I., & Puckett, J. (2007). *Dewey's dream: Universities and democracies in an age of education reform.* Philadelphia, PA: Temple University Press.

BERR. (2008). RDA Finance & Governance. Retrieved November, 2008, from http: // www. berr. gov. uk/ whatwedo/ regional/ regional-dev-agencies/ funding-financial-gov/ page20136. html

Berry, J. (2008, April 1). ASU breaks ground on nursing addition. Retrieved August 8, 2008, from http: // www. azcentral. com/ business/ articles/ 2008/ 04/ 01/ 20080401phxnursing0401-ON. html

Bishop, K., Taylor, M., & Aragno, P. (Eds.). (1997). *Partnerships at work: Lessons learned from programs and practices of families, professionals, and communities.* Burlington, VT: Partnerships for Change.

Blackwood, R. (1968). *Monash: The first 10 years.* Melbourne, AU: Hampden Hall.

Blaney, B., & Caldwell, A. A. (2008, August 19). Oil boom gives boost to Permian Basin. *Lubbock Avalanche-Journal.* Retrieved August 30, 2008, from http://www.lubbockonline. com/stories/081908/bus_320309979. shtml

Blau, P. M. (1964). *Exchange and power in social life.* New York, NY: Wiley.

Boucher, G., Conway, C., & van der Meer, E. (2003). Tiers of engagement by universities in their region's development. *Regional Studies, 37(9),* 887–897.

Boyer, E. L. (1991). *Scholarship reconsidered: Priorities of the professoriate* (4th ed.). Princeton, NJ: The Carnegie Foundation for the Advancement of Teaching.

Boyer, E. L. (1996). *Building community: A new future for architecture education and practice* (1st ed.). Princeton, NJ:The Carnegie Foundation for the Advancement of Teaching.

Briar-Lawson, K., & Zlotnik, J. (2002). *Charting the impacts of university-child welfare collaboration.* New York, NY: Haworth Press.

Bromley, R. (2006). On and off campus: Colleges and universities as local stakeholders. *Planning, Practice & Research, 21(1),* 1–24.

Bronstein, L., McCallion, P., & Kramer, E. (2006). Developing an aging prepared community: Collaboration among counties, consumers, professionals and organizations. *Journal of Gerontological Social Work, 48(1/2),* 193–202.

Bruhn, C. (2006). Higher education as empowerment: The case of Palestinian universities. *American Behavioral Scientist, 49(8),* 1125–1142.

Bulletin of the Texas Technological College. (1935, June). (Vol. 11, No. 4, p. 200). Lubbock, Texas: Texas Technological College.

Bulletin of the Texas Technological College. (1966, May). (Vol. 42, No. 7, p. 66). Lubbock, Texas: Texas Technological College.

Burnheim, C. (2005). Australian universities as sites of citizenship and civic responsibility: Monash University case study. Report for the Australian Consortium of Higher Education, Faculty of Education, Monash University.

Burnheim, C. (2007, November). External engagement and institutional autonomy in higher education. Paper presented at the AARE Conference, Fremantle, AU.

Bussmann, W.(2008). The emergence of evaluation in Switzerland. *Evaluation, 14 (4)*, 499–506.

Byng, M. D.(2008). Complex inequalities: The case of Muslim Americans after 9/11. *American Behavioral Scientist, 51(5)*, 659–674.

Camisón-Zornoza, C., Lapiedra-Alcamí, R., Segarra-Ciprés, M., & Boronat-Navarro, M. (2004). A meta-analysis of innovation and organizational size. *Organization Studies, 25(3)*, 331–361.

Campbell-Hunt, C. (2007). Complexity in practice. *Human Relations, 60(5)*, 793–823.

Campus Partners. (1996). *University neighborhoods revitalization plan: Concept document*. Columbus, OH: Ohio State University Press.

Campus Partners. (2000). *A plan for high street: Creating a 21st century main street*. Columbus, OH: Ohio State University Press.

Campus Partners. (2002). *University/high street development & design guidelines*. Columbus, OH: Ohio State University Press.

Carnoy, M., & Castells, M. (2001). Globalization, the knowledge society, and the network state. *Global Networks, 1(1)*, 1–18.

Chan, H. S., & Chow, K. W. (2007). Public management and policy in western China: Metapolicy, tacit knowledge, and implications. *American Review of Public Administration, 37(4)*, 479–498.

Chatterton, P. (2000). The cultural role of universities in the community. *Environment and Planning A, 32(1)*, 165–181.

Chatterton, P., & Goddard, J. (2000). The response if higher education institutions to regional needs. *European Journal of Education, 35(4)*, 475–496.

Chongqing Statistic Bureau. The Statistics Communiqué on national economy and social development of Chongqing 2007. Retrieved August 12, 2008, from http://www. cqtj. gov. cn/UploadFile/20080328142050156. doc

Chongqing University. (2006.). Devotion for Joint Construction and Efforts made to Develop High-level University—A Report on the joint construction of Chongqing University. Ministry of Education of the People's Republic of China. Retrieved August 29, 2008, from http://www. moe. edu. cn/edoas/website18/58/info23658. htm

Chongqing University Board Statute (1997). Retrieved August 21, 2008, from http://xdh. cqu. edu. cn/zhangcheng. htm

Chongqing University. (2003). Name list of the members of the fourth Chongqing University Board. Retrieved August 9, 2008, from http://xdh. cqu. edu. cn/

chengyuan. htm

City of Columbus, Department of Development, Planning Division. (2006). Weinland Park neighborhood plan (pp. 52–53). Columbus, OH.

City of Phoenix. (2004). Downtown Phoenix: A strategic vision and blueprint for the future. Retrieved July 26, 2008, from ftp: // phoenix. gov/pub/DOWNTOWN/ visiontext. pdf

Clark, B. R. (1998). *Creating entrepreneurial universities: Organizational pathways of transformation*. Oxford, UK: Pergamon.

Coates, R. D. (2007). Social justice and pedagogy. *American Behavioral Scientist, 51(4)*, 579 –591.

Coates, R. D., & Heitzeg, N. A. (2008). Micro-level social justice projects, pedagogy, and democratic movements. *American Behavioral Scientist, 51 (5)*, 595 –598.

Cobb, P. D., & Rubin, B. A.(2006). Contradictory interests, tangled power, and disorganized organization. *Administration and Society, 38(1)*,79 – 112.

Community Properties of Ohio and Community Properties Impact Corporation.(2008). *Annual report*. Columbus, OH.

Community Properties of Ohio Management Services. *Community properties 2004 annual report: A great place to call home*. Columbus, OH.

Cooke, P.(2001). Regional innovation systems, clusters and the knowledge economy. *Industrial and Corporate Change, 10(4)*, 945–974.

Cooke, P., & Piccaluga, A. (Eds.). (2004). Regional economies as knowledge laboratories. Northampton, MA: Edward Elgar Publishing, Inc.

Council on Competitiveness. (2008, March). Cooperate: A practitioner's guide for effective alignment of regional development and higher education. Retrieved July 11, 2008, from http://www. compete. org/images/uploads/File/PDF% 20Files/ Cooperate%20Final. pdf

Cranford, L. (2008, August 26). Texas Tech receives $1M from Workforce Commission to develop wind energy program. *Texas Tech Today*. Retrieved August 30, 2008, from http:// today. ttu. edu/2008/08/texas-tech-receives-1-million-from-workforce-commission-to-develop-wind-energy-program/

Crespo, V.(1993). *Uma Universidade para os Anos 2000*. [A university for the year 2000]. Lisboa, PT: Inquérito.

Crow, M. M. (2003). A letter from Micheal M. Crow. *ASU Vision*, (Fall), 3–4.

Crow, M. M. (2008). Support Letter for C. Peter Magrath Engagement Award Application.

Cutler and Co Pty Ltd. (2008). Venturous Australia: Building strength in innovation. Retrieved November 21, 2008 from http://www. innovation. gov. au/ innovationreview/ Documents/NIS_review_Web3. pdf

Darling-Hammond, L. (2007). The flat earth and education: How America's commitment to equity will determine our future. *Educational Researcher, 36(6)*, 318 – 334.

Davison, G. (2008, May 21). Founding Monash: The university and the promise of modernity. Monash University 50ʰ Anniversary Lecture, BMW Edge.

Dawkins, J. (1997). Higher education: A policy discussion paper. Canberra, AU: Department of Employment, Education and Training.

Deas, I., & Ward, K. G.(2000). From the "new localism" to the "new regionalism"? The implications of regional development agencies for city-regional relations. *Political Geography, 19(3)*, 272–292.

Denis, J., Langley, A. & Rouleau, L. (2007). Strategizing in pluralistic contexts: Rethinking theoretical frames. *Human Relations, 60(1)*, 179–215.

Department for Education, Science and Training.(2002). *Higher education at the crossroads: An overview*. Canberra, AU.

Department of Innovation, Industry and Regional Development.(2008). *Innovation: Victoria's future*. Melbourne, AU.

Department of Innovation, Industry and Regional Development. (2002). *Victorians, bright ideas, brilliant future*. Melbourne, AU.

Department of Premier and Cabinet. (2005). *Growing Victoria together*. Melbourne, AU.

Department of Trade and Industry. (1998). *Our competitive future: Building the knowledge driven economy*. London, UK: The Stationary Office.

Department of Trade and Industry. (2005). *A practical guide to cluster development*. London, UK: Author.

Dobson, I. (2003). University connections to regional engagement: New and old perspectives. Office of the Deputy Vice-Chancellor, Monash University.

Downtown Voices. (2008). ASU planning students getting involved in downtown issues. Retrieved September 5, 2008, from http://downtownvoices. org/2008/02/ 12/asu-planning-students-getting-involved-in-downtown-issues/

Dror, Y.(1968). *Public policy making reexamined*. Scranton, PA: Chandler.

Dror, Y. (1970). *Social science metapolicy: Some concepts and applications.* Santa Monica, CA: RAND Corporation.

Dror, Y. (1983). Basic concepts in policy studies. In S. S. Nagel (Ed.), *Encyclopedia of policy studies* (pp. 3–10). New York: Marcel Dekker.

Duke, C. (2004). Is there an Australian idea of a university? *Journal of Higher Education Policy and Management, 26(3)*, 297–314.

Economics Research Associates. (2005, September 15). Community impact assessments: South campus gateway. (ERA Project No. 16121, prepared for ESIC Realty Partners, Inc.).

Eggleston, F. W. (1932). *State socialism in Victoria.* London, UK: P. S. King & Son.

Egron-Polak, E. (2008, April). Higher education serving economic development: Too much, too little, just right? *IAU Horizons, 14(1)*, 1–2. Retrieved June 14, 2008, from http://www. unesco. org/iau/ newsletters/iaunew14-1-en. pdf

Espinoza, A., & Medina, J. (1997). Reforma Universitaria: El caso de la Universidad de Guadalajara. [University reform: the case of the University of Guadalajara]. Mexico: University of Guadalajara.

Eyler, J., & Giles, D. E. (1999). *Where's the learning in service-learning?* San Francisco, CA: Jossey-Bass.

Ferber, A. L., Herrera, A. O., & Samuels, D. R. (2007). The matrix of oppression and privilege: Theory and practice for the new millennium. *American Behavioral Scientist, 51(4)*, 516–531.

Fitzsimons, P. (2006). Third way: Values for education? *Theory and Research in Education, 4(2)*, 151–171.

Flannery, T. (2008). Now or never: A sustainable future for Australia? *Quarterly Essay*, 31.

Florida, R. (1995). Toward the learning region. *Futures, 27(5)*, 527–536.

Florida, R. (2002). *The rise of the creative class: And how it is transforming work, leisure, community and everyday life.* Cambridge, MA: Perseus Books Group.

Friedman, D. (2008). An extraordinary partnership between Arizona State University and the city of Phoenix. Paper for application for the 2008 C. Peter Magrath Engagement Award.

Garlick, S. (2000). *Engaging universities and regions: Knowledge contribution to regional economic development in Australia.* Canberra, AU: Department of Education, Training and Youth Affairs.

Ghose, C. (2008, February 15). Domino effect: OSU investment driving off-campus development. *Business First,* Commercial Developers Resource section.

Goddard, J., & Chatterton, P. (1999). Regional development agencies and the knowledge economy: Harnessing the potential of universities. *Environment and Planning C: Government and Policy, 17(6)*, 685–689.

Goddard, J., & Puukka, J. (2008). The engagement of higher education institutions in regional development: An overview of the opportunities and challenges. *Higher Education Management and Policy,20 (2)*, 11–41.

Goetz, S. J., & Rupasingha, A. (2005). How the returns to education in rural areas vary across the nation. In L. J. Beaulieu & R. Gibbs (Eds.), The role of education: Promoting the economic and social vitality of rural America. Retrieved August 30, 2008, from Southern Rural Development Center Web site: http://srdc. msstate. edu/publications/ruraleducation. pdf

Gong, J., Yan, H., & Wang, F. (2001). Gao keji chuangxin nengli yu quyu jingji de hudong guanxi tantao. [A study on the relationship between high technology innovation capacity and regional economy]. *Sci-Technology and Management, 12*, 76–79.

Gong, S., & Zheng, L. (2005). Xibu gongzhong de jiankang kechixufazhan. [The sustainable health development of the public in western China]. *Northwest Population Journal*, 03.

González García, C. (2007). Manantlan: Las razones de un descontento indígena. [Manantlán: the reasons for indigenous discontent]. *La jornada,* 5 de Julio de, http://www.lajornadajalisco.com.mx/2007/07/05/index.php?section = opinion&article = 002a1pol, consultada 29 de julio de 2008.

Goodwin, M., Jones, M., & Jones, R. (2005). Devolution, constitutional change and economic development: Exploring and understanding the new institutional geographies of the British state. *Regional Studies, 39 (4)*, 421–436.

Gordon, P. (2005, March 18). The future of the city address [Speech]. Retrieved July 9, 2008, from http://www. mayorgordon. com/news/view. cfm?id = 1762238689

Green, G. P. (2005). Employer participation in School-to-Work programs in rural America. In L. J. Beaulieu & R. Gibbs (Eds.), *The role of education: Promoting the economic and social vitality of rural America*. Retrieved August 30, 2008, from Southern Rural Development Center Web site: http: // srdc. msstate. edu/ publications/ruraleducation. pdf

Greenaway, D., & Haynes, M. (2000). Funding universities to meet national and international challenges. School of Economics Policy Report. University of Nottingham. Retrieved November, 2008, from http://www.nottingham.ac.uk/economics/funding/funding.pdf

Gunasekera, C. (2006a). Leading horses to water: The dilemmas of academics and university mangers in regional engagement. *Journal of Sociology, 42(2)*, 145–163.

Gunasekera, C. (2006b). Reframing the role of universities in the development of regional innovation systems. *Journal of Technology Transfer, 31(1)*, 101–113.

Harkavy, I., & Puckett, J. L. (1994). Lessons from Hull House for the contemporary urban university. *Social Service Review, 68(3)*, 299–321.

Harkavy, I., & Wiewel, W. (1995). University community partnerships: Current state and future issues. *Metropolitan Universities, 6(3)*, 7–14.

Harloe, M., & Perry, B. (2004). Universities, localities and regional development: The emergence of the "Mode 2" university? *International Journal of Urban and Regional Research, 28(1)*, 212–23.

Higher Education Funding Council for England. (2006). Recurrent grants for 2006 – 2007. Retrieved November, 2008, from http://www.hefce.ac.uk/pubs/hefce/2006/06_08/#exec

Hill, K., Hoffman, D., & Rex, T. R. (2005). The value of higher education: Individual and societal benefits (with special consideration for the state of Arizona). W. P. Carey School of Business, Arizona State University. Retrieved September 29, 2008, from http://wpcarey.asu.edu/seid/upload/Value%20Full%20Report_final_october%202005a.pdf

Hollandsworth, S. (2008). There will be Boone. *Texas Monthly, 36(9)*, 114 – 119, 173 –181.

Homans, G. C. (1961). *Social behavior: Its elementary forms*. New York, NY: Harcourt.

Hoon, C. (2007). Committees as strategic practice: The role of strategic conversation in a public administration. *Human Relations, 60(6)*, 921–952.

Horn, P. (1925, October). Greetings from the President to the student body. In *La Ventana*, 1925–26, 27. Lubbock, TX: Texas Technological College.

Horrigan, J. B. (2008, July 2). Home broadband adoption 2008: Adoption stalls for low-income Americans even as many broadband users opt for premium services.

Retrieved August 29, 2008, from Pew Research Center Publications Web site: http://pewresearch. org/ pubs/888/home-broadband-adoption-2008

Housing credit to help fund renovation of Ohio apartment portfolio. (2003, November). *Tax Credit Advisor, 14(11)*, 1–10.

Houstoun, L. (1997). *BIDs: Business improvement districts*. Washington, DC: Urban Land Institute.

Hurley, D. (2004, January 6). Scientist at Work—Felton Earls; On Crime as Science (A Neighbor at a Time). *New York Times*, D1.

Instituto Manantlán de Ecología y Conservación de la Biodiversidad. (2001). Iniciativa local para el manejo integral de la cuenca del Rio Ayuquila: Contribución al programa de desarrollo local sustentable (proders) region Sierra de Manantlán. [Local initiative for the integrated management of the Ayuquila river basin: Contribution to local sustainable development agenda of sierra Manantlán.]. Unpublished manuscript.

Introduction of Chongqing. (n.d.). Retrieved August 21, 2008, from the city government of Chongqing's website http://www. cq. gov. cn/cqgk/

Isserman, A. M., Feser, E., & Warren, D. (2007). Why some rural communities prosper while others do not. Report for the Office of the Undersecretary for Rural Development, U. S. Department of Agriculture. Retrieved July 30, 2008, from http: // www. ace. uiuc. edu/Reap/IssermanFeserWarren_070523_ RuralProsperity. pdf

Jaffe, J., & Quark, A. A. (2006). Social cohesion, neoliberalism, and the entrepreneurial community in rural Saskatchewan. *American Behavioral Scientist, 50(2)*, 206–225.

Jarzabkowski, P., Balogun, J., & Seidl, D.(2007). Strategizing: The challenges of a practice perspective. *Human Relations, 60(1)*, 5–27.

Jardel, P. E., Santana, E., Graf, S., & García Ruvalcaba, S. (2008). Creation of a new N. G. O. to promote nature conservation in western Mexico: MABIO. Retrived on July 2008, http://onlinelearning. unu. edu/ ayuquila/ e-archive/15.pdf

Jay, G. (2000, July-August). The community in the classroom. ACADEME, 33–37.

Jensen, N. M. (2003). Rational citizens against reform: Poverty and economic reform in transition economies. *Comparative Political Studies, 36(9)*, 1092–1111.

Jones, M. (2001). The rise of the regional state in economic governance: Partnerships for prosperity' or new scales of state power? *Environment and Planning A, 33(7)*, 1185–1211.

Keeble, D., Lawson, C., Moore, B., & Wilkinson, F. (1999). Collective learning processes, networking and "institutional thickness" in the Cambridge region. *Regional Studies, 33(4)*,319-332.

Keep pace with the development of Chongqing municipality and serve the economic and social advancement: On the occasion of the 78th anniversary of the founding of Chongqing University. (2007, October 17). *Chongqing Daily.*

Kellogg Commission on the Future of State and Land Grant Universities (1999, February). *Returning to our roots: The engaged institution.* Retrieved August 26, 2008, from National Association of State Universities and Land-Grant Colleges Web site: http://www. nasulgc. org/NetCommunity/Document. Doc?id =183

Kellogg Commission on the Future of State and Land Grant Universities. (2000). *Renewing the covenant: Learning, discovery, and engagement in a new age and different world.* Washington, DC: Author.

Kelly, P. (1992). *The end of certainty: The story of the 1980s.* Sydney, AU: Allen and Unwin.

Kenny, M. et al. (Eds.). (2002). *Learning to serve: Promoting civil society through service learning.* Norwell, MA: Kluwer Academic Publishers.

Kent, F. W., & Cuthbert, D. D. (1986). Making Monash: A twenty five year history. Monash University Gallery, Department of Visual Arts/Department of History, Monash University.

Kezar, A. J., Chambers, A. C., & Burkhardt, J. C. (Eds.). (2005). *Higher education for the public good: Emerging voices from a national movement.* San Francisco, CA: Jossey-Bass.

Kliksberg, B. (2005). Public administration in Latin America: Promises, frustrations and new examinations. *International Review of Administrative Sciences,71(2)*, 309-326.

Laine, P., & Vaara, E. (2007). Struggling over subjectivity: A discursive analysis of strategic development in an engineering group. *Human Relations,60(1)*, 29-58.

Lawson, H., McCarthy, M., Briar-Lawson, K., Miraglia, P., Strolin, J., & Caringi, J. (2006). A complex partnership to optimize and stabilize the public child welfare workforce. *Professional Development: The International Journal of Continuing Social Work Education, 9(3)*, 122-139.

Leander, P. (1991). Högskolan i Luleå 1971 - 1991—en krönika [Luleå University college 1971-1991—a chronicle].

Leitch, S. (2006). *Prosperity for all in the global economy—World class skills.* Norwich, UK: HMSO.

Li, J. (2005). Gaodeng jiaoyu yu difang jingji fazhan. [Higher education and regional revelopment]. *Modern Education Science, 7,* 3-4.

Lowell Bennion Community Service Center. (2008). *Annual report.* Salt Lake City, UT: University of Utah.

Maggio, G. (2004). Multidimensional analysis of poverty dynamics in Great Britain. Working Papers of the Institute for Social and Economic Research. (paper 2004-10). Colchester, UK: University of Essex.

Marginson, S. (2000). *Monash: Remaking the university.* St. Leonards, AU: Allan and Unwin.

Marginson, S. (2007a). University mission and identity for a post-public area. *Higher Education Research and Development, 26(1),* 117-131.

Marginson, S. (2007b). Global position and position taking: The case of Australia. *Journal of studies in international education, 11(5),* 5-32.

Mark, M. M. (2004). The mechanisms and outcomes of evaluation influence. *Evaluation, 10(1),* 35-57.

Martínez, L. M., Carranza, A., García, M., & Cañedo, E. (1998). Reporte de las condiciones de calidad del agua en base a parámetros físico químicos y biológicos en el Río Ayuquila. [Report of the quality of water based on physical chemical and biological agents in the Ayuquila river]. Junio 1996 a diciembre 1997. Universidad de Guadalajara-IMECBIO.

Martínez, L. M., Graf, S., Santana, E., & García, S. (2005). Gestión y manejo del agua en la cuenca del río Ayuquila-Armería. [Administration and water management in the Ayuquila-Armería river]. 1er. Congreso Internacional de Casos Exitosos de Desarrollo Sostenible del Trópico. Memorias. 2-4 de mayo de 2005, Boca del Río Veracruz, México.

Martínez, L. M., Sandoval, J. J., Meléndez, L., & Olguín, L. (2002). Evaluación del impacto del agua residual del lavado de caña del Ingenio Melchor Ocampo En el Riego de los suelos de Las Paredes. [Assessing the impact of waste water from the Melchor Ocampo mill on the irrigation and soil of las Paredes, Autlán, Jalisco]. Municipio de Autlán, Jal. Informe Técnico.

Martínez, L. M., Santana Castellón, E., Iñiguez Dávalos, L. I., & Santana, J. F. (2000). Programa de Acciones del Ingenio Melchor Ocampo para la Restauración del Río Ayuquila. [Action program of Melchor Ocampo mill for the restoration of the Ayuquila River]. Universidad de Guadalajara. Instituto Manantlán de Ecología y Conservación de la Biodiversidad.

Mattei, E. (2008). West Texas panorama. *Texas Highways, 55(7)*, 36–43.

Maurasse, D. (2001). *Beyond the campus: How colleges and universities form partnerships with their communities.* New York, NY: Routledge.

Mayhew, K., Deer, C., & Dua, M. (2004). The move to mass higher education in the UK: Many questions and some answers. *Oxford Review of Education, 30 (1)*, 65–82.

Mazzarotto, N. (2007, September 24). Competition and market incentives in higher education. Retrieved September 6, 2008, from http://ssrn. com/abstract = 1059881

McKernan, S., & Ratcliffe, C. (2002). Transition events in the dynamics of poverty. U. S. Department of Health and Human Services. Retrieved September 19, 2008, from http://aspe. hhs. gov/hsp/poverty-transitions02/

McLennan, G. (2008). Disinterested, disengaged, useless: Conservative or progressive idea of the university. *Globalisation, Societies and Education, 6(2)*, 195–200.

Mead, G. H. (1934). *Mind, self, and society.* Chicago, IL: University of Chicago Press.

Ministry of Education of the People's Republic of China. Higher education in China. Retrieved August 28, 2008, from http://www. moe. edu. cn/english/higher_h. htm

Mintrom, M. (2000). *Policy entrepreneurs and school choice.* Washington, DC: Georgetown University Press.

Morgan, K. (1997). The learning region: Institutions, innovation and regional renewal. *Regional Studies, 31(5)*, 491–503.

Musson, S., Tickell, A., & John, P. (2005). A decade of decentralisation? Assessing the role of the government offices for the English regions. *Environment and Planning A, 37(8)*, 1395–1412.

National Association of State Universities and Land-Grant Colleges.(n.d.). University engagement. Retrieved September 17, 2008, from http: //www. nasulgc. org/ NetCommunity/Page. aspx?pid = 224&srcid = 183

National Governors Association Center for Best Practices. (2003, February). Innovative state policy options to promote rural economic development. Retrieved August 30, 2008, from http://www. nga. org/portal/site/nga/ menuitem. 9123e83a1f6786440ddcbeeb501010a0/

vgnextoid =6ed2303cb0b32010VgnVCM1000001a01010aRCRD

National Governors Association Center for Best Practices. (2003, February). Innovative state policy options to promote rural economic development. Retrieved August 30, 2008, from http://www. nga. org/portal/site/ nga/menuitem. 9123e83a1f6786440ddcbeeb501010a0/? vgnextoid =6ed2303cb0b32010VgnVCM1000001a01010aRCRD

National Institute of Statistics. (n.d.). *Portuguese statistical yearbook.* Lisbon, PT: Author.

Nilsson, J-E., Arbo, P., Dahl, M.S., Dahlum, B., Edvardsson, I.R., & Eskelinen, H., et al. (2006). *The role of universities in regional innovation systems: A Nordic perspective.* Frederiksberg, DK: Copenhagen Business School Press.

Northcott, K. (2008). Electric highways in the sky. *Texas Co-Op Power, 65(2),* 12–14.

Northcott, K., & Hargis, K. (2008). Shedding the light on solar. *Texas Co-Op Power, 65(1),* 9–10.

Nunes, A. S. (2000). *Antologia Sociológica.* [*Sociological Anthology*]. Lisboa, PT: ICS.

Observatory for Science and Higher Education, Ministry for Science, Technology and Higher Education.(n.d.). Statistics on Portuguese education and research. Lisbon, PT: Author.

Ohio State University. (2000, October). The Ohio State University academic plan. Retrieved October 15, 2008, from http: //www. osu. edu/academicplan/Acad _ Plan. pdf

Ohio State University. (2007, December). Report on the freshman class of 2007. Retrieved October 16, 2008, from http://undergrad. osu. edu/classreport/

ONE NorthEast. (1999). *Unlocking our potential: The regional economic strategy for the North East.* Newcastle upon Tyne, UK: ONE NorthEast.

Organisation for Economic Co-operation and Development. (2007). *Four Scenarios for Higher Education.* OECD Publishing. Retrieved December 1, 2008 from www. oecd. org/document/33/0, 3343, en _ 2649 _ 35961291 _ 39378401 _ 1 _ 1 _ 1 _ 1, 00. html

Organisation for Economic Co-operation and Development. (2007). *Higher education and regions: Globally competitive, locally engaged.* Paris, FR: OECD.

Organisation for Economic Co-operation and Development. (2007). *OECD regions at a glance* (2007 ed.). OECD Publishing. Retrieved July 3, 2008, from http://

www. oecd. org/document/61/0, 3343, en_2649_34413_38690301_1_1_1_37429, 00. html

Organisation for Economic Co-operation and Development. (2008). *OECD reviews of regional innovation: North of England, UK*. Paris: OECD.

Ostrom, E. (1990). *Governing the commons: The evolutions of institutions for collective action*. Cambridge, MA: Cambridge University Press.

Ozawa, C. P. (Ed.). (2004). *The Portland edge: Challenges and successes in growing communities*. Washington, DC: Island Press.

Pastor, M., Jr., Dreier,P., Grigsby, J. E., III., & Lopez-Garza, M. (2000). *Regions that work: How cities and suburbs can grow together*. Minneapolis, MN: University of Minnesota Press.

Paton, V. (Fall 2005/Spring 2006). The scope of our country: Expanding access to higher education through community partnerships with Texas Tech University [Special issue] . *Journal of Higher Education Outreach and Engagement, 11 (1)*, 25 – 39.

Percy, S. L., Zimpher, N. L., & Brukardt, M. J. (2006). *Creating a new kind of university: Institutionalizing community-university engagement*. Bolton, MA: Anker Publishing Company, Inc.

Perorazio, T. E. (2001, November). Social contract or state requirement? Economic development and higher education. Paper presented at the annual meeting of the Association for the Study of Higher Education, Richmond, VA.

Perry, B. (2007). The multi-level governance of science policy in England. *Regional Studies, 41(8)*, 1051–1067.

Perry, D. C., & Wiewel, W. (2005). *The university as urban developer: Case studies and analysis*. Cambridge, MA: Lincoln Institute of Land Policy.

Peters, S. J., Jordan, N. R., Adamek, M., & Alter, T. R. (Eds.). (2005). *Engaging campus and community: The practice of public scholarship in the State and Land-Grant University System*. Dayton, OH: Kettering Foundation Press.

Phelps, N. A., Mackinnon, D., Stone, I., & Braidford, P. (2003). Embedding the multinationals? Institutions and the development of overseas manufacturing affiliates in Wales and North East England. *Regional Studies, 37(1)*, 27–40.

Portela, M., Areal, N., Sá, C., Alexandre, F., Cerejeira, J., & Carvalho, A., (2008). Evaluating student allocation in the Portuguese public higher education system. *Higher Education, 56(2)*, 185–203.

Porter, M. E. (1995). The competitive advantage of the inner city. *Harvard Business Review*, (May/June), 55–71.

Potts, G. (2002). Regional policy and the "regionalization" of university-industry links: A view from the English regions. *European Planning Studies, 10 (8)*, 987–1012.

Prasser, S., & Cockfield, G. (2007). Rolling out the regional pork barrel: A threat to democracy? Discussion Paper 22/07. Democratic Audit of Australia, Australian National University.

Prigge, G. W., & Torraco R. J. (2006). University-industry partnerships: A study of how top American research universities establish and maintain successful partnerships. *Journal of higher education outreach and engagement, 11(2)*, 89–100.

Puukka, J., & Marmolejo, f. (2008). Higher education institutions and regional mission: Lessons learnt from the OECD review project. *Higher Education Policy, 21(2)*, 217–244.

Rabrenovic, G., Levin, J., & Oliver, N. M. (2007). Promoting respect for difference on the college campus: The role of interdependence. *American Behavioral Scientist, 51(2)*, 294–301.

Regional engagement: The future for higher education?(2007, September). *IMHE Info*, 1–2. Retrieved March 27, 2008, from http://www. oecd/edu/imhe/newsletter

Reis, J. (1993). O Atraso Económico Português 1850–1930. [Portuguese economic backwardness 1850–1930]. Lisboa, PT: INCM.

Reith, G. (2007). Gambling and the contradictions of consumption: A genealogy of the pathological subject. *American Behavioral Scientist , 51(1)*, 33–55.

Robeyns, I. (2006). Three models of education: Rights, capabilities and human capital. *Theory and Research in Education, 4(1)*, 69–84.

Rojas, R. (2006). Rechazan coadministración de reserva de Manantlán: se intenta privatizar esa área, afirman los consejos asesores de Jalisco y Colima. [Rejection of co-administration of the Manantlán reserve: An attempt to privatize the area, say the advisory boards of Jalisco and Colima]. *La Jornada*, 9 de enero de.

Román, T., & Silva, P. (2006). Combinando esfuerzos y voluntades para la gestión integral de la cuenca del Rpio Ayuquila-Armería. [Combining efforts and will for the integral management of the Ayuquila-Armería river basin]. IV Foro mundial del Agua, México.

Romer, P. (1986). Increasing returns and long-run growth. *Journal of Political Economy, 94(5)*, 1002–1037.

Rudy, A. P., & Konefal, J. (2007). Nature, sociology, and social justice: Environmental sociology, pedagogy, and the curriculum. *American Behavioral Scientist, 51(4)*, 495–515.

Ryman, A. (2008, September 28). State's 3 universities push for more to ear bachelor's degrees. Retrieved October 20, 2008 from http://www. tucsoncitizen. com/ss/ related/97973

Sanderson, I. (2008). Evaluation in complex policy systems. *Evaluation,6(4)*, 433–454.

Santana, E., Navarro, S., Martínez, M., Aguirre, A., Figueroa, P., & Aguilar, C. (1993). Contaminación, aprovechamiento y conservación de los recursos acuáticos del Río Ayuquila. [Pollution, exploitation, and conservation of water resources in the Ayuquila River]. SMBR Jalisco-Colima, Tiempos de Ciencia. no. 30, 29 – 38.

Saxenian, A. (1994). *Regional advantage culture and competition in Silicon Valley and Route 128.* Cambridge, MA: Harvard University Press.

Schneider, M., Scholz, J., Lubell, M., Mindruta, D., & Edwardsen, M. (2003). Building Consensual Institutions: Networks and the National Estuary Program. *American Journal of Political Science, 47 (1)*, 142–157.

Schneider, M., Teske, P., & Mintrom, M. (1995). *Public Entrepreneurs.* Princeton, NJ: Princeton University Press.

Schultz, T. W. (1981). *Investing in people: The economics of population quality,* Berkeley, CA: University of California Press.

Schutz, A. (1932). *The Phenomenology of the Social World.* Evanston, IL: Northwestern University Press.

Schwant, T. A. (2003). "Back to the rough ground!" Beyond theory to practice in evaluation. *Evaluation, 9(3)*, 353–364.

Scott, A., & Storper, S. (2003). Regions, globalization, development. *Regional Studies, 37(6/7)*, 579–592.

Sen, A. (1982). Poverty and famines: An essay on entitlement and deprivation. *International Affairs (Royal Institute of International Affairs 1944 –)*, *58(2)*, 335–336.

Serle, G. (2003). *John Monash: A biography* (3rd ed.). Melbourne, AU: Melbourne University Press.

Simão, J. V., Santos, S. M., & Costa, A. A. (2002). Ensino Superior: Uma Visão para a Próxima Década. [Higher education: A vision for the next decade]. Lisboa, PT: Gradiva.

Soska, T. M., & Butterfield, A. K. J. (2004). *University-community partnerships: Universities in civic engagement*. Binghamton, NY: The Haworth Social Work Press.

Stame, N. (2004). Theory-based evaluation and types of complexity. *Evaluation, 10 (1)*, 58–76.

Stensaker, I., & Falkenberg, J. (2007). Making sense of different responses to corporate change. *Human Relations, 60(1)*, 137–177.

Storper, M. (1995). The resurgence of regional economies, ten years later: The region as a nexus of untraded interdependencies. *European Urban and Regional Studies, 2(3)*, 191–221.

Suarez-Balcazar, Y., Hellwig, M., Kouba, J., Redmond, L., Marinez, L., & Block, B., et al. (2006). The making of an interdisciplinary partnership: The case of the Chicago Food System Collaborative. *American Journal of Community Psychology, 38*, 113–123.

Swan, J., & Scarbrough, H. (2005). The politics of networked innovation. *Human Relations, 58(7)*, 913–943.

Teixeira, P., Rosa, M. J., & Amaral, A. (2006). A broader church? Expansion, access and cost-sharing in Portuguese higher education. In P. Teixeira, B. Johnstone, M. J. Rosa, & H. Vossensteyn (Eds.), *Cost-sharing and accessibility in higher education: A fairer deal?* (pp. 241–264). Dordrecht: Springer.

Texas Tech University. (2008). Wind Science and Engineering Research Center 2007 annual report. Lubbock, TX: Texas Tech University.

Texas Tech University 2008–09 School of Law Catalog. (2008, July). Retrieved August 16, 2008, from http://www.depts.ttu.edu/officialpublications/pdfs/CurrentLawCatalog.pdf

Tomaney, J. (2009). Region. In R. Kitchin & N. Thrift (Eds.), *International encyclopaedia of human geography*. Amsterdam, NL: Elsevier.

Trimble, M. (1986). *Roadside history of Arizona*. Missoula, MT: Mountain Press Publishing Company.

University Neighborhood Partners. (2003). Community partnership guidelines—How we want to work together in partnership. Unpublished document.

University Neighborhood Partners.(2007). *Annual report*. Salt Lake City: University of Utah.

University Neighborhood Partners. (2007). Success stories. Unpublished document.

U.S. Census Bureau.(2000). Census of population. Retrieved August 10, 2008, from http://www. census. gov/main/www/cen2000. html

U.S. Department of Housing and Urban Development. (2002). Lasting engagement: Building and sustaining a commitment to community outreach, development and collaboration. (Vol. 1). Retrieved August 21, 2008, from http://www. oup. org/files/pubs/engagement_vol1.pdf

Uusikylä, P., & Valovirta, V. (2007). Three spheres of performance governance: Spanning the boundaries from single-organization focus towards a partnership network. *Evaluation, 13(4)*, 399–419.

Voigt, K. (2007). Individual choice and unequal participation in higher education. *Theory and Research in Education 2007, 5(1)*, 87–112.

Wahlstrom, K. L. (2008). Leadership and learning: What these articles tell us. *Educational Administration Quarterly, 44(4)*, 593–597.

Watson, D. (2007). The university and its communities. *Higher Education Management and Policy, 19(2)*, 21–29.

Wellin, C. (2008). Telling tales out of school: Dilemmas of race and inclusiveness in the liberal academy. *American Behavioral Scientist, 51(5)*, 686–708.

Weiss, C. H. (1995). Nothing as practical as good theory: Exploring theory-based evaluation for comprehensive community initiatives for children and families. In J. Connell et al. (Eds.), *New approaches to evaluating community initiatives: Concepts, methods, and contexts*. Washington, DC: Aspen Institute.

Wen, R. (2004, February 6). Practice the combination of production, education and research: Ten years of practice. *China Education Daily*, 3.

Westerberg, M., Wincent, J., & Ylinenpää, H. (2007). Triple Helix och utvecklingen av innovationssystem. [Triple Helix and the development of innovation systems], In Laestadius, S., Nuur, C. & Ylinenpää, H.(Eds.), *Regional växtkraft i en global ekonomi. Det svenska Vinnväxtprogrammet. [Regional growth in a globalized economy]* (pp. 237 – 260). Stockholm, SE: Santéreus Academic Press Sweden.

Wiewel, W., & Knaap, G. (Eds.). (2005). *Partnerships for smart growth: University-community collaboration for better public places.* Armonk, NY: M. E. Sharpe, Inc.

Wiewel, W., & Perry, D. C. (Eds.). (2008). *Global universities and urban development: Case studies and analysis.* Armonk, NY: M. E. Sharpe, Inc.

Winter, A., Wiseman, J., & Muirhead, B. (2006). University-community engagement in Australia. *Education, Citizenship and Social Justice, 1 (3),* 211 −230.

Winter, A., Wiseman, J., & Muirhead, B. (Eds.). (2006). *Beyond rhetoric: University-community engagement in Victoria.* Brisbane, AU: Eidos.

World Bank. (2001). *World development report 2000/2001: Attacking poverty.* New York: Oxford University Press.

Yao, S. (2007, August 31). President Hu calls to develop education as priority. Retrieved September 10, 2008, from http: // news. xinhuanet. com/english/ 2007-08/31/content_6640290. htm

Yelland, R., & Pukka, J. (2007, July 27). From denial of place to death of distance: Higher education institutions working for their regions. Pascal Observatory Briefing Note.

Ylinenpää, H., & Lundgren, N-G. (1998, November). Regional dynamics—A comparison of two Nordic regions. Paper presented at the conference "SMEs and districts", Università Carlo Cattaneo (LIUC), Castellanza, IT.